Six years that
shook the world

S.T.L

Six years that shook the world

Perestroika – the impossible project

Rachel Walker

Manchester University Press
Manchester and New York

Distributed exclusively in the USA and Canada by St. Martin's Press

Published by Manchester University Press
Oxford Road, Manchester M13 9NR, UK
and Room 400, 175 Fifth Avenue, New York, NY 10010, USA

Distributed exclusively in the USA and Canada
by St. Martin's Press, Inc., 175 Fifth Avenue, New York,
NY 10010, USA

British Library Cataloguing-in-Publication Data
A catalogue record for this book is available from the British Library

Library of Congress Cataloging-in-Publication Data
Walker, Rachel, 1953–
    Six years that shook the world : perestroika—the impossible
project / Rachel Walker.
        p.   cm.
    Includes bibliographical references and index.
    ISBN 0–7190–3286–5. — ISBN 0–7190–3287–3 (pbk).
    1. Soviet Union—History—1985–1991.   I. Title   II. Title: 6
years that shook the world.
DK286.W35   1993
947.085′4—dc20   92–38069

ISBN 0 7190 3287 3 *paperback* ✓

Reprinted 1995

Typeset in Great Britain
by Northern Phototypesetting Co. Ltd, Bolton

Printed in Great Britain
by Bell & Bain Ltd, Glasgow

Contents

	Preface	vi
1	Russia's two revolutions	1
Part I	**The old Soviet system**	17
2	The system before 1985	19
3	Social context of Soviet politics	40
4	Ideology and political culture	60
Part II	**The politics of *perestroika***	71
5	Understanding *perestroika*	73
6	*Uskoreniye*, prelude to reform	100
7	Political reform	118
8	Collapse of the political system	140
9	The fragile union	164
10	Collapse of the economy	190
11	Foreign policy	210
12	August 1991	222
Part III	**The legacies of *perestroika***	247
13	The unfinished revolution	249
14	The creation of the Commonwealth	289

Preface

The events of recent years on that part of the globe that was once called the Soviet Union have left the world community still breathless with disbelief and amazement. The 'other' great super-power whose continued existence we had all taken for granted suddenly disintegrated not because it was threatened with imme-diate invasion, famine or war but because it crumbled from within. Mikhail Gorbachev, the telegenic politician who came to power in 1985 promising to reform the Soviet system, and who became the only Soviet leader to win the genuine affection and respect of almost everyone outside his country's borders, was transformed almost overnight into the Soviet Union's grave-digger and was ignominiously removed from office. The reform programme that he launched, known as *perestroika*, initiated processes of revolu-tionary change whose outcomes are still frighteningly uncertain and with which no one has yet come to terms.

This book has been specifically designed for the student and the general reader who feel they know little and would like to learn more about the cataclysmic events that brought all this about. Its focus is the fateful six years of *perestroika*. It was during this period that the old Soviet system was effectively destroyed and laid to rest and we are only now beginning to understand why. It was also during this period that many of the most pressing problems now confronting the new states of the former Soviet Union were first created. Most recent textbooks on Soviet and post-Soviet politics have done little to chart the path of well-meaning destruction that was Gorbachev's real legacy to his successors. This book attempts to redress the balance. It also tries to explore and explain some of the developments that have been taking place, particularly in Russia, since the collapse of the USSR in December 1991. The book was finished in August 1992 and takes account of events up to that point.

This book also differs from most others in that it is not a classic textbook. It has adopted a simple, note style of presentation that lays out the crucial issues in a way that makes them easy to follow and that is intended to guide the reader immediately to the important points. Its approach is broadly interpretive and analytical rather than factual. It looks at processes and their underlying causes rather than simply describing what happened because its intention is to provide the reader with the tools for understanding developments, not just a knowledge of events. Consequently, students will derive most benefit from it if they combine its use with wide and informed reading. The general reader, however, will find, I hope, that the book strikes a comfortable balance between fact and interpretation: providing just enough of the first to make sense of the second and just enough of the second to make sense of the first, without overwhelming.

This book has been immensely difficult to write. Writing anything on politics is generally a headache at the best of times because political processes move swiftly and politicians rarely stay the same for long. Keeping up to date with events and taking account of new developments that modify the overall picture present the writer with constant problems. However, writing a book about a revolution in the making has magnified these difficulties by a factor of ten. When this book began life the Soviet Union was still in existence and President Gorbachev was still in charge. By the time it was finished President Gorbachev and the Soviet Union itself had been swept away to be replaced by fifteen new states and a whole set of new political faces. By the time it is read things will undoubtedly have changed again. If the reader comes away from the book able to make more sense of the chaos that has been besetting the countries of the Commonwealth of Independent States since they all became independent then writing it will have been worth the agony.

I owe an enormous debt of gratitude to Neil Robinson, Lucy Walker and Beryl Gell for reading the drafts and for their constructive and helpful comments on how to improve it; to my husband Randy Banks for his unstinting support and the endless cups of coffee; and to the Department of Government at Essex University for finding me the time to write.

Rachel Walker
August 1992

1

Russia's two revolutions

The Soviet state has had a turbulent history which has ended in much the same way as it began. A dissatisfied and discontented population, an economy on the verge of ruin, a political leadership bereft of solutions and new ideas, and a controversial foreign policy all brought the government of the day to its knees.

Of course, one cannot take the analogy too far. Russian society in 1917, backward and overwhelmingly rural, was utterly different from the urban and educated Soviet society of 1991, but both societies experienced revolutions of similar dimensions.

The problems of studying revolution

There is a great deal of uncertainty in the social science literature about how the concept of revolution should be defined and the processes of revolutionary change in a society studied.

The word revolution is used in a variety of different contexts. For instance, people speak of social revolutions, political revolutions, industrial revolutions, information technology revolutions, sexual revolutions and so on. It is also a very political word. Mikhail Gorbachev called his reforms 'revolutionary' because he wanted to galvanise people into action, not because he intended to transform Soviet economic and political structures. Nor is it always easy to distinguish revolutions from associated processes like military coups and civil wars.

Most societies self-evidently change gradually over time, often very

very considerably. For example, Soviet society in the 1990s is very different from what it was in the 1930s under Stalin. Consequently, distinguishing between change and revolution, continuity and discontinuity frequently presents a problem.

There is some measure of agreement however that in order for an event or a process to be called revolutionary there must be a transformation in any given set of relations, a discontinuity with the old order. This transformation may be sudden or relatively gradual, or both, but it must involve:

1 changes in the holders of political and economic power.
2 changes in political and economic institutions.
3 changes in the relationship between government and governed.

These transformations may involve violence. They may also be followed by attempts at social engineering, but they need not be. The revolutions of 1989 in the countries of Eastern Europe brought about transformations in all three areas but they were mostly non-violent, hence the name 'Velvet Revolution'. And most of the engineering that the new governments have subsequently attempted to bring about has been economic rather than social. Although it is, of course, always difficult to draw a neat dividing line between the two, since economic change usually has considerable social consequences.

The problem of prediction

The making of a revolution usually involves such a large number of interrelated variables that it is almost impossible to predict in advance that a revolution is going to take place. These variables include:

1 the mood of different sectors of the population, workers, business people, farmers, students, politicians.
2 the levels of popular organisation and of public protest. And in particular the presence of articulate and clever opposition leaders.

3   the loyalty of the armed forces and the police to the purposes
    of the government and the head of state.
4   the flexibility of political institutions and the intelligence and
    ability of leading politicians.
5   the state of the economy and people's expectations about their
    standards of living and the future of their children.

Equally, it is difficult to judge in advance to what extent any given
set of state institutions will be strong enough to withstand the
social and political pressures coming from below. In 1989 the
Chinese Communist Party was quite successful in crushing a
peaceful student rebellion with military force, while its counterparts in Eastern Europe capitulated without a murmur when
people took to the streets.

However, even if it is impossible to predict the precise moment
when a revolution is likely to begin, it may be possible at least to
estimate whether an upheaval of revolutionary potential is on the
cards.

Systemic crisis

All societies periodically experience crises of greater or lesser
severity.

Economic crises

These may be the result of attempts at rapid internal reform;
government incompetence, and/or changes in the world economy
that affect the domestic economy of a country adversely. They
may be very severe and may strike more than one country simultaneously, as in the case of the Great Depression of 1929. Or they
may be much less severe, localised crises. For example, the
economic recessions in Britain during the 1990s, which have hurt
some sectors of the population very badly but others much less so.

Political crises

These may also be the result of attempts at internal reform. Or
they can be the product of rapid changes in the social structure.
They usually involve popular anger at the inadequacies of

particular institutions of government and lack of access to policy-making. The upheavals in Europe during 1968 when young people occupied buildings and took to the streets as a reaction to perceived government unrepresentativeness and unresponsiveness is an example.

Legitimacy crises
These occur very rarely because they are generally the result of prolonged economic and/or political crisis. They usually involve a general loss of faith in the institutions of the state and in the ability of government to govern, whatever its political make-up. The social consensus that underpins the authority of the government and of the state, begins to break down. People lose their respect for the law and law enforcement agencies. They lose their respect for society's leaders and they begin to question the established order.

Generally, such crises come singly, do not affect the whole population equally, and are therefore manageable. The Great Depression of 1929 did not lead to the general collapse of the capitalist system, partly because some sectors of the population, those with jobs, did very well out of it. But mostly because, despite the weakness of the economic system, the institutions of state and government remained strong and continued to inspire the confidence of the majority. Indeed, it was massive government intervention during the 1930s that put the capitalist economies of the United States and Europe back on an even keel. Equally, the youth rebellions of 1968 were easily controlled because the economies of the European countries remained strong and continued to meet most people's needs. Nor was there any great crisis of confidence amongst the majority in the fundamental nature of each country's political institutions.

However, on those rare occasions when such crises occur together and are sufficiently intense as to affect the majority of the population then one can foresee the possibility of revolution.

We should note that revolutions often happen when attempts to reform existing institutions are already underway. Reform brings new social forces into play, people's expectations are raised and increasing demands are made of the system which it cannot yet meet. Moreover, reform tends to weaken the institutions of government and undermine their effectiveness.

A revolution may still not take place. The armed forces may be strong and ruthless enough to shore up the existing power structures; and/or the opposition may lack adequate organisation and leadership and consequently may be too weak and divided to take power.

Nevertheless, when a crisis in the economy fails to ensure the adequate distribution of necessities to the general population, the political system is seen to be unrepresentative and fails to inspire confidence and there is a general loss of faith in the institutions of the state, then one can speak of a crisis of legitimacy and a situation of chronic instability. In such circumstances only the continued use of maximum force or a revolutionary transformation can be the outcome.

1917 and 1991

Both the Russian revolution of 1917 and the botched and bungled coup of August 1991 which effectively brought the Soviet federal state to an end were the consequence of such a coincidence of crises. The exact circumstances were not the same, but the underlying dynamics were rather similar. In each case the old system underwent catastrophic collapse which created a power vacuum. The chaos and confusion that resulted necessitated extraordinary measures which in the modern case are still going on.

Economic crisis

In early 1917 the tsarist state was suffering the consequences of Russian participation in the First World War. The economy, backward to begin with relative to its European neighbours, was devastated. The small industrial base could not produce enough munitions, manufactures and clothing to supply the troops or the population. The transport system was too inadequate to cope with both the shipment of troops and of supplies. The agricultural system, overwhelmingly dependent on manpower, horses and ploughs for food production, crumbled as men and horses were drafted to the front. Hundreds of thousands of people died of cold, hunger and disease or were slaughtered at the front without adequate weapons or supplies. Unsurprisingly, Russia was losing the war.

In August 1991 the Soviet economy was not suffering from 'hot war' but it was suffering the physical consequences of:

1 a very prolonged 'cold war' with the capitalist countries. This had involved the massive long-term diversion of most of the country's resources from the civilian economy into an endlessly escalating arms race and an enormous military–industrial complex whose central purposes were to defend the country and to keep itself in business.
2 a disastrous series of structural reforms which had originally been introduced in order to try and overcome the most pernicious effects of the cold war.

The old system of administered central planning that Mikhail Gorbachev inherited in 1985 was never very efficient or productive, except in the military sphere. It was wasteful, cumbersome and slow. It failed to meet any but the most basic needs of the population and was enormously backward relative to the advanced economies of the USA, Japan and Germany. Many people were convinced, including Gorbachev himself, that this system would collapse of its own accord under the strain of international competition if no attempt were made to reform it. However, the system did work after a fashion – as long as no one interfered with it. Everyone knew the rules of the game and how to play them.

Unfortunately, Mikhail Gorbachev's economic reforms, collectively known by the slogan *perestroika* (reconstruction), disrupted this system of administered planning and distribution without replacing it. Established economic relations between factories, shops, farms, villages, cities, regions and republics were thrown into chaos. People were told to stop working in the old ways, but they were given few incentives to change and few ideas about how to work in new ways. By 1990 there was much talk amongst politicians about the need to move to the market. But since no one really understood what the market was, nor how to go about creating one, this talk achieved very little. As a consequence the economy began to grind to a halt. Production and distribution collapsed and factories, farms, urban and rural communities across the vastnesses of the Soviet sub-continent were forced to barter what they could where they could in exchange for what they needed or could get hold of. People were not dying of hunger or living in holes in the ground as they had been in 1917. But after seventy-odd years of striving and failing to build a new society and after six years of being told that things were going to get better, they were appalled to find themselves staring hunger and depriva-tion in the face.

When the State Committee for the State of Emergency, as the coup leaders called themselves, usurped legitimate government on 19 August it cited the catastrophic state of the economy and the consequent possibility of massive social unrest as one of the main reasons for its attempt to take power.

Political crisis

Russian society, although economically backward relative to its neighbours, had not stood still in the years before 1917. Several of the Russian tsars, starting with Peter I (the Great) at the turn of the eighteenth century, had initiated state-led modernisation pro-grammes. Conscious of the economic and military gulf between their sprawling country and more developed neighbours like Britain, Germany, France, these reforming tsars encouraged the technological modernisation of the economy and one or two of the more enlightened ones also sought to improve the educational and social lot of their people.

However, economic modernisation did not lead to significant political reform. The tsars continued to rule as absolute monarchs until 1917. Inevitably, therefore, the results of modernisation were mixed and, as it turned out, explosive. Modernisation set in train new social forces that the tsarist state would not recognise and could not control.

Industrialisation and the gradual expansion of the educational system that accompanied it led to the emergence of:

1   a small but highly concentrated and literate working class
    which increasingly resisted the terrible conditions in which it
    was forced to work;

2   highly educated professional classes, doctors, teachers, law-
    yers, and a growing 'sub-class' of students, most of whose
    members were dedicated to improving society and who
    resented, increasingly bitterly, their lack of rights and their
    lack of access to any sort of modern political process;

3   a small but fairly rapacious and well-educated commercial
    bourgeoisie which wanted greater freedom from the state to
    engage in commercial activity.

Modernisation did not, however, greatly improve the lot of the
peasantry, which constituted the overwhelming majority of the
population. It gave many of them access to a rudimentary education, which improved their ability to organise themselves. It also
allowed a small minority to get rich. But the economic condition of
the vast majority remained one of destitution and appalling
exploitation. Starved of land and burdened with debt the
peasantry grew increasingly resentful of a lazy and incompetent
aristocracy and of a greedy state which exported their grain in vast
quantities in order to pay for modernisation but gave them little in
return.

Violent unrest shook the social fabric several times before 1917
and the events of 1905, often called the failed revolution, would
have warned a more intelligent monarch than Nicholas II that real
political change could no longer be postponed. However,
Nicholas II did not heed the warning. He conceded some civil
rights and the formation of an elected parliament, the Duma, to
the protesting population, but increasingly curtailed them so that
by 1917 the Duma was both unrepresentative and without power.
Needless to say, this did nothing to alleviate the social pressures
that had given rise to the events of 1905. If anything, these
half-hearted political gestures exacerbated them. The Duma provided the intelligentsia with an open forum for criticism and
debate and it acted as a reminder both of what could be gained by
popular protest and of how much remained to be achieved. However, the vast majority of the population remained disenfranchised

and politically repressed. The potential for revolution in the country therefore continued to grow unabated. It needed only a spark, as Lenin was to remark.

By August 1991 the Soviet political system was effectively labouring under the opposite problem. Mikhail Gorbachev's political innovations were remarkably successful in unleashing the repressed social forces in Soviet society; in transforming people's behaviour and enabling them to speak out, but remarkably unsuccessful in creating appropriate political institutions to cope with and channel this behaviour.

The policy of glasnost

The policy of *glasnost* – often translated as 'openness' – resulted in the abolition of censorship and political control in the media, education, the arts, the social sciences and over society generally.

The lifting of political controls increasingly unleashed a torrent of debate, criticism, complaint, opposition and demands for change both great and small from all sectors of the public. Society no longer consisted of inarticulate peasants, but of highly educated elites and a literate and educated public who were well able to challenge state authority once the fear of coercion was lifted from them.

This did not happen all at once of course. It took a little time for people to become convinced that the lifting of political repression was genuine. But by 1989 and 1990 not only were they convinced, the chaos of voices and the deluge of demands had become so overwhelming that the system could not cope with them.

For the first time in Soviet history people could speak out without fear. Unfortunately, however, it is not clear that they could always make their voices heard or that they could have any influence in the making of policies that affected their lives. In order to be heard and have influence people need regularised channels of access to the institutions that govern their lives. On the whole, these did not exist and the Gorbachev reforms did very little to create them.

Democratisation

As the word implies, democratisation encompassed a set of policies which were intended to increase popular participation in the system. This, it was hoped, would give ordinary people a greater vested interest in actively helping to modernise and streamline the economic and social system. However, the process of democratisation was very half-hearted and therefore tended to have the opposite effect.

First of all, the powers and political prerogatives of the Communist Party which had dominated the Soviet system for seventy-odd years were not significantly challenged until 1990. Its members continued to dominate in the new institutions, particularly at the all-union (federal) level, and many of them did their best to hamper the process of democratisation. This led to a great deal of anger and cynicism both amongst ordinary people and politicians who had come to despise the Communist Party and its privileges. It also hindered the creation of new institutions, such as a multi-party system, which might have acted to aggregate and reconcile the divergent interests and demands of different sectors of the population which were now being articulated with increasing vociferousness.

Secondly, no attempt was made, until it was far too late, to rethink the nature of the relationship between the all-union government in Moscow and the fifteen union republics of which the old federal Union of Soviet Socialist Republics (USSR) was made up.

For most of their seventy years these republics had been thoroughly subordinated to Moscow and were governed by largely compliant, party-dominated elites.

In 1989 and 1990 all this changed. The first semi-competitive elections ever held in the Soviet Union produced nationalist governments in a number of republics: in the Baltic republics of Lithuania, Latvia and Estonia in 1989, followed by most of the rest in 1990. As the process of democratisation unravelled, the central government continued to insist on republican subordination to central commands. The republican governments, increasingly jealous of their rights, refused to comply. This became known as the 'war of laws'. The result was stalemate followed by a creeping disintegration as one republic after another attempted to resolve the stalemate by declaring its sovereignty from the centre. The federal institutions in Moscow could not mediate between the republics, or arbitrate on the conflicts of interest between the republics and the central government, because they were too closely associated with the Communist Party and the old system. The consequence was an upsurge of irreconcilable demands and a series of often bloody battles which undermined the authority and legitimacy of the central authorities completely. Gorbachev's failure to address this problem until it was forced on him by republican non-compliance resulted in a power vacuum and the eventual disintegration and formal abolition of the Soviet federal state in December 1991.

Thirdly, the new institutions that were established at the all-union level, the Congress of People's Deputies, the Supreme Soviet, the executive presidency, were unrepresentative, lacked effective power and rapidly lost their authority. The Congress of People's Deputies which raised such hopes in 1989, when virtually the whole Soviet population stayed at home to watch its televised debates, was soon dismissed as nothing more than a 'talking shop' which is fundamentally all it was. The executive presidency, which was granted a great deal of formal power during the course of 1990, quickly lost credibility as the 'war of laws' and the 'war of sovereignty' with the republics gathered momentum. Gorbachev's popularity sank to an all-time low.

Finally, within the republics the situation was no better. Not all the republican governments were necessarily representative of their populations. Many minorities, for example Poles and Russians in Lithuania, Ossetians in Georgia, increasingly felt themselves to be excluded from the political process and became resentful of what they considered to be a new nationalistic suppression of their rights. The result has often been bloody and insoluble conflict. Nor have all the republics succeeded in creating new structures of government. The Communist Party has continued to be a powerful and obstructive force in some republics, particularly the Central Asian republics, and in almost all the republics there has been a bitter and vicious political struggle going on between the forces of left, right and centre for control of the levers of power.

Meanwhile, economic disintegration continued to accelerate while people, including politicians at the very top, spent their time politicking in smoke-filled rooms or agitating on the streets.

Crisis of Legitimacy

The revolution in 1917 did not begin with the Bolshevik takeover of power in October. It actually began with the abdication of the tsar, Nicholas II, in February. Ignorant of the needs and wishes of his people, ignorant of the real situation prevailing in the country and unwilling even to take advice from his ministers, Nicholas II made a series of disastrous decisions concerning the prosecution of the war. As a result everyone, from his closest advisers to the armed forces, lost confidence in him. He was left with no alternative but to abdicate.

The Bolsheviks took power in October 1917 not because a cruel and vindictive government had to be overthrown but because government had effectively ceased to exist. Power did not reside with the Provisional Government, which was established by the Duma immediately after the tsar's abdication, because it lacked popular support and refused to take vital decisions. It did not properly reside with the new Soviets of Workers, Soldiers and Peasant deputies. These institutions began life as workers' strike committees in 1905. They re-emerged again in February 1917 when they rapidly turned into organs of democratic popular self-government. They had enormous influence within the army and in the urban centres, but they could not control the vastnesses of the countryside and did not have the resources, human or material, to organise the life of society as a whole.

The Bolshevik Party was by no means the only party with organisation and leadership at the time but its leaders, and most obviously Lenin, were the only people to recognise the emergence of a power vacuum. As they saw it, they either had to take power, and that meant taking control of the bureaucratic machinery of the old tsarist government, or watch the country disintegrate. Or, worse, see the restoration of some form of monarchical or military rule.

The attempted coup of August 1991 had its historical antecedent in the attempted coup of August 1917 when General Kornilov, at the head of the remaining monarchist military and political forces, tried to take power. Both coups failed because they lacked organisation, popular support and because the levers of power – the police, the army, state institutions – had themselves begun to disintegrate.

The Bolsheviks were able to take power not because they themselves were powerful but because the old system had already collapsed under the weight of war, economic disintegration and the disaffection and hostility of virtually the whole population towards the old system.

By August 1991 the disintegration of the state and popular disaffection towards the institutions of central government were probably even greater.

1   The institutions of government were in complete disarray and quite unable to govern.
2   Those who had wanted to conserve the old system as much as possible, largely because it had given them power, were outraged as one bastion of the old system after another had come under attack. These people had sought to hamper the reforms in any way they could and they continued to resist the processes of disintegration that Gorbachev's reforms had set in motion.
3   The democratic forces who had wanted to accelerate the process of political and economic change had become increasingly dismayed by Gorbachev's vacillations and the half-heartedness of his reforms.
4   Those in the centre who had wanted gradual and prudent change found themselves cast adrift without any sort of coherent programme as the system disintegrated around them and Gorbachev dithered.
5   Even the paramilitary institutions of the state – the army, the police, the secret services – were divided in their allegiances and beliefs between those who wanted to conserve the system and those who wanted change.

6   Ordinary people had already transferred their allegiance to their ethnic group and/or their republican government.
7   Above all, however, people in all walks of life were exhausted by the endless conflicts, disillusioned by the failure of the reforms, and appalled by the state of the economy which appeared to be sliding into the abyss while the politicians bickered endlessly but did nothing. As a consequence people completely lost faith in the system.

Even so the coup of August 1991 was not without its supporters. What is remarkable about the defence of the Russian government building in Moscow (the White House) is not that people came out into the streets to defend it against the junta but that so few people did so. In their heart of hearts many people were fed-up and wanted the restoration of some sort of order. However, the coup failed ultimately because central power and central authority had already effectively ceased to exist.

A government can continue to control the governed without authority, that is to say without the willing obedience and respect of the citizens, provided it has enough obedient and well-armed troops at its disposal. However, once it is deprived of guns and gunmen it has no means of imposing its will.

The result in the Soviet case was a genuine revolution as the governments in Russia and the other fourteen republics of the old Union took control of their own destinies and the central institutions simply petered out of existence. However, this new revolution is, in many respects, only just beginning.

Conclusion

Clearly, revolutions are not events but long and complex processes. Russian and Soviet history suggests that revolutions necessarily involve at least two stages:

1   the disintegration and collapse of the old social system;
2   followed by a prolonged period in which the construction of a new system is attempted.

Such a sequence inevitably means that the second stage will be confused, contradictory, highly conflictual and probably not very successful. Politicians will be too busy trying to manage the consequences of the collapse of the old economic and political system to be able to spend much time or give much thought to the creation of new institutions, especially if they intend those new institutions to be more democratic and efficient than the old ones. In fact, it is possible to argue that the crisis measures needed to mitigate the worst effects of the first stage, to prevent the population from starving for example, are inevitably bound to undermine any subsequent attempts to move towards a more open and democratic society. Because the management of crisis generally demands instant responses there is a tendency for old authoritarian structures to reassert themselves. Moreover, once new leaders have adopted authoritarian measures to overcome crisis they are generally reluctant to give up their new-found power. Having overcome crisis, such leaders tend to think that they have the best solutions and are psychologically reluctant to delegate or co-operate with others.

Are the peoples of the old Soviet Union condemned to a vicious cycle of crisis, revolution and new authoritarianism? The jury is still out on the answer but we must think about the question.

When Mikhail Gorbachev set out to reform the Soviet system in March 1985 he clearly did not intend to destroy it. He wanted to modernise it. So, we have to ask, what went wrong?

Only a survey of Soviet history, Soviet politics and Soviet society will enable us to answer that question.

Part I examines the key features of the old Soviet system that Mikhail Gorbachev inherited in order to put his reforms in context. This will enable us to explain why his reforms were necessary and, at the same time, unlikely to succeed.

Part II explores *perestroika* in some detail. It seeks to explain what Gorbachev thought he was attempting to achieve and to examine the disruptive political, economic and social processes that were the result of his contradictory aims and desires.

Part III looks briefly at developments in the first year after the coup of August 1991 and, in particular, at the first eight months of independence for the new states that emerged out of the rubble of the old system.

Further reading

Calvert, Peter, *Revolution* (Key Concepts in Political Science), Pall Mall & Macmillan, 1970

Frankel, E. R., Frankel, J., Knei-Paz, B., *Revolution in Russia: Reassessments of 1917*, Cambridge University Press, 1991

Hosking, Geoffrey, *A History of the Soviet Union*, Fontana Press, 1990

McAuley, Mary, *Politics and the USSR*, Penguin, 1977

McAuley, Mary, *Soviet Politics 1917–1991*, Oxford University Press, 1992

Reed, John, *Ten Days that Shook the World*, Penguin, 1977

Riazanovsky, Nicholas, *A History of Russia*, Oxford University Press, 1984, 4th ed

Questions

1   How would you define the concept of revolution? Is it a useful concept for studying social change?

2   How would you explain the Bolshevik seizure of power in 1917?

Part I

The Old Soviet system

2

The system before 1985

In order to understand the reasons for *perestroika* and its failure, and to grasp the nature of the problems confronting the collection of countries that made up the Soviet Union, some knowledge of the old system and its problems is essential. *Perestroika* was introduced in order to overcome these problems. It failed because, as it turned out, the Soviet system could not be reformed, it could only be transformed.

Part I therefore examines the system that Gorbachev inherited when he became General Secretary of the Communist Party of the Soviet Union (CPSU) on 11 March 1985.

Pre-crisis

Gorbachev himself was of the opinion, and a great many members of the Soviet elite agreed with him, that Soviet socialism had reached what he called a 'pre-crisis' situation by 1985, although they sometimes disagreed about the causes.

The key factors that had promoted this slide towards crisis were as follows.

First, although the Soviet Union had long had the status of a global superpower on the international arena and possessed a formidable military arsenal, its domestic economy was manifestly failing to meet the needs of the ordinary consumer. Almost everything was in short supply and the goods that were available were generally of extremely poor quality. Endless queueing for goods had become an endemic feature of Soviet existence and the general quality of life for most people was pretty awful. This was particularly so in rural areas and the more remote parts of the country where lack of housing and lack of proper sewage and water facilities and other social amenities often reduced people to very primitive ways of living.

Second, the political system was almost completely unresponsive to the needs, demands and interests of ordinary people.

1   The Communist Party dominated all decision making at national and local levels and its full-time officials (the *apparatchiki*) were extremely unresponsive both to the needs and opinions of the party's own members as well as to those of the population as a whole.

2   The soviets (*soviet* is a Russian word meaning 'council'), which functioned both as popularly elected legislative assemblies and as popularly elected organs of local government, lacked power. They were thoroughly dominated by the interests of Communist Party officials, the interests of government ministries, and were subordinated, above all, to the demands of the central authorities in Moscow. Local government therefore barely functioned.

Third, as a result of its gross inefficiency the official 'planned' economic system was riddled with corruption and crime. It had also given rise, over time, to the development of an enormous 'black market' or 'second economy' which almost rivalled the official economy in size. Top officials exploited their position in order to get their hands on luxury goods (especially from abroad). Factory and farm managers had to wheel and deal to get their hands on the resources needed to keep their enterprises working. Ordinary people exchanged goods, services and access to scarce resources on a 'personal favour' basis so as to get by (see Chapter 3). As Gorbachev publicly complained in May 1985: 'Try to get your flat repaired: you will definitely have to find a moonlighter to do it for you – and he will have to steal the materials from a building site.'

Fourth, by the late 1970s and early 1980s the inefficiency, corruption and unresponsiveness of the economic and political system had given rise to an enormous degree of cynicism, contempt and alienation amongst ordinary people. These expressed themselves in chronically high levels of alcoholism; terrible labour discipline; and the complete loss of any sense of collective or individual responsibility. People simply did what they were told, no matter how irrational the order, without any thought for and regardless of the possible consequences. This is not because people were innately irresponsible but because the system actively discouraged personal responsibility. Anyone who resisted or complained about the stupidity of what they were asked to do (and many did) was marked out as a 'trouble-maker' and usually persecuted (loss of job, failure to get promoted, etc.). In these circumstances, it took a very brave person to buck the system (see Chapter 4). The economic and social consequences were terrible.

Under Leonid Brezhnev's leadership (1964–82) none of the above problems were ever publicly acknowledged. The media, heavily controlled by the CPSU, painted a rosy picture of Soviet life for the most part and any statistics which might have suggested otherwise were simply kept secret or not collected in the first place.

After 1985, the policy of *glasnost* (openness) not only allowed these problems to be revealed but increasingly enabled people in all walks of life to discuss their causes. Most people, accustomed to assuming that the problems they were experiencing were mostly local in origin since they had very little real news about life elsewhere, were shocked to discover just how appalling the situation was across the country, and just how backward the Soviet Union was in comparison to the West. It did not take long for a great many people to come to the conclusion that the primary cause of all these problems was 'the system' itself, or 'the administrative command system' as it became known.

The system

The Soviet system was a profoundly contradictory and paradoxical one. It combined opposing principles in a fragile balance which was just about sustainable as long as no one tried to interfere with it in any way. Lenin and Stalin created this system. Khrushchev tried to reform it, quite successfully insofar as he managed to eliminate Stalinist mass terror as an instrument of rule, but he was removed from office in 1964 before he could do it any lasting damage. Brezhnev tinkered with the system but basically allowed it to drift. Chernenko did likewise. Andropov began to speak about the need for change but it was Gorbachev who finally acknowledged the need for root-and-branch reform.

However, Gorbachev, a good party man himself, had no way of knowing that serious reform in any one of the elements described below was bound to create chaos in all the rest. Or, put another way, he had no way of knowing that the Soviet system was balanced like a house of cards – any movement in one card risked the collapse of the whole structure.

The system's contradictions were to be found in the opposition between theory and practice, between democracy and control.

The theory

Democracy

The Communist Party came to power dedicated to the creation of a revolutionary democracy. Lenin, in his most idealistic moments, argued that every educated person, every 'educated cook' as he put it, was capable of becoming directly involved in the running of society's affairs. In his vision of revolutionary democracy the state, with its bureaucracies, its paramilitary arms (the police, the army), its ministries, and its government 'bosses' would wither and eventually disappear. It would be replaced by direct democracy and the immediate and personal involvement of ordinary people in the management of their own affairs. This utopian vision was not to be realised, but the CPSU never ceased to speak the language of democracy or to boast about the democratic nature of the system it had created. The original commitment, and the constant lip-service that was subsequently paid to it, gave rise to institutions which *could* have been democratic had they been able to function properly from the start (although perhaps they would not have been very efficient).

1   *A federal system* of great complexity (see Chapter 9) in which almost every group (with some exceptions) had its own territory and its own local government. In which each Union Republic (the largest federal unit) had its own constitution; its own elected representatives at the level of the Union (i.e. federal) government in Moscow; and the right to secede from the federation if it so chose.

2   *A federal constitution* (rewritten several times) which, among other things, contained commitments to the classic democratic rights and liberties of the individual: freedom of speech, belief, and so on and also enshrined equal rights for women.

3   *A complex and extensive system of law* and a comprehensive legal system to adjudicate it. This had democratic input at the lowest levels through the people's militia and the people's courts.

4   *A democratic structure of government* which was based on the principle that the whole population should be able to participate in the management of society's affairs. It was therefore rather complex.

The soviets of people's deputies

The soviets functioned at all levels of the system as both popularly elected legislative assemblies and as organs of government. Legally speaking, each soviet was master within its own territory 'making all the necessary decisions to run local affairs, subject to confirmation by the next higher soviet' (Hill, 1985, p. 102), according to the principle of democratic centralism (see below).

All soviets were directly elected. The people's deputies (the elected representatives) were subject to recall. That is to say, their electorate could demand their removal at any point in their term of office if their performance was not up to par.

All soviets also combined legislative and executive functions to a certain degree. Lenin and the Bolsheviks had been suspicious of the separation of legislative and executive power (as in the United States for example) because they argued that a separate executive would always be able to cut itself loose from legislative control and get the upper hand. Lenin's view was that decisions and laws were best implemented by those who made them (i.e. the fusion of powers). Only in that way could one guarantee that the popular will would be done. All soviets therefore had executive com-mittees (rather like mini-'cabinets') of their own, (called the 'Presidium' at the top levels), which were responsible for the day-to-day management of the soviet's affairs and for overseeing the activities of the government proper (see below).

1   *The USSR Supreme Soviet* (i.e. the federal Supreme Soviet) was the 'highest body of state authority' and the supreme legisla-tive body in the land. It had two chambers: the Soviet of the Union, directly elected by the Soviet population as a whole; and the Soviet of Nationalities, elected proportionately by the USSR's many nations (USSR: Union of Soviet Socialist Republics). It was responsible, in principle at least, for:

(a)   making all laws in areas of federal jurisdiction;
(b)   appointing the ministers of the government (the USSR Council of Ministers), and overseeing the activities of the government;
(c)   ratifying the decisions of the republican Supreme Soviets below it.

However, because it only met in full session twice a year (normally in June and December) for a few days at a time, the day-to-day functions of governing the country were carried out by its executive committee: the USSR Supreme Soviet Presidium which met regularly throughout the year and had wide-ranging powers to act in the Supreme Soviet's name (subject to ratification at the next full session of the Supreme Soviet). These included appointing and dismissing government ministers; declaring states of emergency; ratifying treaties. Inevitably, the Presidium rapidly became the more powerful body of the two because the full Supreme Soviet met too infrequently to monitor current affairs effectively (Hill, 1985, p. 102ff.).

2   *Republican Supreme Soviets.* Each of the USSR's fifteen Union-republics had its own Supreme Soviet, elected by the population of the republic. So did each of the USSR's twenty

autonomous republics. These, in turn, had their own Presidium. The Union-republican Supreme Soviets were subordinate to the USSR Supreme Soviet in all matters of federal jurisdiction and were obliged to implement all the laws of the USSR. The Supreme Soviets in the autonomous republics were similarly subordinate to the Supreme Soviets of the Union-republic in which they were located. In everything else, however, all republican Supreme Soviets were supposed to have independent authority on their territory. This was supposed to include appointing the members, and monitoring the activities, of the republican government (Council of Ministers) as well as ratifying the decisions of the regional, city and district soviets below them. In most respects, the republican Supreme Soviets functioned exactly like the USSR Supreme Soviet.

3 *Local soviets*, at regional, city and district level were directly elected by the regional, city and district populations respectively. They had roughly the same internal structure as the soviets above them: full sessions of elected deputies which met relatively infrequently; and executive committees (the *ispolkoms*) which were responsible for day-to-day affairs in between. Local soviets were obliged to implement all the legislative decisions that were made by the soviets above them, although they were supposed to have autonomy in their area. The functions of local soviets were largely concerned with the provision of local services (education, health, municipal lightings, etc.), although they were also supposed to have considerable powers to monitor and control the activities of local industry and agriculture. In practice, though, their room for manoeuvre was almost non-existent.

The hierarchy of the soviets was therefore like a pyramid, with the USSR Supreme Soviet at the pinnacle, and the numerous districts soviets forming its base. Power (what there was of it, see below) effectively flowed from the top down.

The Councils of Ministers and the executive
The Councils of Ministers were the highest administrative and executive bodies of state authority. They existed at the all-union, Union-republican and autonomous republic levels. They were

largely responsible for managing the day-to-day operation of the economy and they were, in principle, appointed by, and accountable to, the appropriate Supreme Soviet.

1   *The USSR Council of Ministers* had executive responsibility for the administration and management of the Soviet economy and social affairs. Its members were the ministerial heads of the big all-union ministries which operated across Soviet territory; or the heads of the various State Committees (see below). In principle, ministers were supposed to be appointed by the USSR Supreme Soviet and they were supposed to account regularly to USSR Supreme Soviet deputies for their activities.

2   *The republican Councils of Ministers* were supposed to have independent executive authority on their territory to run the economy of their Union or autonomous republic. In addition to the big all-union ministries there were also numerous republican ministries which either functioned jointly with the all-union ministries or were subject, in principle, to purely republican jurisdiction. The last two were nominally the responsibility of republican Councils of Ministers. The republican Councils of Ministers could also rescind the decisions of, or give instructions to, the executive committees of the soviets at regional level and below, because at these levels the soviets, in addition to their legislative functions, were also supposed to have considerable responsibility for the local economy. However, the republican Councils of Ministers were themselves subject:

(a)   To the decisions of the Council of Ministers above them, which they had to obey following the principle of democratic centralism (see below).
(b)   To Soviet law and the republican law laid down by the relevant Supreme Soviet.

The executive arm of the state was therefore also shaped a bit like a pyramid, with the USSR Council of Ministers at the pinnacle overseeing a vast network of all-union ministries that penetrated all parts of the USSR; with the Union-republican Councils of Ministers below it and largely subordinate to it; below them the

Councils of Ministers of the autonomous republics; and below them the executive committees of all the local soviets. Again, power flowed from the top down.

This system could be horribly confusing even for the people trying to operate within it, but its essential principle was that it was supposed to guarantee the democratic participation of the whole population in the management of society's affairs.

It certainly did involve a great deal of participation of a sort. For example, at any one time there were over two million deputies involved in the activities of the soviets. There was something like a 50 per cent turnover rate at each election which means that in any period of ten years about five million people would have experienced deputy service – a remarkably high proportion of the population (Hill, 1985, p. 99). However, this participation was often rather formal. Very few deputies could actually exert any influence because the whole democratic process was grotesquely and thoroughly undermined by the system of planning and, above all, by the central role of the CPSU.

The practice

Planning
Planning was introduced by Stalin in the late 1920s as the fastest means to achieve industrial development and economic growth. It was a very extreme form of planning. Everything was controlled and directed by the USSR State Planning Committee (*Gosplan*) in Moscow: finance and budgets, the sort, quantity and quality of goods, the allocation and distribution of resources and so on. And all production was organised through huge hierarchical state ministries whose ministers sat on the USSR Council of Ministers and took their orders from *Gosplan* and the party (see below). It has been called 'command planning' because the planning instructions issued by *Gosplan* and by the ministries below it to the factories and farms under their control had to be obeyed. The plans were law and to disobey them was an offence.

This system inevitably undermined the democratic institutions.

1   The autonomy of the Union Republics (and smaller federal

units) was severely constrained by the fact that their budgets were largely dictated to them by the all-union *Gosplan* and by the fact that most of the industrial production that took place on their territory, often up to 90 percent of it, was controlled by ministries with their administrative headquarters in Moscow.

2   The same applied to the soviets. They had little control over the money they received or even what they could spend it on. The ability of republican and local soviets to meet the needs of their local populations was therefore practically non-existent unless those needs fell within 'the plan'. Instead of representing the needs and interests of their electors, they largely became agents of central government, responsible for the unquestioning fulfilment of central government policy in their area.

3   The executive arm of the state became massively enlarged because running the economy effectively became a central function of government.

The state therefore acquired all sorts of bodies which simply do not exist in capitalist systems. For example, in 1984 there were twenty-two state committees which were responsible, among other things, for planning (*Gosplan*), setting wage levels across the country, fixing prices for millions of different commodities, organising and co-ordinating supply systems, encouraging technological development in industry. All activities which in a market system would be carried out by private firms themselves in response to market movements. The government consisted of fifty-nine federal ministries which controlled every major branch of industry and agriculture and foreign trade, as well as those activities we more usually associate with government – defence, foreign affairs, health. And this figure does not include those ministries with joint federal–republican jurisdiction, and those with republican jurisdiction only, some eight hundred ministries in all! However, these effectively had very little autonomy from Moscow.

As David Lane has remarked, 'The student has to make a mental leap to conceptualize the scope of . . . Soviet government' and to grasp the magnitude of the size of the Soviet bureaucracy

(Lane, p. 35). Reliable figures are difficult to come by, but by the mid-1980s the administrative bureaucracy taken as a whole employed about 14 million people, or some 12 percent of the workforce. And an additional 11 million people were employed in administrative jobs in factories and farms (Sakwa, 1990, pp. 296–7). Gorbachev was a frequent critic of what he called this 'bloated administrative apparatus' which on his reckoning (in 1989) was costing some 40 billion roubles a year to maintain (or approximately 420 million dollars at 1989 exchange rates).

The soviets, with their frequent turnover of personnel and their limited powers, had no hope at all of monitoring the huge monopolistic empires which the ministries had become. They had no control over the state committees, no control over budgets, no control over the planning process.

The law and the legal system became equally toothless. The directives of 'the plan' frequently contravened other laws and regulations, but because 'the plan' was paramount these other laws were ignored. And the ministries simply disregarded any laws which got in the way of their activities (for example, environmental pollution controls of which the old USSR had an enormous amount, all equally worthless in practice).

In fact, by the 1970s no one was able to control this vast bureaucratic empire, not even the party. As Gorbachev himself complained in mid-1986: 'For *Gosplan* there exist no authorities, no General Secretaries, no Central Committees. They do what they want'. (Sakwa, 1990, pp. 363–4).

The CPSU

The Communist Party's role and place in society was always ambiguous. According to the 1977 constitution it was supposed to 'lead and guide society' towards its communist future. But it was never clear even to the party's own politicians exactly what that was supposed to mean. Party leaders, from Khrushchev on, frequently criticised the party for becoming too involved in the activities of state institutions. However, they never successfully managed to do anything about it because they always insisted that only the party knew what was in the best interests of society. Party officials consistently had a very paternalistic attitude towards society: 'the party knew best', what was good for 'its people'. This attitude inevitably gave rise to a constant temptation to interfere in the activities of all non-party institutions. Such interference, from the earliest days, turned into a central institutional feature of the Soviet system. In practice, therefore, the party's 'leading and guiding role' came to mean party rule and party domination over society.

Many specialists have tried to make a distinction between 'ruling' and 'governing'. They have argued that the CPSU 'ruled' but the state 'governed' society (see e.g. Hill and Frank). However, this distinction is dubious given the extent to which the party penetrated state institutions. Governing and ruling effectively came to mean the same thing and it therefore makes more sense to talk about a unified 'party-state'.

Nevertheless, it is very important to note that the party and the state institutions (the hierarchy of the soviets, the Councils of Ministers and the ministries) retained their own organisational identities and existed as separate entities. The party controlled state institutions by ensuring that its members dominated all the key positions (see below). But party and state structures did not all become part of the same huge organisation. It is vital to bear this in mind because once the party lost its ability to control the key positions in society as a result of Gorbachev's reforms (see Part II), it also lost its control over these state institutions which were therefore able to emerge as independent centres of power. This was a crucial factor in the disintegration of the system.

How did the party undermine the democratic processes of which it claimed to be so proud? It had a number of mechanisms at its disposal (see Hill and Frank for a useful discussion):

1   *Democratic centralism*, a contradiction in terms if ever there was one, was the key organisational mechanism that underpinned the functioning of all institutions and that held the Soviet state together. It was supposed to enable the combination of democratic discussion with efficient decision-making. In practice, however, only one of its rules was ever taken seriously. This rule stated that the 'decisions of higher bodies are always binding on lower

bodies'. This meant that everyone had to do what they were told by their superiors (on pain of punishment) regardless of what their electors wanted or what they themselves thought it most advisable to do. This principle on its own removed all accountability, responsibility and democracy from the system.

2 *The nomenklatura*. A personnel recruitment and appointment system through which the party controlled access to all the key leadership positions in the party, the state and society (including the legal system) regardless of whether these positions were elective or not. Only those people who were loyal to the party (although not necessarily party members), and who the party itself considered to be capable could fill these designated posts and get access to the privileges that went with them (see Chapter 3). The existence of the *nomenklatura* was never publicly discussed until well after 1985. No figures were ever published but it is estimated that it covered several million posts throughout society. It also became an extremely important social institution (see Chapter 3).

This mechanism effectively undermined:

(a) all electoral processes – party and soviet. Elections did not serve as an instrument of popular sanction, as they do (however imperfectly) in democratic countries. They merely provided a veneer of popular approval to what were in practice party appointments.

(b) all relations of accountability. For example, every single member of the federal and republican Councils of Ministers was appointed through the *nomenklatura*, not by the relevant Supreme Soviet, as was supposed to happen according to the constitution. Ministers therefore owed their allegiance and were accountable only to the party. The legislative organs of the state had no power to call them to account for their actions.

(c) the implementation of the law. Most judges were party appointees and usually did what the party told them. The phenomenon became known as 'telephone law', because a judge would get on to his or her party committee for 'advice' about a case, and the party secretary would indicate his or her (usually his) preferred outcome.

3   *Parallelism and podmena*. The party functioned as the real
centre of government. Its internal organisation paralleled the
internal structures of the soviets and duplicated the managerial
activities of the ministries at all levels. The party's 'government'
departments effectively supplanted and undermined those of the
state (this is the meaning of *podmena*). The party's top internal
policy-making body, the Politburo, was also the top policy-making
body for the country as a whole. Its decisions took precedence
over, and were effectively 'law' for, all party and state institutions.
And its leader, the General Secretary, was the supreme leader of
the country. Policies and decisions (even quite small ones) were
not made by the people, or by their elected representatives in the
soviets, but by the party's officials.

4   *Interlocking membership*. At the height of its power the CPSU
had a total of just over 19 million members, some 10 percent of the
adult population. A small proportion worked within the party
itself. The vast majority were spread throughout society where
they earned their living as state employees. (*Note*: almost all
property was owned by the state. Consequently, almost everyone
was an employee of the state, see Chapter 3). Most people joined
the party not because they believed in its programme and goals but
because it was the best way of making a career. As a consequence:

(a)   The ordinary membership of the soviets, at all except the very
      lowest levels, was dominated by party members who
      organised themselves into 'factions' within these nominally
      elective state bodies in order to co-ordinate their activities.
      For example in 1984, 71.4 percent of the deputies elected to
      the federal Supreme Soviet were party members.

(b)   Almost all the party's full-time officials, the *apparatchiki*, also
      had elective positions as deputies within the soviets. For
      example, all the members of the Politburo were also 'elected'
      deputies of the federal Supreme Soviet. And the party's
      General Secretary generally also occupied the post of Presi-
      dent (formally speaking, the Chair of the Supreme Soviet).

(c)   Many key state officials were also members of party com-
      mittees. For example, one or two of the most important state

ministers were also members of the party Politburo (this
varied since the Politburo was in practice self-selective). And
many ministers had seats on the party's Central Committee.

Effectively, therefore, although the party and the state as institutions could be formally identified as having separate structures,
they were welded together into one entity through the overlapping
of their personnel.

5   The CPSU was *above the law*. Party members caught in illegal
acts were not subject to the civil law but only to party discipline. At
the extreme this might mean expulsion from the party, in which
case the individual could then be prosecuted. Usually, however, it
meant no more than a reprimand or demotion, in which case the
individual remained beyond the law. The party's consequent
contempt for the civil law may well be imagined.

Conclusion: A balance of paradoxes

1   *The system was supposed to be planned but it became increasingly
unplanned and chaotic* particularly at the most important level, the
level of production in factories and farms.

In order for the system to work, the policy makers in the
Politburo, the central planners in *Gosplan* and the ministries, and
those in the bureaucratic ranks below them, had to know exactly
what was going on and what was needed at all times and in all
places. They were therefore dependent on everyone below them
for the provision of accurate information. These were impossible
conditions to meet.

(a)   Co-ordinating the activities of 25 million administrators and
planning the production and distribution of anywhere around
20 million products could not be done even with the best
computers and the best will in the world.
(b)   Everyone in the system except those at the top had a vested
interest in supplying false or distorted information about
their needs and activities because they wanted easy plan
targets or more resources, or because they had failed to meet

their previous plan targets, etc. But most importantly because no one in the system wanted to transmit bad news to their superiors. Bad news meant that the system was not working properly and this was not a message that the party leaders wanted to hear or to convey to the rest of the world. Consequently, people, including party members, lied to their superiors (who in turn misinformed their superiors and so on up the system) about what was really happening on the ground. The result was a vicious circle of misinformation and an arbitrary and grotesquely inefficient economic system. The more out of touch the central authorities became the more people below them had to lie to protect themselves and so on.

Under Stalin sheer physical terror (death or exile might well be the reward for failure) and the simplicity of the economic system kept people in line and enabled the system to work. Once the terror was lifted by Khrushchev however, and the system became more complex, it began to spin out of control. It only worked as long as it did because, first of all, everyone developed their own informal mutual protection and supply networks. Second, the 'planning' process actually turned into a bargaining process: *Gosplan* bargained with the ministries about what they could produce and the ministries bargained with the factories, farms, shops, distribution networks, etc. under their control. Third, the basic rule was 'do what you always have done only a bit more of it'. Keep producing the same old products in slightly greater quantities to show improvement (even if these goods are not wanted) and things are much less likely to go wrong. This became known as the 'ratchet principle': each year just a little bit more was produced in order to 'demonstrate' progress.

Radical innovation and change was poison to this system because it had no way of coping with them. A new product could be introduced here, a more modern production method there, but the whole process of introducing new techniques and working practices was extraordinarily bureaucratic, cumbersome and slow. Innovation along Japanese or US lines was utterly unthinkable.

Note: The exception was the military economy which was vastly more efficient because missiles have to work and the arms race necessitated rapid innovation. However, in order to achieve this the military economy received the lion's share of the country's best resources and its most highly skilled personnel. Its only return to the civilian economy, which was immensely drained as a result, was that many defence factories also produced those consumer goods – for example, televisions, fridges, washing machines – which need to be made reasonably well in order to work at all.

2 *The CPSU was all-powerful but became increasingly powerless* to control the system, and for much the same reasons.

In order to function the party required honesty, diligence, commitment and obedience to orders on the part of its members. These qualities were constantly promoted by the party's leaders as the qualities of the 'good communist', but they were precisely the qualities that party members could not afford to exhibit if they wanted to survive.

Party members were not just party members. They were also low-level managers, factory workers, etc., and top state officials who got their positions through the *nomenklatura*. They were all equally subject to the imperatives of 'the plan' and therefore under the same pressures as their non-party colleagues in addition to the pressures imposed on them by the obligations of party membership. The right of the party to rule in the eyes of the population depended very greatly on its ability to deliver the goods. It had come to power promising to improve the economic lot of the ordinary people. The performance of party members and party officials was consequently judged to a great extent on the economic performance of the enterprises in their area. They were therefore obliged to engage in the same practices as everyone else. Members of the *nomenklatura*, in particular, had even more of a vested interest than most in making it *look* as though the system was working. They risked losing their sought-after positions and their privileges if they did not.

The result was that the party's own internal organisation began to undergo the same processes of disintegration that the economic system was suffering from. The perpetual shortages, the constant and all-pervasive disinformation turned all political and economic processes into a subterranean struggle for survival and control over dwindling resources – subterranean because these processes seethed and bubbled away beneath the glacier of censorship and coercive control.

The party's leaders could discipline and punish individuals, but they could not change these behaviour patterns without fundamentally changing the ways in which the whole system worked.

However, although the party could not actually control the system, the party was nevertheless vital to its maintenance because party and *nomenklatura* officials, and less-exalted party members down the line, used their power, their contacts, their interpersonal relations and their control of the law to keep the system working. They were the crisis managers. They also informally provided the horizontal lines of communication between the party, the soviet and the huge ministerial hierarchies which the practice of democratic centralism had eliminated. Put another way, the mechanisms of democratic centralism, interlocking membership, the *nomenklatura*, increasingly became the only ties which kept the various parts of the system from flying apart. They continued to be coercive. But instead of providing the party with instruments for directing society, they became the only means of preventing its disintegration.

As Gorbachev was to discover the party was the linchpin of the system. To undermine it, which is what began to happen after 1987, was to undermine the system as a whole.

3 *The party prided itself on its revolutionary credentials yet revolution was the very thing it could not allow* because this threatened the party's political dominance.

The CPSU came to power as a party which was committed to permanent revolutionary endeavour. In principle the revolutionary process would only end once communism was achieved – one thing which the CPSU never claimed to have done. It was this goal which was supposed to drive the whole system forward. Even under Stalin's leadership the party constantly exhorted people to be creative, to take the initiative, to be actively involved in the management of society's affairs, to engage in revolutionary 'daring-do'. It constantly exhorted them to be constructively critical of their peers and superiors, and self-critical of their own actions. And yet it prevented these exhortations from having any great effect by maintaining a system of almost glacial political control: through censorship of the media and society's intellectual life; through control of the processes of socialisation (education, youth organisations, etc.). And persecuting anyone brave enough to try and take it at its word. This was because any *real* change, and certainly any genuinely revolutionary change, would have threatened (and in the end did destroy) the power of the party. The party therefore had a vested interest in preventing meaningful change. This was something that Gorbachev never understood.

The CPSU did not stifle all debate and criticism. Its leaders increasingly needed sources of intelligent and reasonably accurate information as the system grew more complex. During the 1960s and 1970s specialists (economists, foreign policy experts and so on) were increasingly invited into the policy-making process by the top party leadership and were allowed to engage in limited public debate about the system's problems. But debate and criticism had to remain within the limits set by the party leadership. Subjects that it did not want discussed could not be discussed and no one was allowed to criticise party policy – the 'party line' – or the nature of the system as a whole. Anyone who tried to was subject to political or economic harassment: driven into emigration abroad, deprived of their job, incarcerated in mental hospitals, labour camps or prison. This deprived the system of intelligent criticism without which any society will atrophy.

The result was that an enormous gulf developed between what the party *said* it wanted to achieve, and what was actually achieved. The Soviet world became a world of opposites. The party of revolution became in practice the party of stagnation and stasis. Soviet planning became the antithesis of planning, a sort of chaotic and coercive 'anti-planning'. Soviet democracy became the antithesis of democracy: a great deal of state-sponsored activity but very little voluntary participation.

However, because the party constantly paid lip-service to its revolutionary and democratic commitments this gulf between words and deeds (which party politicians were constantly saying they had to do something about) remained perpetually visible. The existence of potentially democratic institutions like the soviets, like federalism, and the idea of planning gave people a measure of just how far the party was failing to live up to its own words. People were constantly reminded of what they did not have.

Federalism enshrined the idea that national groups of all sorts and all sizes were entitled to autonomy over their own affairs.

The soviets enshrined the idea that people should participate in the decisions that affected their lives.

The many peoples of the Soviet Union who had never experienced democracy and had no history of democracy, learned the language of democracy from the party itself.

Nor was the party itself immune to these paradoxes. In practising coercion and preaching democracy and revolutionary creativity it was able to contain within its ranks both conservatives like Brezhnev and reformists like Gorbachev. These divisions remained hidden as long as nobody rocked the boat. But they became clearly visible during the years of *perestroika*.

Some questions

Could the Soviet 'administrative-command' system have survived if Gorbachev had not tried to interfere with it? Some people thought so, notably the opponents of *perestroika* within the Soviet Union. But it is doubtful that it could have survived long. The system teetered on a knife-edge because it rested on institutionalised hypocrisy and the habit of fear. No modern industrialised society can function effectively on this basis for any length of time.

Could it have worked better if it had been more democratic? Again one suspects that the answer is no. Soviet central planning was based on the idea that only the planners at the centre of the system knew what was in everyone's best interests. They were therefore never particularly interested in knowing what ordinary people wanted or thought. This is not a good basis on which to try and build a democratic system of any sort.

Further Reading

Friedgut, Theodore,*Political Participation in the USSR*, Princeton University Press, 1979

Goldman, Marshall, *USSR in Crisis: the Failure of an Economic System*, Norton, 1983

Hill, Ronald, *Soviet Union: Politics, Economics, Society*, Frances Pinter, 1985

Hill, Ronald, and Frank, Peter, *The Soviet Communist Party*, Allen & Unwin, 1986 3rd edn

Hough, Jerry and Fainsod, Merle, *How the Soviet Union is Governed*, Harvard University Press, 1979

Jacobs, Everett, *Soviet Local Politics and Government*, Allen & Unwin, 1983

Lampert, Nicholas, *Whistleblowing in the Soviet Union: Complaints and Abuses under State Socialism*, Macmillan, 1985

Lane, David,*Soviet Society under Perestroika*, Unwin Hyman, 1990

McAuley, Mary, *Politics and the Soviet Union*, Penguin, 1977

Sakwa, Richard, *Gorbachev and his Reforms, 1985-1990*, Philip Allan, 1990

Sakwa, Richard, *Soviet Politics: an Introduction*, Routledge, 1989

Shmelev, Nikolai, and Popov, Vladimir, *The Turning Point*, I. B. Tauris, 1990

Taubman, William, *Governing Soviet Cities: Bureaucratic Politics and Urban Development in the USSR*, Praeger, 1973

Yeltsin, Boris, *Against the Grain: an Autobiography*, Jonathan Cape, 1990

3

Social context of Soviet Politics

Most books on politics and most politics courses make some reference to the social environment in which the political system operates. The reasons are simple. In democratic countries the political process is very much about the interplay of interests between social groups: the conflicts between them for resources, status, power. In this context governments are often seen as trying to arbitrate and balance the different interests which exist in society. Democratically elected governments do not make policy in a vacuum but in response to the cross-cutting demands that different interest groups make upon them. Consequently, it is important for the student to know something about what those interests are and how they relate to the political process.

This was never so obviously the case in the study of Soviet politics.

As we suggested in Chapter 2, Communist Party rule was based on the idea that only the decision-makers at the centre knew what was in the best interests of society. Consequently, the system was not really designed to take popular interests into account.

(a) Prior to 1985 the Communist Party's leaders insisted that there were no conflicts of interest in Soviet society. The whole population was unified around the 'common' (i.e. the party's) goal of 'building socialism'. Consequently, there were no legitimate channels through which interests counter to the 'party line' could be expressed. Nor were there any channels though which the conflicts of interest which existed between different social groups could be resolved. All such interests were repressed.

(b) The institutions of popular representation, the soviets, had ceased to play any meaningful role as channels for the expression of social interests and needs.

(c) The party-state leadership was not immune to the pressures of different interests, but only the most powerful institutional interests, for example, the big industrial ministries, the armed forces, had access to the decision-making process. And the party-state leadership could pick and choose who it listened to. It did not *have* to listen to anyone because it was not subject to the sanction of elections and could impose its will coercively if necessary, even if this coercion was not particularly successful in changing general patterns of behaviour.

Consequently, the party-state leadership made policy in something of a vacuum. It only had very limited knowledge of the real condition of society, and was almost entirely ignorant of the enormous conflicts of interest which were latent within it. The potential for ethnic conflict was the best example of this.

This general situation did not change a great deal in the years after 1985.

Gorbachev's administration acknowledged that Soviet society contained many economic, political and social interests which were often in conflict with each other and which the country's leaders had to pay attention to. However, Gorbachev himself remained convinced, even when the system began to disintegrate in 1989–90, that the party could continue to manage these interests in what *it* considered to be the best interests of society as a whole. Gorbachev assumed that the CPSU could become a genuinely popular party which would rule by popular consent rather than coercion. However, he continued to insist until 1990 that it alone would rule and that it alone could give an adequate voice to all the different interest groups which had emerged onto the political arena. Consequently, although people were allowed to speak out there was still no guarantee that their interests would be translated into policy and they were still expected to keep to the limits set by the party. As we will see, one of the reasons for the failure of *perestroika* was the woeful ignorance that Gorbachev displayed about how the Soviet system *actually* worked. In this respect he was like every other Soviet leader before him.

The policies of *glasnost* and democratisation opened the way for the emergence of genuine political pluralism. They led to the legalisation of independent interest-group activity and to the introduction of the first semi-competitive, and therefore the first reasonably genuine, elections. These developments greatly undermined the party's hold on society. This, in turn, undermined the old political system but did not lead to the creation of a new one. The result instead was political and social fragmentation. Thousands of groups sprang to life voicing a thousand-and-one demands which no authority, central or local, was equipped to deal with.

The new governments which have been trying to cope with the consequences of fragmentation and disintegration since August 1991 have not always been particularly sensitive to popular interests. In some of the former Soviet republics, Georgia for instance, a new nationalist dictatorship replaced the old party dictatorship. In others, for example Russia, the need to stave off complete economic collapse has necessitated hard decisions.

These are matters that we shall be returning to in later chapters.

The lack of correspondence between politics and society in the Soviet Union pre- and post-1985 does not mean that the social context of politics is of no relevance. The old Soviet system created a particular structure of interests which became visible during the years in which the battle for *perestroika* was fought out. *Perestroika* challenged powerful vested interests in the system, as became evident in the failed coup of August 1991. It is therefore useful to know something about who was for, and who was against, reform between 1985 and 1990. It is also useful to try to gauge who has most and who has least to gain from the system building and the misguided dash to the market that has been going on since 1991. Governments may, or may not, govern in the interests of their people when there is a crisis on. But gauging the extent of popular support or hostility to their policies is an indicator of how far they are likely to succeed in what they are trying to achieve.

Social diversity

Soviet society on the eve of *perestroika* was not the homogeneous and unified society that the most dogmatic of the party's politicians liked to think it was.

Ethnic diversity

The vast continent that was the Soviet Union has one of the most diverse and heterogeneous populations in the world. It has 140 different ethnic identities. Some of these have enormous populations. For example, the Russians with 145.07 million people in 1989 constitutes the largest group at 50.78 percent of the total population on ex-Soviet territory. Others are tiny tribal groups of no more than a few hundred people. The old Soviet Union was not called 'the last of the great empires' for nothing. Most of these peoples had nothing in common with each other. Several of them had experienced independent statehood at some point in their history, for example, Georgia, the Baltic republics (now independent sovereign states once more). And they were ruled from the centre in Moscow in what can only be described as a colonial, or imperialist, fashion. This applied as much, if not more, to the huge Russian nation as it did to the other smaller nations. We will be returning to this important issue in Chapter 9. Here it is important to note:

The marked regional differences in the standard and quality of life, and the level of development, between republics and within republics between urban and rural areas.

1 For example, the central Asian republics (e.g. Tadjikistan, Kirgiziya now Kyrgyzstan, Uzbekistan) are still predominantly rural, agricultural and industrially under-developed by comparison with the central European republics like Russia and the old Baltic republics of Lithuania, Latvia, Estonia. This has caused a great deal of resentment, particularly against the Russian republic, which dominates the continent and which contains most of its natural resources. This was an important factor in the struggle for power that took place between the republics after August 1991 when central power collapsed.

2   Rural areas, and particularly very remote villages, have suffered from a relative lack of investment in social amenities, cultural and educational facilities compared to the towns and cities. The rural quality of life, on the whole, is extremely poor. In Tadjikistan, for example, many country people still live in clay huts without running water, electricity, sewage facilities, adequate health provision or adequate roads. This also caused a great deal of resentment, both against the central government in Moscow and against the local urban elites.

These social and economic differences were repressed during the first flush of post-independence euphoria when the various national groups were united in their hostility to Moscow and their demands for sovereignty. However, the distribution of resources between rich and poor and between the different ethnic minorities within the new independent states will unavoidably become a crucial issue as economic realities begin to bite.

Stratification
Seventy years of rapid industrialisation created a differentiated and stratified society that was not so very different in its general outline from that of the capitalist industrial societies at the turn of the century. In 1917 Russia was an overwhelmingly peasant society. By 1985 the Soviet Union had an educated and relatively stable industrial labour force which was becoming increasingly differentiated according to social background, status and reward.

This development was achieved at enormous cost in human suffering particularly during the Stalinist period of accelerated industrialisation. For example, it is estimated that approximately 7 million peasants died, and another 13 million were deported to labour camps or Siberia, as a result of Stalin's policy of collectivisation which effectively eliminated private farming from the system. The terror and upheavals of the Stalinist period were burned into the psyche of the Soviet population and they continued to have lingering effects into the 1990s (see Chapter 4). However, the processes of modernisation were not completed by the time the USSR collapsed. Urbanisation was still underway and many peasant communities still lived extremely traditional ways of life which were largely untouched by the official culture of the Communist Party.

Class

The nature of the class system in the Soviet Union was always a matter of considerable disagreement. The argument hinged, in particular, on whether there was such a thing as exploitation in the Soviet system.

The CPSU itself argued that there were only two classes in society – the working class and the collective farm peasantry, plus the stratum of the intelligentsia – and that these two classes lived in harmonious relations with each other. It censored any attempts to discuss alternative interpretations. This official position was not accepted outside the Soviet Union.

East European critics of socialism, most famously Milovan Djilas, argued that socialist societies in general had produced a new ruling class which was able to exploit the working population through its control over the centrally planned economy and the distribution of resources.

British and other observers were more inclined to argue that a class structure was only in the process of formation in the Soviet Union because of high (but declining) social mobility and other peculiarities of the Soviet system (see below).

The argument partly depends on how one defines the term 'class'. But the evidence certainly suggests that critics like Djilas were right.

Note: Soviet statistics are notoriously inaccurate and difficult to deal with. Most of the figures below are therefore approximate.

Additionally, for those who would like to know the sterling equivalents for the income figures that follow, the rouble-sterling exchange rate before 1985 was set artificially by the state at 1 rouble to 1 pound. After 1985, however, the value of the rouble fell by leaps and bounds as a result of inflation, so sterling equivalents are very difficult to estimate and actually meant very little in the domestic context. For example, by January 1992 the average wage of 350 roubles per month was worth precisely £1.60 (one pound and sixty pence). In any case, as we will see shortly, official incomes revealed very little about *actual* standards of living.

The upper class   The upper class could certainly be identified with the *nomenklatura*. Its members received higher official salaries than the rest of the population (the maximum for top state salaries was supposed to be 1,200 roubles per month, which compares with an average wage of about 200 roubles per month). They received a whole range of hidden privileges which were not available to the rest of the population. And they were able to exploit their positions in order to get privileged access to the best schools, the best jobs, and so on for their children. Certainly, in the Soviet context, to become a member of the *nomenklatura* was to become a member of the Soviet Union's most rich and powerful class and was a sought after prize. So much so that the term '*nomenklatura*' has now become identified in Russian with 'them', 'the ruling class', 'the privileged bosses', 'the establishment'.

The middle class   The middle class is more fluid and much less easily defined, but could be identified with the growing numbers of educated white-collar workers, the professional groups, and many of the middle-level managers in the vast industrial hier-archies. By 1987 the Soviet economy was employing 34.6 million specialists of one sort or another in a variety of highly skilled and skilled technical, managerial and executive positions (out of a total working population of approximately 130.8 million people), a great many of them in the military economy. Not all of these people would have been included in the middle class as this is conventionally understood, but many of them had considerable political awareness and considerable ambitions to improve their 'market positions'.

The working class   The working class was the largest class in Soviet society, constituting 62.7 percent of the working popu-lation in 1987. It was becoming increasingly differentiated according to skill, education, status and income. The numbers employed in what we would call the old traditional 'smokestack industries' – mining, heavy industry, energy production – were gradually declining relative to those employed in the service sectors. Those in the traditional occupations were also gradually losing out in the income and status stakes to the 'modern' working class occupations in high-tech industries like electronics (mostly poorly developed except in the military economy). Wages varied considerably from more than 300 roubles per month for highly skilled workers and factory or farm managers, to less than 80 roubles per month for unskilled manual labourers. There was also a disparity between workers, whatever their skill, who worked in the civilian economy and those working in the military sector, where pay tended to be better.

The under class   There were considerable and increasing levels of poverty in the system which became greatly exacerbated as a result of *perestroika* and its failures. The groups most at risk were those which are vulnerable in any industrial society: pensioners, single-parent families, people with disabilities, war veterans, unskilled manual labourers. In the late 1980s about half the Soviet population was living in households with an income of 100 roubles a month or less. And according to official figures issued in June 1989 some 40 million people were living below the official poverty line of 75 roubles a month. (The basic minimum pension was only 70 roubles a month). In short, there were enormous levels of poverty in the system, a fact that was not publicly acknowledged until after 1985.

Distinctive aspects of the social structure

State ownership
Virtually all property was owned by the state, i.e. the means of production, land, buildings, machinery. The exceptions were:

1   Personal private property belonging to the individual.
2   The collective farm sector (the *kolkhozy*). The land was owned by the state, but the activities of the collective farms were controlled (in principle, at least) by the collective farmers who owned and ran them as co-operatives. In practice, the activities of collective farms were almost as heavily controlled by 'the plan' as the activities of state farms (whose employees were classified as state workers). However, because of their status as independent farmers, collective farmers were denied

social benefits, like pensions, until the mid-1970s.

3   The private plots. All farmers (collective and state) were
     allowed to own small plots of land where they could engage in
     private farming. This private farming was extremely pro-
     ductive. For example, in 1975 it contributed about 12 percent
     to the marketed output of the agricultural sector. Farmers
     were allowed to sell the produce from their private plots in the
     private (and legitimate) *kolkhoz* markets that existed in most
     towns and cities. They were often the best (and on many
     occasions the only) places where city dwellers could get access
     to fresh fruit, vegetables, good meat and dairy produce. The
     prices were almost always higher than in the state shops –
     where fresh fruit and vegetables, etc., however, were usually
     unobtainable.

The fact that the state owned most property and controlled the
economy through central planning meant that:

1   Virtually all Soviet citizens were employees of the state. They
     were therefore dependent on the 'party-state' for their jobs,
     their income and rewards. No one was allowed to have any
     sources of wealth independent of party-state control (at least
     in principle, see below) which meant, in turn, that no indivi-
     dual had a source of power independent of the party-state.
     Keeping one's income (and privileges if any) depended on
     hanging onto one's job. Not to have a job was an offence
     (called 'parasitism'). Everyone therefore had a vested interest
     in doing what the party-state told them to do, however much
     they might privately disagree with, or however contradictory,
     the orders. This was a powerful instrument of economic,
     political and social control.

2   The state, in the form of the relevant state committee, could
     and did intervene to adjust income differentials across the
     economy according to prevailing party policy. For example,
     Khrushchev wanted to reduce differentials and create a more
     egalitarian society. Gorbachev wanted to achieve the opposite.
     State bodies acted accordingly. This did not mean, however,
     that incomes were fully under state control. There was a great

deal of drift at local levels as a result of the general bargaining process that planning had become by the 1960s and 1970s. For example, factory managers short of labour found their own ways of increasing incomes. In addition, many people could earn unofficial incomes on the black market (see below).

3 The party's policy makers and the state officials responsible for implementing their policies had a certain amount of direct control over social development. Consequently, these officials were able to manipulate the distribution of income and wealth and the distribution of services between different groups within the population, usually to their own advantage. This suggests that they were the equivalent of a 'ruling class' even though they did not have independent sources of wealth and power and no legal means of passing their privileges on to their children (the classic arguments against there being a ruling class in the USSR).

Another paradox

However, the whole question of who got what in the Soviet Union was always a very complex one because it reflected contradictions in the CPSU's policies and goals which it was never able to reconcile.

On the one hand, the CPSU maintained a lingering commitment to *egalitarianism* because it came to power dedicated to improving the economic lot of the ordinary working person and to eliminating all classes and all exploitation. This was an ideological commitment that the party could not easily abandon because it justified the party's right to rule in the eyes of the population. This commitment resulted in:

1 Cradle-to-grave state welfare provision. Although the quality of the services provided was usually poor and there was never enough of them to meet the demands of an ever-growing population, this did sustain the worst off.

2 A policy of full employment, even if this meant people doing jobs that did not need doing, or being over-qualified for the jobs they did do.

3   The periodic manipulation of wage levels to prevent differences in the *official* incomes received by those at the top of the social pyramid and those at the bottom from becoming too great. The difference between top incomes and average incomes was never as great in the USSR as it is in capitalist societies (see e.g. Lane, *Soviet Society*, p. 147).

4   A certain amount of ideological unease towards the idea of material incentives. That is to say, the use of really substantial income differentials or huge money bonuses in order to motivate workers and managers to do their jobs more effectively and efficiently. This was because material incentives appeared to cater too much to personal greed. Consequently, although material incentives were unavoidable (see below), they were never large enough, particularly for professionals (who were very poorly paid compared with skilled workers), to provide anyone with a real incentive to work hard. Instead, party leaders, notably Khrushchev, often promoted the idea of 'moral incentives'. Essentially, this meant persuading people that they should work better not because they would make more money, but because it was good for society and good for the collective and therefore, ultimately, good for themselves. However, moral incentives were never terribly successful except in the very early days when people still believed in the revolutionary goals of the system. And they became less and less effective as the system began to degenerate.

5   A high level of popular support for the general idea of egalitarianism that made large sectors of the population resentful of anyone who earned more or who had access to special privileges.

On the other hand, the CPSU was also historically committed to the goals of *industrialisation and modernisation*. These goals required the introduction of material incentives (i.e. income differentials) in order to encourage labour mobility and labour productivity, particularly in the early stages under Stalin. They also resulted, inevitably, in the development of a complex division of labour. People became socially and economically differentiated in terms of their social status, their rewards and their power according to the job they performed and the amount of knowledge, skill and training it required.

The party therefore found itself having to promote the idea of material incentives and income differentials in order to generate industrial growth. This frequently produced campaigns against the idea of wage egalitarianism, or what was known as *uravnilovka*, or wage levelling, particularly on the part of those party leaders, Stalin, Brezhnev and Gorbachev, who were most concerned with economic growth and who therefore wanted to increase income differentials.

The outcome of these contradictory goals and commitments was a paradoxical incomes policy that tried to combine a residual commitment to egalitarianism with anti-egalitarianism with the result that neither was achieved. By the 1970s, the system lacked adequate material incentives to encourage the high levels of labour productivity that were required to sustain economic growth. This was reflected in the standard Soviet joke: 'They pretend to pay us, we pretend to work.' At the same time, there were just enough differentials, both in terms of incomes but especially in terms of unearned privileges (see below), for it to be quite clear that this was not the egalitarian workers' state that the party claimed to be building. As another Soviet joke ran: 'Full communism has been achieved in the USSR: for the party elite' (see Yeltsin, p. 128).

To complicate matters further, money incomes did not always count for a great deal in conditions of chronic shortage where what mattered was not so much money, or how much one had of it, but access to scarce goods and over-stretched services. Differential access to scarce goods and services, rather than differences in official incomes, therefore became the real source of social inequality. This resulted in the following distinctive characteristics.

Hidden privileges

In order to bind the country's elites to the regime and to circumvent the problem that elite incomes could not officially rise too high in what was supposed to be a socialist state, the CPSU introduced a system of hidden privileges (systematised under Stalin). Members of the *nomenklatura* were systematically provided with secret and exclusive access to networks of special, high-grade services subsidised by the state: good housing, private medical facilities, hotel and holiday facilities, fleets of official cars (in a country where cars are in high demand and in very scarce supply), and special shops where (often imported) foodstuffs, clothing, furniture and so on were provided at low prices that were inaccessible to the rest of the population.

For example, when Boris Yeltsin became a member of the Politburo he and his wife were allotted 'three cooks, three waitresses, a housemaid, a gardener, and a whole team of undergardeners'; and a *dacha* (holiday home), previously occupied by Gorbachev, that had 'marble walls, countless outsize rooms, and its own cinema' (Morrison, p. 48). As Morrison notes, this might not have seemed much by Western standards, but in the context of pervasive and country-wide shortages of most goods 'even modest privileges' acquired 'a high relative value' (Morrison, p. 49).

Not everyone in the *nomenklatura* benefited equally. It was not a homogeneous elite. Privileges were carefully graded according to one's position in the bureaucratic pecking-order. However, the standard of living of members of the *nomenklatura* were substantially better than those of the rest of the population, and the people at the top of the system were seriously wealthy by Soviet standards.

As Morrison points out, this manipulation of shortage became a powerful instrument of political and social control particularly during the Brezhnev period (Morrison, p. 49). Yeltsin described the mechanism in his autobiography: 'The higher one climbs up the professional ladder, the more there are comforts that surround one, and the harder and more painful it is to lose them. One becomes therefore all the more obedient and dependable' (Yeltsin, p. 127). And he subsequently notes: 'The joke is that none of this belongs to those who enjoy these privileges. All these marvellous things – [*dachas*], rations, a stretch of seaside fenced off from everyone else – belong to the system. And just as the system has given them, so it can take them away. It is an idea of pure genius' (Yeltsin, p. 130). Everyone was vulnerable in this system, including the top leader, the party General Secretary himself. It was therefore an extremely effective means of control.

Although the party was banned shortly after the August events of 1991 and with it the *nomenklatura* system of appointments and privileges, the *nomenklatura* as an identifiable social group still exists in all the old Soviet republics, and it is the object of much popular hostility and criticism. Despite the fact that many of its members opposed Gorbachev's reforms because they appeared to threaten *nomenklatura* power and privileges, the *nomenklatura* is actually in the best position to benefit from moves towards privatisation and the market. It is the only group in society with sufficient wealth, knowledge, power and organisation to buy up property and turn this ownership to its own advantage and it has been doing so with great alacrity since the Soviet Union's collapse (see, e.g., Steele).

'Sector' privileges

Special treatment was not quite the exclusive reserve of the *nomenklatura*. The big ministries and individual industries were able to provide their employees (according to rank) with exclusive access to special works canteens, supplies of good quality food which was mostly unavailable in the state shops and their own housing stocks. Workers in high-priority industries (i.e. those with the highest levels of investment, especially in the military sector) could therefore achieve somewhat higher standards of living than workers in low-priority industries, regardless of income. As a consequence, workers very often moved from one factory to another not because they wanted better pay but because they stood a better chance of getting a decent flat. These networks, particularly the food supplies, became crucial lifelines for many people when economic collapse and disintegration became realities in 1990.

The second economy

The second economy, a general name for the USSR's extensive black markets, was another, very substantial, cause of social inequality. Black markets exist in most societies, but they became all-pervasive in the Soviet Union because of the hopeless inefficiency of the official state economy, hence the name second economy. By 1985 it had become very difficult to survive without some involvement in black market activities.

The second economy was a source of inequality because it operated like a market. Anyone with skills to sell, or access to scarce goods could do rather well. For example, according to one survey conducted in the mid-1980s, doctors and dentists earned only 1.21 roubles per hour in their official jobs, but were able to earn 32.96 roubles per hour on the side treating private patients (Lane, *Soviet Society*, p. 150). Even unskilled manual workers could earn a great deal more selling their labour on the black market than in official jobs (from 0.96 roubles per hour official pay to 18.9 roubles per hour for unofficial work). In addition, almost everybody stole from their places of employment, because state property was 'no one's property', for subsequent sale or exchange. Counter staff working in retail food shops could do particularly well because they could siphon-off and hide the best cuts of meat or the best fruit, etc., from deliveries for sub-sequent under-the-counter sale to favoured customers who could, in turn, provide them with desired goods stolen from their own places of work. The result was a generalised system of bartering favours, bribery and string pulling (known in Russian as *blat*) which ensured that most people could get access to goods and services (carpenters, plumbers, car mechanics, etc., also did particularly well) that were otherwise scarcely obtainable officially. By contrast, those with nothing to sell and no access to goods did very badly. This meant that, at one extreme, members of the *nomenklatura* were able to exploit their positions, very often through very corrupt means, to expand their wealth and access to scarce resources. While at the other extreme, the disadvantaged groups – cleaners, street-sweepers, old age pensioners, people with disabilities – were unable to profit and had to rely on their very inadequate state benefits.

The second economy provided a real, if illegal, source of independent wealth (sometimes considerable wealth. The exist-ence of a small group of 'rouble millionaires' was always rumoured). This wealth did not necessarily translate into political power. But it did produce a sort of 'positional power' which

increased the higher up the bureaucratic hierarchy one pro-
gressed.

From about 1989 when Gorbachev's attempts to democratise
society and limit the functions of the CPSU began to have serious
effects on the ability of the official planned economy to function at
all, the black market began to expand enormously. This exacerbated 'market' inequalities. It led to a serious decline in the
quality of life for most people as shortages grew worse and
necessities became more difficult to find. While it greatly
increased the positional power of those with access to scarce
goods and services. People began to make real fortunes. This gave
rise to serious popular dissatisfaction with the course of *perestroika*
and serious worries about the possibility of social unrest which has
remained an ever-present problem.

The pattern of interests

It is not easy to establish the pattern of social interests in the old
Soviet system where information was either secret or inaccurate,
and opinion polling was frowned on. Nor is it easy to establish in
the *perestroika* and post-*perestroika* periods. Although the quality
and quantity of information grew enormously after 1985, and
opinion polling became very popular, the lines of social division
and people's beliefs about the system became more and more
uncertain and fluid as the system itself began to disintegrate.
However, it is possible to say the following.

Although there was a general feeling in Soviet society on the eve
of *perestroika* that the country was ripe for change there was,
inevitably, considerable uncertainty about the direction and scope
of change.

1 *The groups that were most resistant to change* because they got
enormous power and resources from the old system were:

(a) The managerial elite, and to some extent the workers, in the
country's vast military-industrial complex. This absorbed the
lion's share of the country's resources (up to 70 percent of
Soviet national income according to estimates in 1991),

worked reasonably efficiently, and its leaders wanted no more than to streamline and improve the civilian economy. The military–industrial complex has continued to put up enormous resistance to change even after the collapse of the Soviet Union in 1991.

(b) The executive elite in the party, the state planning and control agencies, the ministries, and the agricultural sector who derived their power from the old planning system.

(c) The older generations in the party, the ministries, the KGB, the armed forces (much like the older generations in the population at large) who had invested most of their lives in building up the system and could see no future for themselves if the system changed radically.

These groups wanted only minimal change – a streamlining of the old system to make it more efficient. This, in fact, is all Gorbachev sought to do between 1985 and 1987. They put up increasingly vigorous resistance as *perestroika* became more radical and a wholesale move towards a market economy began to look like a real possibility. It is no coincidence that the leaders of the failed August coup represented this establishment almost exactly – the military-industrial complex, the party, the KGB, the armed forces, the collective farm sector were all represented. The military-industrial complex and the armed forces continued to be an unknown quantity, and potential opponents to change, in the months after August 1991. They were the only institutions to retain their trans-republican organisational structures after the federation collapsed at the end of 1991. They had an awful lot to lose from the destruction of the old system. At the time of writing however it remained to be seen whether they would or could do anything about it.

2   *The following groups had much more to gain* from change:

(a) The national elites in the republics, although bound to the centre through their membership of the party, their membership of the *nomenklatura* and their economic privileges, resented central interference in local affairs and frequently did their best to resist it. They had a great deal to gain from radical reform. Democratisation and decentralisation gave them an opportunity to become rulers in their own right, rather than having to be dependent on, and subject to, central rule from Moscow.

(b) The ever-expanding groups of specialists, professionals, intellectuals, scientists, artists also had a great deal to gain from radical reform. It was these groups, the intelligentsia, that were quietly pushing for reform even before Gorbachev came to power, and that initially provided him with his main base of support.

They wanted greater access to the political process and decision making. Under the old system they lacked the freedom to exchange information, to travel, and constantly had to subordinate professional standards to the political and economic demands of the party.

Many of them were aware of their lower standard of living relative to their counterparts in the west. They could do little about this under the old system because the state controlled a large part of what they could earn. Consequently, these groups advocated the introduction of a market system not just because it might prove to be more economically efficient but because it would also enable them to realise their market 'value'. For example, several of Russia's leading writers are now earning enormous sums in foreign currency publishing in foreign markets. Their standard of living has increased enormously in the post-*perestroika* years (foreign currency, especially dollars, will buy anything in the new Commonwealth of Independent States).

3 *Inevitably, some groups were more uncertain* about change because they had much to lose as well as gain:

(a) The majority of the population benefited from the old system. The state provided it with cradle-to-grave welfarism in the form of free education, health and basic social security. It heavily subsidised the prices of necessities: the cost of rents, utilities (gas, electricity), public transport, and many basic foods were kept artificially low. And it consistently followed a policy of full employment. The standard of living was not high but it was guaranteed. Radical *perestroika* and above all the move to a market system threatened all of this. A market system might have benefits in the long term: independence from suffocating state control; marked improvements in the quantity, quality and range of consumer goods; much greater power for the consumer. But it also threatened people with unemployment, high prices, much wider pay differentials and therefore greater inequality, and all the human costs of economic restructuring.

(b) Factory managers, managerial personnel with direct responsibility for production also benefited in some ways from the old system. Command planning deprived them of a great deal of control but it also absolved them of a great deal of responsibility. They were told what to do and had to make the best of it. Decentralisation and marketisation forced them to take direct responsibility for managerial decisions. They had to learn to work in entirely new ways.

Conclusion

In the event, the rapid disintegration of the Soviet state overtook everyone, whatever their views on reform, and the immediate future does not look bright for the average citizen. New, and much more extreme, forms of inequality are going to emerge as subsidies disappear, prices increase and property is privatised. The fittest will survive and the weakest are very likely to go to the wall. In these circumstances, those who were powerful before, notably the *nomenklatura*, will be in the best position to protect their interests and to become powerful again.

Further reading

Kerblay, Basile, *Modern Soviet Society*, Methuen, 1983

Lane, David, *The End of Social Inequality? Class, Status and Power under State Socialism*, Allen & Unwin, 1982

Lane, David, *Soviet Society under Perestroika*, Unwin Hyman, 1990

Lewin, Moshe, *The Gorbachev Phenomenon: a Historical Interpretation*, Hutchinson Radius, 1988

Matthews, Mervyn, *Class and Society in Soviet Russia*, Penguin, 1972

Matthews, Mervyn, *Poverty in the Soviet Union: the Lifestyles of the Under-privileged in Recent Years*, Cambridge University Press, 1986

Matthews, Mervyn, *Privilege in the Soviet Union: a Study of Elite Lifestyles under Communism*, Allen & Unwin, 1978

Morrison, John, *Boris Yeltsin: from Bolshevik to Democrat*, Penguin, 1991

Nove, Alec, 'Is there a ruling class in the USSR?', *Soviet Studies*, Vol. 27, No. 4 (October 1975), pp. 615-38

Nove, Alec, 'The class nature of the Soviet Union revisited', *Soviet Studies*, Vol. 35, No. 3 (July 1983), pp. 298-312

Sakwa, Richard, *Soviet Politics: an Introduction*, Routledge, 1989, Chapter 11

Simis, Konstantin, *USSR: Secrets of a Corrupt Society*, Dent, 1982

Steele, Johnathan, 'The Lazarus Act of the Nomenklatura', *Guardian*, 30 May 1992, p. 19

Yanowitch, Murray, *The Social Structure of the USSR*, Westview Press, 1987

Yeltsin, Boris, *Against the Grain: an Autobiography*, Jonathan Cape, 1990

Zemtsov, Ilya, *Private Life of the Soviet Elite*, Crane Russak, 1985

Questions

1 To what extent has inequality in the Soviet Union been the result of social engineering by the party-state?

2 Was there a ruling class in the Soviet Union? Does it matter?

3 To what extent would you consider social inequality to be inevitable and desirable?

4

Ideology and political culture

Ideologies are about the ideas that people bring to their understanding of society. They usually combine philosophical propositions, for example, about human nature and the proper relationship between government and the individual, with practical ideas about how things should be done. The term ideology has been used to describe a number of things: the beliefs of individuals and groups, religions, nationalism, the programmes of political parties. But what these usages share in common is the notion that ideologies provide individuals, groups and society as a whole with a framework of general ideas for understanding the world; a set of preconceptions about how the world works and some very general guidelines about how to behave and act.

All societies need to have some sense of collective identity: a broad consensus, however vague it might be, about society's goals and about how society and its institutions should function. This systemic identity (conveyed, for example, by the ideas of 'capitalism' or 'socialism') provides society's governing institutions with some of their authority in that citizens are much more willing to obey them voluntarily if they are mostly all agreed that things like parliament, elections, the legal system and mechanisms of law enforcement, etc., are a 'good'. It also provides people with a general sense of who they are, their place in the system, and what they should be striving for. In the absence of such a general consensus a society is liable to disintegrate into warring factions very quickly.

The study of political culture is broadly concerned with the relationship between a political system and people's beliefs about and attitudes towards it. It therefore includes ideology. Its central premise is that what people think of their political system, and how they react to the demands that the system makes of them, can make a great deal of difference to the ways in which the system actually works, especially when a society is trying to reform itself. Consequently, although it is often difficult to find out what people's real beliefs and attitudes are it is nevertheless important to know something about them. The modern obsession with opinion polling is a good indication of this.

Soviet political culture

Like so much else in the old Soviet system, its ideology and political culture were deeply contradictory. The party's ideology did provide Soviet society with a general sense of what it was supposed to be about, but the ways in which this was conveyed meant that people could not really identify with it, except in some isolated respects. The result, as Gorbachev was to acknowledge, was that there was a considerable gulf between the official vision of society and how it actually worked. This greatly affected people's behaviour. It also had important implications for reform.

Official political culture was schizophrenic in the view of many Russians. The official culture promoted by the CPSU had an 'ideological face' and a 'real face'. It created a public culture and a private culture (actually many private cultures). And it produced, what one Soviet dissident (in the old days) called 'visible man' and 'hidden man'.

The ideological face that the CPSU presented to the world in many respects bore very little relationship to the realities of the Soviet system. It was populated with ideal types. The cult of Lenin depicted a superhuman, omnipotent revolutionary hero who almost single-handedly (it seemed) brought the new socialist state into existence. The 'new Soviet person' was a model of honesty, diligence, hard work, efficiency, and selflessly dedicated to the communist cause, just like the model Communist. The Soviet state was a model of socialist development (although its leaders were increasingly willing to acknowledge that not everything was perfect as yet). The cults of the party leaders in their lifetimes painted them as direct descendants of the 'hero Lenin' and liked to pretend that they were also (almost) superhuman. It made a great deal of Soviet democracy and of socialist legality. It painted a picture of Soviet citizens as active participants in the management and development of Soviet society. It painted a picture of the party as a selfless and unified organisation dedicated to the well-being of the people and the achievement of communism.

In short, the party's ideology was rather like a fairy story (Alexander Solzhenitsyn, a famous dissident, called it 'The Big Lie'). It described the Soviet system as the party wanted it to be, not as it was.

The real face of the official political culture was, however, almost exactly the opposite of this 'story' because it was part of the realities described in Chapter 2.

The party's official ideology made no sense in the context of everyday life. Indeed, to many, particularly the young, it seemed like a cruel joke and many young people were extremely alienated from it as a result. How could people be honest, diligent etc. when the political and economic system obliged them to cheat, lie, steal in order to survive and make the system work? When anyone who actually tried to talk about the everyday realities of the system, e.g. the dissidents in the 1970s, was ruthlessly persecuted by the party? The result was:

1   The 'visible man' who publicly conformed. In public everyone paid lip-service to the party's ideology. They repeated the party's phrases parrot-fashion and quite literally pretended that the system worked in the ideal ways that the party said it did, whatever they thought in private. As we noted in Chapter 2, the rules of survival for 'visible man', the public person, became 'don't stick your neck out', 'don't rock the boat'. In party meetings, meetings in the soviets, public meetings generally, individuals simply voted with the majority without even thinking about it, and the majority always voted for whatever the local party secretary told them to. This produced public irresponsibility on a massive scale.

2   Public conformity went hand in hand with an all-pervasive sense of fear and a high degree of public intolerance of anything or anyone who was different. This had its origins in the Stalin years. Party ideology was underpinned by constant warnings about the 'enemies of socialism': the capitalist and imperialist threat, the 'enemies within' – bourgeois spies, troublemakers, anti-Soviet agitators. This generated a habit of suspicion and mutual distrust between individuals which was constantly reinforced by the ways in which the system worked. Everyone was on the make. Everyone had to fiddle the books, break some law or other, to make central planning work (or to make it look as though it worked). Consequently, everyone was perpetually vulnerable to the possibility of getting caught. Cross someone (most especially your boss) and they might shop you to the authorities. Suspicion and mutual distrust went hand in hand with bribery and endless deals of the 'you scratch my back, I'll scratch yours' variety, and slavish obedience to the will and whims of one's superiors.

3   A political culture of officialdom that was based on 'slavish toadying' to superiors, cronyism and what one Soviet emigre called a 'feudal psychological complex' (Efim Etkind, p. 10). That is to say, a combination of unconditional subordination to one's boss in the hierarchy and of unconditional despotic authority over one's subordinates. Because the power and privileges of officials depended entirely on retaining their official positions in the party and the state, they always had to stay in their boss's good books but at the same time had the same control over those below them. This culture promoted mediocrity (no boss wants to be outsmarted by a subordinate) and a slavish despotism: 'you can often spot in the facial expression, the habits and the voice of the Soviet manager a striking mixture of humility and despotism, bootlicking and bullying' wrote Etkind in 1978 (see also Barghoorn and Remington, p. 51).

4   A faceless political system that instilled a deep sense of powerlessness within ordinary people. Policy making was a hidden process which went on behind the doors of the party committees and was never publicly discussed. Decisions were

handed down from on high with no explanation, no justification, no discussion, and no indication of who had actually made them (those responsible were never named). The party consequently appeared rather like a dark and mysterious force, an elemental force of nature, especially to the millions of people who lived thousands of miles away from Moscow, and hundreds of miles away from the nearest big city. Party orders, and their often chaotic effects, had to be endured, rather like one endures a natural event like storm or drought – they control one's life but one cannot reason with them. This sense of powerlessness generated a great deal of popular resignation, apathy, weariness and the type of stubborn resistance and will to survive that people experience in the face of natural forces. They must simply endure.

5   Yet there were also some aspects of the system with which people could identify. Its commitment to economic growth, state welfarism and a certain degree of egalitarianism coincided with people's desires for a better life for themselves and their children. Its emphasis on patriotic and nationalist themes coincided with a genuine popular pride in the Soviet Union's achievement of superpower status against overwhelming odds, and genuine fears and uncertainties about Western intentions. Above all, it gave everyone a sense that society was going somewhere. People were sustained by the belief, and the hope, that all the suffering and indignity might be worth it if it ultimately produced a wealthy, fair and more egalitarian society from which their children could ultimately benefit.

The result was a political culture which, in Stephen White's words, was 'a blend of conformity and dissent, of genuine commitment to the Soviet system and pride in its achievements combined with considerable cynicism with regard to those presently responsible for its management' (White, p. 111). However, this only tells half the story.

Private cultures

In order to survive this system of institutionalised hypocrisy, many people retreated into what might broadly be called 'internal emigration'. They were honest in private where they could not be in public. In consequence, they did not so much support the political system as put up with it and avoid it where they could.

Individuals sought refuge in personal beliefs, e.g. religious beliefs; in their ethnic identity – as Kazakhs or Armenians; or in sub-cultures, which mushroomed during the 1970s particularly among the urban young – many of them alternative lifestyles which borrowed heavily from the West.

People also found all sorts of ways to opt out of the system or to reduce the pressures it imposed on them. For example, Martin Walker describes the son of a general, fluent in four languages, with a good degree, who took a job as a caretaker at a 100 roubles (about £100) a month so that he could concentrate on writing poetry and avoid the official system altogether. This was a common phenomenon among the urban young, the would-be rock musicians, writers, poets and the generally disaffected (Walker, p. 87).

Similarly, there was a migration of highly qualified engineers and technicians into skilled manual jobs because the pay was better, there was no responsibility and less stress. There is survey evidence to suggest that managers in the system tried to avoid promotion because top jobs involved too much stress (see Martin Walker, p. 88).

Soviet humour, which became legendary abroad, provided a powerful means for humanising and ridiculing the official system. Ironic comments about the various party leaders, and endless jokes about queues, told the truth about the system and relieved the social pressure. It is interesting to note that Soviet humour has gone into something of a decline since the years of *perestroika*.

The private social networks provided by family and friends provided a strong source of support for individuals and a means of defence against the public system. The resources of each individual (official connections, access to goods, etc.) were pooled and put at the disposal of family and friends. People got drunk around the kitchen table and complained about the realities of the system.

And people did try to organise themselves. Informal groups, the '*neformalnye*', existed in Soviet society long before Gorbachev came along and legalised such activity. The most famous abroad were the human rights groups and the dissident movement, mostly organised by intellectuals. But there were others, less visible: nonconformist religious groups, nationalist groups. There was even an unsuccessful attempt to form an independent trade union.

These groups had to operate in the underground. They were subject to constant harassment and were therefore unable to organise effectively. However, like the tip of the iceberg, they indicated the amount of social energy that was pent up beneath the glacial control of the party and that was waiting to be tapped.

At the same time official political culture and the party's ideology was so detached from the realities of everyday life that it left many traditional cultures virtually untouched. The Muslim Islamic traditions of the peoples of the central Asian republics, or the traditional culture of machismo and vendetta in Georgia, or the clan traditions of the nomadic tribes in Siberia continued to be celebrated in much the same ways as they had always been beneath the superficial veneer of official conformity. Or, they combined with elements of the official culture in ways that subverted it. For example, local party officials were frequently ticked off for attending the religious and other ceremonies of their native group. In the more remote parts of the country 'communism' was scarcely even a rumour. Mary McAuley narrates the story of a TV journalist in 1990 who 'finding herself in a village where a bedraggled poster still proclaimed the building of communism, in vain asked toothless old women and grinning lorry drivers if they knew what communism was. Eventually, a man, carrying heavy parcels, stood and pondered the question before venturing, doubtfully, 'isn't there a party of that name?' (unpublished).

Implications for reform

The influence of this 'schizophrenic' political culture on the progress of Gorbachev's reforms was considerable and inevitably paradoxical.

On the one hand, people were initially rather cynical. Gorbachev was yet another party leader with bright ideas that would not work. Many people therefore adopted a 'wait and see' attitude to his reforms. They were extremely reluctant to be the first to show their heads above the parapet despite Gorbachev's exhortations that *perestroika* would only work if people actively participated to bring it about. They were not certain if Gorbachev would last and they were only too well aware that their livelihoods depended not on Gorbachev but on local party officials and on their own immediate bosses, many of whom had nothing to gain from changing their ways. In particular, as Gorbachev was to discover, the 'feudal psychological complex' of the average party *apparatchik* proved impervious to change.

At the same time, the atmosphere of mutual suspicion and fear of difference that pervaded Soviet society took some time to change. This meant that it was enormously difficult for individuals to strike out in the new directions that Gorbachev wanted them to. For instance, the entrepreneurs in the new private co-operative business sector that began to emerge after 1986–7 faced considerable hostility from both local party officials and the ordinary public. The former resented the fact that they were not supposed to exercise control over this new independent sector. The latter resented their individualism and their ability to make huge profits out of a situation in which almost everyone was suffering from the chronic shortages of goods.

On the other hand, once it became clear in about 1988 that Gorbachev really was serious in his desire to reform the system and was willing to challenge society's power structures in order to achieve it, the social explosion that resulted proved impossible to control.

1 The party's ideological myths crumbled almost overnight in an accelerating and 'compulsive orgy of truth-telling' (Morrison, p. 2) about the realities of the Soviet system and its history. The status of the party and its ability to control society dwindled rapidly as a consequence.

2 The private cultures of individuals, groups and nations emerged into the daylight in a celebration of difference that rapidly turned into a torrent of conflicting demands that the party-state could not cope with.

3 Society became increasingly polarised between those who

thought reform had gone too far and those who thought that it had not gone far enough. It also became increasingly fragmented: groups could unite against what they hated in the system, but they could not agree on what they wanted to achieve.

In short, Soviet society lost its sense of self or, rather, discovered that it had never really had one. This contributed to the eventual disintegration of the system.

A note about terms

The descriptive terms 'right' and 'left' to denote someone's place on the political spectrum have been an indispensable part of political discourse since the French Revolution.

In Western usage 'right' refers to those who want to preserve the status quo. It is therefore generally associated with 'conservatives' or parties that promote the capitalist system. Whereas 'left' refers to those who want change. It is therefore applied to those parties promoting some variety of socialism.

However, in the Soviet and post-Soviet context these meanings are reversed. The 'right' still refers to those who want to preserve the status quo but this means maintaining state controls and a return to socialism. Whereas the 'left', i.e. those who want change, advocates private property and a free market (see Morrison, pp. 16–17 for a useful discussion).

This can get very confusing unless one bears in mind that the meaning of 'right' and 'left' is always dependent on the political context in which they are used.

To simplify matters, 'right' and 'left' in this book refer generally to those who want to preserve the status quo versus those who want change.

Further reading

Barghoorn, Frederick C. and Remington, Thomas F. *Politics in the USSR*, Little, Brown & Co., third edition, 1986, Chapter 2
Brown, Archie, (ed.), *Political Culture and Communist Studies*, Macmillan (St. Antony's Series), 1984

Etkind, Efim, *Notes of a Non-Conspirator*, Oxford University Press, 1978

Hosking, Geoffrey, *The Awakening of the Soviet Union*, Heinemann, 1990

Morrison, John, *Boris Yeltsin: from Bolshevik to Democrat*, Penguin, 1991

Sakwa, Richard, *Gorbachev and his Reforms, 1985–1990*, Philip Allan, 1990, especially Chapter 5

Shipler, David, *Russia: Broken Idols, Solemn Dreams*, Times Books, 1983

Vitaliev, Vitali, *Dateline Freedom*, Hutchinson, 1991

Walker, Martin, *Martin Walker's Russia*, Abacus, Sphere Books, 1989

White, Stephen, *Political Culture and Soviet Politics*, Macmillan, 1979

Wilson, Andrew and Bachkatov, Nina, *Living with Glasnost*, Penguin, 1988

Part II

The politics of *perestroika*

5

Understanding *perestroika*

Part II examines what happened between March 1985 when Gorbachev came to power and August 1991 when the abortive coup effectively ushered in the end of the Soviet state. This chapter provides an overview of the different stages of reform and of some of the issues raised by the reform process. Subsequent chapters will look at the different aspects of *perestroika* in more detail.

Mikhail Gorbachev

Mikhail Gorbachev was fifty-four years old and the youngest member of the Politburo when he became General Secretary of the CPSU on 11 March 1985. Unlike his three predecessors, Leonid Brezhnev, Yuri Andropov and Konstantin Chernenko, Gorbachev was vigorous, active and healthy. This was a radical change in itself. As one of the first jokes about him commented, 'What support does Gorbachev have in the Kremlin?' Answer: 'None – he walks unaided' (see White, p. 8). He was a solid party *apparatchik*. But he was also a trained professional, a lawyer, unlike most of his predecessors. His wife Raisa was a trained sociologist and, unlike most of her predecessors, took an active interest in politics. In short, they were both representatives of the modern Soviet intelligentsia, described in Chapter 3. And like most of their contemporaries they had had enough of the corruption, inefficiency and incompetence of the Soviet system.

They wanted change.

Gorbachev's goals: questions and dilemmas
There has always been some uncertainty about whether
Gorbachev knew what he wanted to achieve at the outset and
about whether he had a plan.

Evidence for   Some analysts cite the following circumstantial evidence to support the suggestion that Gorbachev did, at least, have
a general idea about what he wanted to achieve.

1   Gorbachev was always very clear that he wanted to achieve a
    massive improvement in economic performance and
    accelerated economic growth, although as time passed it
    became less and less clear that he had any idea about how to
    achieve this.
2   In a speech on ideological matters presented to a party meet-
    ing on 10 December 1984 Gorbachev made references to
    perestroika and *glasnost* (see White, p. 17).
3   Gorbachev has also given an account of a private conversation
    between himself and Eduard Shevardnadze (his radical
    Foreign Minister and a close friend) which took place in
    December 1984 in which they both agreed that life in the
    Soviet Union 'had all gone rotten'. In Gorbachev's words, 'We
    began looking for an answer to the question: How should we
    live? . . . And we put forward a simple formula: more demo-
    cracy, more *glasnost*, more humanity. On the whole, everything
    must develop so that the person in this society feels like a
    human being' (see Goldman, pp. 82–83).
4   Gorbachev's big speech to the 27th Party Congress in 1986
    made reference to the need for electoral reform and a more
    effective political system.

Evidence against   However, the actual record of *perestroika* overwhelmingly suggests that even if Gorbachev thought he knew
what he wanted to achieve, he certainly did not have a plan.

1   Many of his policies were mutually incompatible and mostly

achieved quite the opposite of what he intended. As a consequence *perestroika* did not actually reform the system, but instead
resulted in its chaotic disintegration.

2 There were at least three radical shifts in direction in 1987,
1990 and 1991 which indicate quite clearly that Gorbachev
changed his mind about the nature of the system's problems and
what had to be done to resolve them. This suggests that *perestroika*
is probably best understood as a rapid learning process for both
Gorbachev and his immediate advisers.

3 Gorbachev's policies were profoundly confusing for domestic
public opinion. All too often there seemed to be a gulf between
what Gorbachev said, the policies he promoted and what actually
happened. As a result:

(a) Many of those on the conservative wing of the political
spectrum, i.e. who wanted to preserve the system largely
intact, were already becoming convinced by 1988 that
Gorbachev had no idea where he was going. For example, at
the Nineteenth Party Conference in 1988 Yuri Bondarev, a
well-known conservative writer, compared *perestroika* to
taking off in a plane without having the faintest idea of where
it was going to land. They were increasingly of the conviction,
rightly as it turned out, that Gorbachev's 'half-baked policies'
were leading to the disastrous disabling of the old system.

(b) Democrats on the left of the political spectrum, i.e. those who
wanted much more radical change, became increasingly convinced, on the other hand, that *perestroika* was a giant confidence trick. Gorbachev frequently talked in terms of bringing about a 'revolution' in the system as his policies became
more radical. Yet, by 1990 and 1991 many elements of the old
'administrative command' system were still in place, and
although a great deal had changed, a great deal more had not.
As Ilya Zaslavsky, a well-known radical politician, remarked
in 1990: 'Personally I'm against *glasnost* and *perestroika* and
for freedom of speech and democracy.' By March 1991,
Boris Yeltsin, then head of the Russian republic (RSFSR),

was declaring publicly that *perestroika* had nothing to do with reform or revolution but was merely the last stage in the process of the system's stagnation. It was basically the command system's dying gasp.

(c) Ordinary people increasingly felt cheated. They had been promised an economy that worked and that put the consumer first, and a political system that listened to them. What they got was economic and political chaos and a political leadership that didn't seem capable either of listening to anyone properly or of being decisive.

The outcome was growing cynicism, anger and conflict on all sides.

In fact, there was a certain logic to Gorbachev's ideas and goals as they developed over time, on paper at least. He seems in the end to have believed that it was possible to create a new 'democratic socialism' by combining the best of planning with the best of the market, limited popular sovereignty with one-party rule, decentralisation within a highly centralised federal system. However, these ideas rested on hopelessly unrealistic assumptions about the nature of Soviet society: in particular, that there was a basic social consensus on the benefits of socialism, and a basic popular loyalty and commitment amongst all the peoples of the USSR to the party and its ideals.

Because these assumptions were fundamentally wrong, what Gorbachev actually ended up with was the worst not the best of all possible worlds.

Stages of reform

Different observers periodise *perestroika* in slightly different ways depending on how much emphasis they want to put on the more subtle shifts in Gorbachev's policies and the spontaneous changes occurring in Soviet society. However, the simplest way is to divide it into four periods:

1   from 1985 to the end of 1986;
2   from January 1987 to January/February 1989;
3   from March 1989 to February 1990;
4   from March 1990 to August 1991.

This is because each of these periods marks a radical shift in direction.

1985–6, *uskoreniye* (acceleration)

The period of 'acceleration' was not about reform but about the rationalisation of the 'administrative command system'. Gorbachev's only goal was to achieve 'accelerated growth' (hence the slogan). However, he was convinced at this stage that the Soviet system was basically sound. The problem was that people were not behaving as they were supposed to. Consequently, he used some very traditional methods to try and improve performance:

1 Disciplining individuals to work properly rather than changing institutions.
2 Streamlining the 'administrative command' system to make it work faster and more efficiently.
3 Achieving accelerated economic growth on the basis of old economic priorities and by imposing an overly ambitious five-year plan (the twelfth five-year plan).

The buzz words of this period were actually *uskoreniye* (which means 'acceleration'), 'intensification' and 'discipline', not *perestroika* or reform, words which were barely mentioned.

There were some slight economic innovations. For example, in November 1986 the Law on Individual Labour Activity was passed (although it did not come into effect until May 1987). This legalised very small-scale private activity in the service sectors. However, as we shall see in Chapter 6, this did not amount to very much and was in fact undermined in classic Soviet fashion by a campaign against 'unearned incomes'.

There was limited talk of 'improving the political system', but political change during this period consisted almost entirely in the massive replacement of old Brezhnevite party officials by Gorbachev's own appointees.

Glasnost

Glasnost, on the other hand, did become a slogan of Gorbachev's almost from the beginning. However, as we will see in Chapter 6, its purposes at this stage were very limited. It was certainly not intended to result in the more general public free-for-all that it was subsequently to become. The long official silence surrounding the catastrophic explosion of nuclear reactor no. 4 at Chernobyl in April 1986 was an indication of how limited *glasnost* was.

The record

The record of these two years was abysmal. They did not result in 'accelerated economic growth' but in continued decline and some profoundly negative long-term consequences. The measures adopted severely exacerbated the shortages and imbalances in the Soviet economy and contributed enormously to the explosive growth of the Soviet budget deficit. They also alienated large sectors of the population.

These factors undermined Gorbachev's public credibility as a reformer from the start. They also created entirely the wrong sort of environment for institutional reforms when these did occur.

1987–9, revolution from above

The failure of these early measures prompted Gorbachev to change direction.

It began to dawn on the party's reformers that the problems besetting the Soviet system were much more complex and deep-rooted than they had realised. That official corruption and irresponsibility were the result of absolute power and lack of public accountability, not simply the product of sloppy discipline and loose morals on the part of individuals. That economic decline and low productivity were a consequence of the extraordinary over-centralisation and secrecy of the 'command' system, not simply a matter of laziness, drunkenness and lack of will on the part of the workers.

It also began to dawn on Gorbachev that the system needed a new source of legitimacy in order to rekindle the population's commitment to the system. This meant basing party rule on a genuinely popular mandate rather than on party-inspired myths about Lenin, the revolution and the coming of communism.

The way to overcome these distortions and deformations of the system, according to Gorbachev, was to democratise it. This would give ordinary people a greater personal investment in the system and force party-state officials to be more accountable for their actions.

The result was the gradual emergence during the course of 1987 and 1988 of a *four-pronged strategy*. The fundamental purpose of this strategy was:

1 To place limits and controls on the enormous executive power of the party-state bureaucracies.
2 To bring about a limited transfer of executive and legislative power and authority from the party to state institutions.
3 To enable greater public participation in all spheres of Soviet life.
4 To bring about a radical democratisation of the CPSU so that it could continue to 'lead and guide' Soviet society with the consent and willing support of the people.

It is very important to note that Gorbachev fully intended that the implementation of this strategy would remain under the complete control of the party and the central authorities (most importantly himself). It was to be a 'guided' reform process which by combining central guidance 'from above' with effective mechanisms for control 'from below' (e.g. elections), would enable Gorbachev to bring the party and ministerial bureaucracies under control and force them to reform themselves without actually destroying them. It was a hopelessly unworkable project.

Economic reform involved the transfer of some executive power:

1 from the CPSU to the bodies properly concerned with economic matters;
2 from the central authorities to the republics; and
3 from planning authorities to the factories and farms actually doing the producing.

Political reform involved the transfer of executive and legislative power from the CPSU to the soviets and, through the soviets, to the people. It also involved heavy emphasis on the rule of law and the creation of what was called a 'socialist law-based state'. However, the CPSU was to retain its 'leading role' as a political party charged with the overall direction of Soviet society.

Glasnost was to be deepened and broadened to enable much greater public debate and the much freer expression of different points of view, even where these were not supportive of party and government policy. This became known as the 'socialist pluralism of opinions'. Gorbachev also opened the way for a far-reaching public examination of Soviet history and the nature of socialism. However, Gorbachev still intended that *glasnost* would remain within overall limits set by the party.

This strategy was supposed to be implemented in stages. In fact, it was implemented very haphazardly and very little, if any, thought was given to the knock-on effects that political reform might have on economic reform, and *vice versa*; or to the effect that the reform process as a whole might have on the functioning of the system. The result was the emergence of social forces and of political, economic and social processes that rapidly became impossible to control and led to accelerating chaos.

Institutional reform

The economy   Reform in the economy was the first process to get off the ground.

1   In line with policies begun in 1985-6 the central planning and ministerial apparatus continued to be reduced in size and scope although their functions remained the same.

2   The links between the all-union ministries and the republican ministries were reduced, confused and sometimes cut altogether by a decree of July 1987 which allowed republican governments relatively free rein during the course of 1988 to reorganise and reduce the union-republican ministerial structures. This reduced the powers of the all-union ministries considerably. It also had political consequences (see Chapter 9).

3 The CPSU Central Committee approved Gorbachev's radical economic reform proposals in June 1987. These included the Law on State Enterprises which was to be a central plank in the economic reform process. This was intended to give 'real economic independence' to industrial enterprises in Gorbachev's words. It also included an element of industrial democracy that enabled workers to participate in the election of their managements. This was supposed to give them a much greater sense that the factories belonged to them and therefore a much greater personal interest in working more productively. This law came into effect on 1 January 1988 with the gradual transfer of all industrial enterprises to the new regime over the course of 1988 and 1989.

Related reforms of planning, pricing, finance and credit, and the material and technical supply systems were all to follow later, but to be completed by 1991 (which in the event they never were).

Agricultural reform was to follow in 1989. Its central plank was the leasing of land long-term to private farmers. However, very little was done to change the basic nature of the collectivised system. Consequently, agricultural reform did not get very far.

4 One other potentially very radical law was adopted in May 1988. This was the new Law on Co-operatives. This legalised the development of small and medium-sized businesses that could set their own prices, fix their own wages and produce directly to market demand. In principle, this was a really radical move in the direction of private enterprise. In practice, however, the co-operatives that were created found themselves hedged about by all sorts of state restrictions. Consequently, their development was slow. By January 1990 there were only 193,100 co-operatives in operation in the USSR, mostly in the service sectors.

These developments did not eliminate the 'administrative command' system but they certainly began to undermine the co-ordination of its central structures and the power and control that they could exert over the economy. This had rather serious economic consequences (see Chapter 10).

The political system   Reform in the political system took much longer to get off the ground and did not really begin until the end of 1988. Moreover, when it did start to take place it failed to deal with crucial issues like federal reform. This was a grave error on Gorbachev's part because he had led people to expect that political reform would occur much sooner than it did; and that it would be much more radical than, in fact, it was.

The CPSU Central Committee had already approved the idea of 'democratisation' as a general principle in January 1987. This was accompanied by a great deal of rhetoric from Gorbachev about the need for a 'profound democratisation' of Soviet society. The Central Committee meeting of January was followed by the first experimental multi-candidate elections to local soviets in June 1987 in about 5 percent of constituencies. These developments, plus moves on the economic front, inevitably raised a great many hopes and expectations. However, the detailed programme for political reform was not actually approved until a whole year later at the Nineteenth Party Conference in June 1988. This generated a great deal of public frustration and anger. The political reform programme that was finally approved generated even more public outrage because it simply did not go far enough. It contained nothing on federal reform. Moreover, it was clear to everyone that its proposals for electoral reform and new democratic structures had been badly compromised by right-wing opposition within the party. It was from this point that Soviet public opinion became seriously politicised and began to polarise.

As a result of the Nineteenth Party Conference a number of constitutional amendments were adopted that, among other things, provided for:

1   New electoral laws.
2   The creation of a new two-tier parliamentary structure at the all-union level: the directly elected Congress of People's Deputies the primary function of which was to elect the new semi-permanent Supreme Soviet which was to be a proper working parliament (unlike the old one).
3   A proper division of functions between legislative and government bodies (this laid the basis for the creation of a 'law-based state'); and between the party and the state – there was to be no

more *podmena* (see Chapters 2 and 7).

These amendments were ratified by the USSR Supreme Soviet on 1 December 1988 and began to be implemented in 1989. Their effects on the system were revolutionary, although not in the ways that Gorbachev had intended.

The CPSU Change also took place within the CPSU. In late September 1988, the Central Committee Secretariat, i.e. the party's top permanent 'civil service' in Moscow, was formally reorganised. Its departments (including those that had monitored government activities, see Chapter 2) were reduced in number from twenty to nine, and six commissions were established to develop party policy on key issues like the legal system, agriculture, foreign affairs and to monitor the internal activities of the party. This reform was also adopted at republican level.

Its purpose was to weaken the power of the party's 'civil servants' while increasing the participation of elected Central Committee members through the activities of the commissions. It was also intended to remove the party's control over economic management. In practice, the new commissions never really got off the ground, and the party secretariat continued to function much as it had done before. However, because the secretariat was greatly reduced in size and number and rather disorganised as a result of this reform, its control over policy and decision making, particularly in the economic sphere, was considerably weakened as intended. The reform also helped Gorbachev to out-flank the conservative opposition to his policies in these organs.

Political and social processes

The launching of democratisation and greater *glasnost* in 1987 led to rapid changes in the general political climate. They unleashed *spontaneous processes* which ultimately proved impossible to control.

1   Gorbachev's reform proposals inevitably generated enormous opposition from within the party apparatus and the *nomenklatura* who stood to lose most from these changes. By the time of the

Nineteenth Party Conference in June 1988 the party was already visibly dividing into:

(a) 'Conservative' anti-reformers who were almost universally identified with the top party apparatus. This wing was associated with Politburo member Yegor Ligachev.
(b) Gorbachev supporters, mostly identified with the lowest (and least powerful) ranks of ordinary party members who had a quite a lot to gain from greater democracy, and the ordinary public.
(c) Radical 'pro-democracy' reformers who wanted to go much further and faster than Gorbachev was prepared to go. This wing was associated with Boris Yeltsin.

These divisions widened and grew increasingly antagonistic as *perestroika* proceeded.

2   The reforms also lit the fuse of the slow burning but unstoppable 'revolution from below'. People began to organise to defend and promote Gorbachev's plans against the opposition of the conservatives, and, more importantly, to promote their own interests. Thousands of groups, large and small, sprang up across the country. Most importantly, 1988 saw the emergence of:

(a) Radical pro-democracy and pro-independence coalition movements in the Baltic republics. These were known as the Popular Fronts and they quickly became very effective. The idea of the Popular Front also spread quite rapidly to other parts of the country after 1988.
(b) The first embryonic political parties (although these were still 'illegal' at this point).

3   *Glasnost* and *democratisation* also gave rise to militant republican nationalism and ethnic conflict that was to blow the country apart after 1990.

Glasnost allowed long-standing enmities to bubble to the surface. For example, the conflict between Azerbaijan and Armenia over the territory of Nagorno-Karabakh began in

February 1988 and rapidly escalated out of control.

However, a great deal of the republican nationalism that was later to emerge was Gorbachev's fault. One of the most notable omissions from his programme for political reform was the issue of reforming the federation. This generated an enormous amount of avoidable hostility (see Chapter 9). It should have been the key to democratisation not the after-thought that it was.

4   Finally, *glasnost* gave vent to growing popular dissatisfaction with the deteriorating state of the economy, and the fact that *perestroika* only seemed to be making things worse. By the end of 1988 rationing systems were being used in many parts of the country for basic items like meat, sugar, potatoes and soap. Many people began to compare the situation with living conditions during the war. The resulting popular outrage was forceably brought home to Gorbachev on his walkabouts when people began to harangue him in no uncertain terms about their appalling living conditions.

1989 to February 1990, revolution from below

By the end of 1988 society was already beginning to bubble and seethe with spontaneous popular activity particularly in the big towns and cities. But until this point the CPSU remained largely in control of events. However, from the beginning of 1989 on the CPSU and Gorbachev in particular rapidly began to lose control over the reform process, so much so that by the end of 1990 both Gorbachev and the party had become more or less irrelevant to the spontaneous revolution that was sweeping through Soviet society.

The key to this loss of control were the elections that took place in 1989 and 1990 and the activities of the USSR Congress of People's Deputies.

National elections
The national elections to the new USSR Congress of People's Deputies took place in March 1989. These were multi-candidate elections conducted by secret ballot. They were not properly

competitive because the CPSU still retained enormous control over the process, particularly over how candidates for election were selected. Nevertheless, the outcome of these elections was explosive.

1 They provided a focus for:

(a) Popular hostility to the CPSU apparatus which was visibly seen to be interfering with and hampering the democratic process.

(b) Intense popular organisation amongst the 'democratic forces' as they came to be known, in support of independent candidates, particularly in the big cities, some of whom did succeed in winning.

2 They resulted in some spectacular defeats for Communist Party candidates who had taken their election as deputies to the Congress for granted. This was a powerful and humiliating blow to the arrogance of the party apparatus across the country.

3 They also demonstrated the contradiction in trying to combine popular sovereignty with one-party rule. The people could defeat party candidates for deputy but they could not vote the party itself out of power.

This fuelled an increasingly angry public debate about the constitutionality of the CPSU's leading role and led to demands for the abolition of the article guaranteeing this leading role in the Soviet constitution (article 6).

The USSR Congress of People's Deputies

This body which met for the first time for fifteen days from 25 May to 9 June 1989 was ultimately a rather ineffective body as a parliament. Its constitutional powers remained unclear. It was badly organised, and radical democrats were in a minority because of the rigging of the 1989 elections. Nevertheless, it transformed the political landscape irreversibly.

1 The very existence of a popularly elected national assembly

marginalised the party's apparat and top policy-making bodies. These could serve no useful function once control over legislation and policy-making had been taken away from them.

2 Its deputies had parliamentary immunity and the radicals in particular used it to push back the frontiers of *glasnost* in all directions. There were fierce debates between radicals and conservatives; fearless denunciations of government policy, the KGB, the bureaucracy, the economic crisis, and all sorts of issues were raised that had previously been taboo.

3 These debates were televised which meant that they were brought directly into virtually every Soviet home.

All this had revolutionary effects on public political consciousness and political activity. As one leading radical Anatoly Sobchak (later to become mayor of Leningrad) put it: 'The political awareness of people changed more in three weeks than in the preceding fifty years' (see Morrison, pp. 96-7). For example, this first session of the Congress was a catalyst for the mass miners' strikes which shook the country during the summer of 1989. It gave people courage to express long suppressed grievances.

Elections to the republican Supreme Soviets and local soviets
This process began at the end of 1989 and proceeded throughout most of 1990. These elections were much freer and consequently much more democratic than the elections of 1989 because the republics were left to decide how and when to conduct them. This resulted in the removal of many of the 'anti-democratic filters' as the Russians called them, that had enabled the CPSU to retain control over the electoral process in 1989. The consequences were also revolutionary because these elections resulted in:

1 *The genuine transfer of political power* from the party to sovereign legislatures in many areas. For example, in the Baltic republics anti-party Popular Front candidates achieved landslide victories in elections to the Supreme Soviets and local soviets, forcing CPSU deputies into a minority in the republican Supreme Soviets. And across the country local party organisations lost

control over many local soviets particularly at city level.

By the beginning of 1990 the Baltic results alone had made a mockery of the party's constitutionally guaranteed 'leading role'. In February 1990 the CPSU Central Committee and Gorbachev himself were forced to bow to the inevitable and recommend its removal from the constitution. This was ratified by the Congress of People's Deputies in March.

2   *The effective abolition of democratic centralism.*

(a) The 1989–90 elections finally put popular sovereignty into practice. The consequence was that republican and local politicians were no longer responsible to Moscow but to their electorates. Even in areas where party rule was not significantly challenged by the elections, party politicians had a vested interest in promoting popular demands for greater democracy, sovereignty and independence because they risked being displaced by more radical forces if they did not. Consequently, they increasingly began to disobey the Moscow authorities unless it suited them to do otherwise. This process was to accelerate from the end of 1989 onwards.

(b) By the end of 1989 the party itself had begun to split irrevocably into different ideological 'platforms' with different political programmes as a result of these developments. This fatally undermined the operation of democratic centralism within the party; and consequently turned the party from being a relatively unified executive organisation into an arena for savage political battle with enormous consequences for the functioning of the Soviet system as a whole.

This general situation resulted in the gradual collapse of executive power throughout the system. Increasingly, there were lots of local bodies with elected authority but no one with the power to get anything done.

Disintegration
The overall effect of the reforms in 1989–90, therefore, was to

promote the disintegration of the political system. The CPSU was the only unifying political and executive force in the country, and once it was undermined there was nothing else to hold the system together.

Disintegration of the political system also meant the gradual disintegration of the economic system. The central planning authorities and the remaining ministries continued to try to exert control despite the economic reforms that had been introduced. But they increasingly lacked the coercive power to make anyone obey them. The result was that they were increasingly disregarded as economic collapse dictated the adoption of local strategies for survival and the republics began to assert their independence.

Popular dissatisfaction with spiralling economic collapse erupted in the summer of 1989 in mass strikes in the mining regions of the country where the lack of soap and washing powder (no joke for people doing one of the filthiest jobs in the world) was the last straw. The miners were eventually coaxed back to work with unrealistic government promises which could not be fulfilled, only to strike again in 1990 and 1991. Other vital groups, like railway workers, also struck or threatened to strike in 1990. Serious labour unrest continued to rumble on into 1991.

By the end of 1989 and the beginning of 1990, therefore, Gorbachev's four-pronged strategy of controlled and directed political and economic reform was in tatters: undermined by the very processes that it had set in motion.

1990–1, crisis management

The period from March 1990 to August 1991 was packed with events, hasty policy reversals and several radical shifts in political direction as Gorbachev twisted and turned in his efforts to find solutions to the country's mounting problems and the crisis in his own authority and power.

The establishment of a new executive presidency in March 1990 was Gorbachev's overall attempt to stem the crisis. The reasoning behind it was, first of all, that it would replace the collapsing executive power of the party with a new centralised executive authority legitimately vested in the state. And, secondly, that only a strong state leader with extraordinary powers could pull the country back from the brink of collapse.

It also secured Gorbachev's personal position because it meant that even if the party's conservatives succeeded in ousting him as party General Secretary he could continue to rule as President.

However, the authority of this new executive presidency was fatally undermined by:

1 *The lack of a new constitution*, which was still being drafted in 1990. This meant that:

(a) the relationship between the new presidency and the other institutions of government were very unclear. Increasingly no one knew who was responsible for what;
(b) there were no checks and balances on the power of the presidency; but
(c) the president had no administrative structures or clear chains of command at his disposal through which to govern. Both the USSR Congress of People's Deputies, the USSR Supreme Soviet and the old USSR Council of Ministers had their own sources of authority and operated independently of the president.

Gorbachev tried to overcome this problem by demanding ever-greater powers from the Supreme Soviet (which the obedient majority were willing to give him); and unilaterally abolishing the Council of Ministers, sacking the government of Prime Minister Nikolai Ryzhkov (originally a Gorbachev appointee) and replacing them with bodies like the new Cabinet of Ministers which were directly responsible and accountable to him alone. This occurred in November and December 1990.

However, none of this did anything to help re-establish Gorbachev's control over the country.

2 *The republican challenge to the centre*. By the end of 1990:

(a) all fifteen Union-republics had popularly elected govern-ments that had a great deal more legitimacy than the central authorities;

(b) every Union-republic, and even some smaller federal territories, had declared themselves autonomous, independent or sovereign in one way or another; and

(c) every Union-republican government, many smaller territories, and even local government, was fiercely resisting the demands of the centre and, in particular, President Gorbachev's attempts to impose executive control. Gorbachev could not get his decrees implemented. The USSR Congress of People's Deputies and the Supreme Soviet could not get their laws implemented. And the economic authorities increasingly could not get their plans implemented. At the republican level, this became known as the 'war of laws'. It was a war that the central authorities were ultimately to lose.

Gorbachev's unprecedented accumulation of powers – in December 1990 Boris Yeltsin accused him of having more 'legally formulated power' than even Stalin had acquired – could not stop this process. On the contrary it frightened the republican governments into demanding more autonomy than they might otherwise have done. At the end of 1990 there were real fears that the foundations for a new dictatorship were being created.

3 *Gorbachev's failure to stand for popular election* and his refusal to give up the post of CPSU General Secretary.

(a) He persuaded the Congress to elect him as President in March 1990 on the basis of an uncontested ballot, rather than going to the country, thus undermining his own rules.

(b) He continually resisted popular calls that he should resign his party post and refused to recognise the fact that combining the two was placing him in an impossible position. As Alexei Kiva, a leading political scientist, noted, 'The General Secretary serves first and foremost his Party and its structures. The President should serve the citizens, society, the state ... Gorbachev thus finds himself in the grip of an insoluble conflict' (Morrison, p. 251). Gorbachev had to

choose between preserving the party or promoting democracy. His inability to do so compromised him fatally.

As a result, he lost what was left of his authority in the country at
large, and his bargaining position with respect to the democratically elected presidents of the republics was fatally undermined.

Tactical political manoeuvring

Gorbachev also tried to shore up his position by manoeuvring
between the conservatives and the 'democratic forces' which had
now become very polarised and both of which were piling on the
pressure. This was something he had always done (and been very
good at) in order to keep both the 'right' and the 'left' off balance.
And for the first three years or so of *perestroika* it worked. Now,
however, it became extremely dangerous and destabilising
because it resulted in a catastrophic lack of political and economic
direction at the centre at a time of real crisis. It also lost Gorbachev
the trust of both 'right' and 'left'. And drove even his few remaining supporters into opposition against him.

It left him without power, authority or support from any
quarter.

During the course of 1990 Gorbachev came under increasing
pressure from conservatives in the party-state apparatus who were
appalled at what was happening to the party and the power system.
The government under Nikolai Ryzhkov (until its abolition) was
increasingly asserting its independence and becoming reluctant to
implement policies that threatened what remained of the 'administrative command system' and therefore the government's main
power-base.

In addition, a new Russian Communist Party was formed in
June 1990 under the leadership of an arch-conservative (Ivan
Polozkov). Unlike the other republics in the Union, Russia (the
RSFSR) had never had its own party (see Chapter 9). It now
acquired its own communist party. This immediately became the
largest organisation within the CPSU with 58 per cent of the
CPSU's total membership – because of the overwhelming size of
Russia. This new party gave the conservatives and the party

apparatchiki an independent power base that Gorbachev could not control in the way that he had controlled the all-union Politburo and Central Committee. They used it to harry him and organise against him.

Gorbachev was also coming under pressure from the democratic and liberal 'left'. The 'democratic forces' were not nearly as well-organised as the conservatives and lacked ideological cohesion. However, their interests were informally represented by a powerful and immensely popular leader in the shape of Boris Yeltsin. Yeltsin had all the popularity and legitimacy that Gorbachev did not have. He was democratically elected as President of the RSFSR in June 1991 in a Russia-wide competitive election (as opposed to being elected to the post by the Russian Congress of People's Deputies as he had been in 1990). He was also President of the largest and most powerful republic in the Union. And he ruled from the Russian parliament building (the White House) which was just down the road from Gorbachev's Kremlin headquarters in Moscow. Yeltsin was a powerful critic of Gorbachev from the 'left'.

During the summer of 1990 Gorbachev initially aligned himself with Yeltsin and the 'left', on the question of economic reform.

By this time everyone was afraid that the economy was on the point of real disintegration. An astonishingly rapid consensus had also been reached, amongst reformers at any rate, that the only solution was to make the transition to a fully fledged market economy. However, there were profound disagreements about how this transition was to be accomplished.

Gorbachev and Yeltsin collaborated to put together a team of radical economists who were charged with the elaboration of a programme for this transition. The result was the '500-day programme', also known as the 'Shatalin Plan' after the man who headed the team.

However, by this time, Gorbachev was too powerless and still too conservative in his aims to follow through. When the government under Nikolai Ryzhkov refused to implement this programme, partly because it advocated the rapid decentralisation of enormous economic power to the republics, Gorbachev himself refused to support it. As a result the programme was abandoned.

To make matters worse, the USSR Supreme Soviet refused to accept Ryzhkov's alternative because it was too conservative.

The consequences were:

1   A catastrophic lack of economic direction which no amount of institutional change (like sacking the Ryzhkov government) or of effort to find a compromise could disguise.
2   The alienation and defeat of the 'democratic forces'. Yeltsin and the Russian government felt betrayed. And all of Gorbachev's reformist supporters who were in positions of power within the party or the government either resigned or were quietly pushed out of office. The alienation of the democratic 'left' was highlighted by Eduard Shevardnadze's dramatic public resignation as Foreign Minister in December 1990 amid dire warnings of impending dictatorship.
3   Gorbachev's inevitable swing to the right.

During the late autumn of 1990 Gorbachev promoted a number of conservative hard-liners to prominent positions in the government: the very people, like Boris Pugo as Interior Minister, Valentin Pavlov as Prime Minister, or Vice President Gennadi Yanaev, who were subsequently to stage the coup against him. This resulted in something of a reversion to old-style coercive party methods during the winter and spring of 1990–1. Attempts were made to clamp down on the press, to restrict the rights to strike and demonstrate. Troops were sent in to the Baltic republics to harass and undermine their governments and peoples, most notoriously in Lithuania where thirteen people were killed by Soviet army tanks in the capital Vilnius in January 1991.

However, this did nothing to restore order or to re-establish the centre's power, quite the opposite. This new 'right-wing' government was bereft of ideas and used force and repression simply to 'treat' the symptoms of the crisis. It did not try to come up with an alternative political and economic programme for treating its causes. As a result its measures greatly exacerbated political tensions in the country and intensified the struggle between the centre and the republics, almost all of whom now refused to co-operate with the central authorities at all. This threatened not just economic collapse but the collapse of the Union itself. This forced Gorbachev to change direction yet again.

In April 1991, under pressure from Boris Yeltsin and the presidents of eight other republics, Gorbachev left his hard-line government to its own devices (instead of replacing it, a fatal mistake) and engaged in intense negotiations with this group of republican leaders. These became known as the 'Nine Plus One' talks. During these talks Yeltsin and the other eight presidents managed to convince Gorbachev that he would have to co-operate with them if the Union was to be saved in any form at all. The result was a new set of negotiations that would have resulted in the genuine decentralisation of power to the participating republics (although it is doubtful whether even this would have saved the Union) had the coup of August 1991 not intervened to disrupt the process.

Everyone agrees that Gorbachev bears indirect responsibility for the coup because of the way he promoted conservatives to power at the end of 1990 and then left them in power after he swung to the 'left' again in the spring of 1991: although as it turned out these conservatives were actually powerless because by mid-1991 the central institutions no longer had any power or authority. They had effectively ceased to exist in anything but name.

Conclusion

It is almost impossible to come up with a comprehensive explanation for this extraordinary period of contemporary history. It was only six-and-a-half short years. Yet it combined vision and ineptitude; skilled political infighting and incredible political naivete to an astonishing degree.

However, the following points are worth bearing in mind.

Gorbachev was, above all, the supreme leader, the General Secretary, of the Communist Party of the Soviet Union. He had spent his career in the party and he was a product of the party. Gorbachev was not, however, a machine politician, a party *apparatchik* like Brezhnev, committed only to lining his pockets, increasing his power and preserving his skin. He was a committed socialist from the 'creative wing' of the party (see Chapter 2) who really did believe that a unique form of Soviet 'democratic socialism' was both possible, desirable and desired by the majority of the Soviet population.

These two factors had the following consequences.

1   Gorbachev's position and background suggest that he was profoundly ignorant of how the system actually worked, for all the reasons cited in Chapter 2. He knew a lot about the system, and learned a great deal more during his period in office. But, one suspects, that he never really grasped what made it tick, how people related to each other on a day-to-day basis.

His reforms tried to change the system as he *thought* it worked, not as it actually worked. They treated the system as though:

(a) it really *was* centrally planned;
(b) the party *did* have a meaningful political role to play and that it really did guide and control society as it claimed to;
(c) democratic centralism *was* about democracy as well as centralism;
(d) federal centre-republican relations *were* harmonious and based on co-operation;
(e) the Soviet people *were* united behind the party and its socialist goals and would use the new democratic opportunities he offered them to promote those goals not to undermine or oppose them.

This explains, e.g., his total inability to understand the social forces that his reforms unleashed. Or the effects that competitive elections would have on the power structure and on federal relations.

By contrast, his reforms did nothing constructive to alter the vast networks of informal relations (not all of them corrupt) on which the continued functioning of the system actually depended.

As a result, *perestroika* disrupted these established patterns of behaviour but did nothing to replace them with viable alternatives. People were told that they had to change. But they were not told how to change or given the environment in which they could change their behaviour. It disrupted the 'administrative command system' (which, of course, was not planned at all) without replacing it. It fatally undermined democratic centralism (which, of course, had nothing to do with democracy) but did not replace it with new mechanisms for integrating society. In short, it resulted in the thoroughly inept and messy dismantling of the old system but prevented the creation of a viable alternative to it. The Russian word *rasstroika*, which means deconstruction or destruction, would actually have been a better description of Gorbachev's reforms than *perestroika*.

2 For all the apparent radicalism of some of his measures Gorbachev had a very narrow vision of what was actually needed to transform the system, and of the ultimate objectives of such a transformation. As a result his institutional reforms were very narrowly conceived.

His one clear goal throughout was to create a modern industrial economy and achieve a transformation in economic performance. As he declared at the Twenty-seventh Party Congress in February 1986, economic growth was the 'key to all our problems, immediate and long-term, economic and social, political and ideological, domestic and foreign'. And this remained his basic conviction.

Accordingly, his political reforms were never ends in themselves but were only a means to this end. For example, democratisation was not about creating a democracy, but about making Soviet society more democratic than it was in order to improve the ways in which it functioned. It therefore had nothing to do with introducing the idea of political *choice* into the system, for example, giving people the right to choose who would govern them, but was fundamentally about checking and preventing the abuse of power by those who held it and would continue to hold it. It never even occurred to Gorbachev that democratisation would automatically raise the thorny issue of political choice. Consequently, measures that appear to be extremely radical *to us*, like the elections, did not appear to be that radical to Gorbachev, because with his background he simply could not grasp their full implications.

In sum, it is possible to argue that Gorbachev remained impaled on the contradictions of the old system described in Chapter 2.

Like Khrushchev before him he tried to marry the totalitarian forms of control represented by the party's monopoly of political power (its leading role) and by his own enormous powers as party General Secretary, with the democratic forms of participation represented in principle by the soviets, federalism and the party's constant lip-service to democracy and creativity. He tried to do this by combining these institutions in new ways and by trying to bring about a psychological revolution that would energise ordinary people into overcoming the terrible inertia and stasis that was the inevitable result of this system. To the end of his days in power Gorbachev was never able to shake off his basic conviction that it was the people who ran it, not the system itself, that was causing all the problems. Even by the end of 1990 he was still insisting that people mattered more than structures and that the 'most important revolution' was not the institutional revolution but the 'revolution in our minds, in our heads, in us ourselves'. Like all the party's leaders before him, going right back to Lenin, he fundamentally believed that the system's problems could be overcome by the sheer force of the human will. However, because he also believed that the human will deeply desired socialism he never anticipated the possibility that the psychological revolution would overwhelm the limited institutional reforms that had set it in motion.

Gorbachev's reforms were, perhaps, the culmination of the Communist Party's paradoxical attempts over seventy years to 'make a socialist system' in that they were simultaneously both deeply orthodox and conservative and extremely radical, more radical than anything that had preceded them. In this respect, Gorbachev tried, once and for all, to resolve the problems that the CPSU had been grappling with for most of its history. However, all he succeeded in doing was to demonstrate the essential unworkability of its whole revolutionary project. One can therefore agree with Yeltsin that *perestroika* was the 'administrative command system's death rattle.

Consequently, Gorbachev is best understood as a transitional leader. He saw out the old, but was quite incapable of seeing in the new.

Further reading

Goldman, Marshall, *What Went Wrong with Perestroika*, W. W. Norton & Co., 1991

Morrison, John, *Boris Yeltsin: from Bolshevik to Democrat*, Penguin, 1991

Sakwa, Richard, *Gorbachev and His Reforms, 1985–1990*, Philip Allan, 1990

White, Stephen, *Gorbachev and After*, Cambridge University Press, 1991

6

Uskoreniye, prelude to reform

Gorbachev's clear and overriding goal from 1985 to the beginning of 1987 was to achieve a *rapid turnaround* in economic performance. Steps were taken towards the more long-term reform of the economy but in 1985 Gorbachev wanted instant results. The combined demands of high levels of defence spending, the costs of modernising industry and, above all, Gorbachev's own desire to achieve rapid improvements in the satisfaction of people's consumption needs could only be met in the short term by a rapid acceleration (*uskoreniye*) of economic growth.

Unfortunately, the measures actually adopted to achieve this accelerated growth had the opposite effect:

1. they exacerbated the structural problems of the Soviet economy rather than alleviating them;
2. set economic forces in motion that quickly became difficult to control;
3. and made it infinitely more difficult, if not impossible, to achieve the institutional reforms that were to follow.

The traditional approach

Gorbachev was highly critical of the system's deficiencies from the beginning and made no bones about saying so in public. As people were fond of remarking at the time, he sounded more like a dissident of the 1970s than the General Secretary of the CPSU.

As we noted in Part I he was aware that there was a great deal of corruption, inefficiency and waste in the system. However, his understanding of what caused these problems was very limited and rather traditional at this stage. He clearly believed that it was the attitudes and behaviour of management and workers that were to blame rather than the Soviet system itself which was at fault. Consequently, his policies treated the symptoms not the causes of economic decline. These policies were based on the assumption that central planning worked and that the way to achieve growth was to put coercive pressure on the system. This would squeeze out all the hidden reserves and motivate people to work properly. The real key to rapid growth was to ensure that 'everyone works honestly, conscientiously and effectively at his place of work'. Gorbachev called this 'activating the human factor' and constantly stressed its importance.

This was not an entirely implausible attitude to have in 1985. The Soviet 'administrative command' system had achieved some startling successes over the course of seventy-odd years, taking the Soviet Union from feudal backwardness to world superpower status within a generation, as party officials never tired of pointing out. It therefore seemed credible to argue that it was Brezhnev's hands-off attitude to economic management that had caused the problems not the system itself. And that there was nothing wrong that a stiff dose of discipline, some streamlining of the system and a generalised attack on corruption could not solve. However, it resulted in a very traditional approach to the problems of economic growth and economic management which, in the circumstances of the mid-1980s was disastrously inappropriate.

Activating the human factor

To begin with, Gorbachev was convinced that the key to 'activating the human factor' was the introduction of a greater measure of social justice into economic relations. By this he meant the following:

1 Creating proper incentives to encourage high-quality work and ensuring proper remuneration for a job well done; from

which it followed that income differentials had to be increased and adequate reward given for skill, training and experience.

2 Re-establishing a proper work ethic that emphasised profes-sionalism, honesty, decency and commitment and gave people back a sense of pride in their work. This involved greater work discipline and clamping down on drunkenness, laziness and cheating in all its forms.

3 A generalised attack on corruption and illegality to stop people from stealing state property and making fortunes not because they worked hard but because they could exploit their positions.

4 Overcoming the terrible alienation of the Brezhnev years that had caused all this corruption and lack of discipline and produced a massive over-bureaucratisation of the system.

However, the policies that were actually introduced in order to bring this transformation about tended to have the opposite results.

Highly ambitious plan targets

One obvious solution to the problem of low growth and poor labour productivity was to give everyone much higher plan targets to fulfil.

The five-year plan for 1986–90 was being formulated when Gorbachev came to power. He took the opportunity (against the better judgement of the planners in *Gosplan*) to inflate all the plan's growth targets by absurd amounts. His reasoning was that obliging people to achieve difficult plans would squeeze all the laziness, slackness and inefficiency out of the system and force people to work more productively and effectively. Everyone would be obliged to pull their weight and put in a decent day's work for their wages. The new twelfth five-year plan that was the result certainly put the economic system under enormous pressure but this in turn only served to make its structural problems worse.

1 The new plan bore even less relation to what was practically possible than the old 'Brezhnev' plans had done. Shortages and

supply bottlenecks got worse as factories, farms, etc., struggled to find the extra resources to meet their targets by whatever means they could. And useless products simply got churned out at a faster rate. So the ordinary consumer did not benefit. On the contrary, the supply of consumer goods, if anything, deteriorated.

2 The new plan undermined the bargaining process that 'central planning' had actually become during the Brezhnev era. Gorbachev sent the draft of the plan back to *Gosplan* three times in order to get the changes he wanted inserted. *Gosplan* was then obliged to impose it on the rest of the economy. This could only exacerbate the already high levels of non-compliance with central commands as republics, ministries, departments, factories, farms, struggled to protect their own interests. People had even greater incentives than before to ignore what the central party leadership was ordering them to do and to lie to their superiors about what they had achieved. This also undermined the new policy of *glasnost* (see below).

3 This plan was in operation for almost the whole period of *perestroika*. It created the wrong sort of climate for the economic reforms that were to follow. People cannot learn new rules or change their behaviour if they are working flat out using the old methods in their old jobs. Major reorganisation requires time and effort and people's workloads have to be temporarily reduced correspondingly. Gorbachev did not give anyone this breathing space. This undermined the chances of long-term institutional change and meant that the reforms that were introduced in 1987 and after simply added to the burdens of an over-stretched and labouring economy. By 1988 radical Soviet economists were arguing that *perestroika* simply would not work if something was not done to change the plan. The most radical economist, Nikolai Shmelev, even advocated abandoning the plan altogether (see White, pp. 118–19).

Streamlining the system

Gorbachev was highly critical of the 'bloated administrative bureaucracy' that had turned the central planning system and the ministries into top-heavy, inefficient and insensitive machines that were riddled with all sorts of vested interests that opposed change. This machinery was a brake on economic growth because it was too cumbersome and poorly co-ordinated to operate properly. It also alienated people by drowning them in red-tape. Gorbachev's solution was to try and streamline the system by:

1   *Concentrating even more power at the top* through the creation of a number of 'superministerial' bodies which were charged with the co-ordination of a number of related ministries. For example, a Bureau for Machine-Building (attached to the USSR Council of Ministers) was set up in October 1985 to co-ordinate the activities of twelve or so civilian machine-building ministries. About five of these bureaux were created in all.

2   *Reducing the number of ministries* by merging related ministries into 'superministries' and reducing the numbers employed. This was initially tried in the agricultural sector which was overwhelmed with red tape (in 1985 there were thirteen all-union ministries and state committees in charge of what was known as the 'agro-industrial complex'). In November 1985 five 'agro-industrial' ministries and one state committee were merged into a 'superministry' called *Gosagroprom* and their central staff (approximately 7,000 people) was reduced by some 47 per cent. The same sort of thing was also tried within the construction industry and education.

3   *Reducing the numbers of people employed at the centre*. Beginning in 1986 people were simply sacked, retired or redeployed. For example, the staff of *Gosplan* (the State Planning Committee) was gradually cut by more than half from 2,650 in 1986 to 1,095 by 1988. The staff of the all-union ministries was reduced by 46 per cent from 1.6 million in 1986 to 871,000 by 1989 (Aslund, p. 196).

4   *Encouraging local initiative* through, for example, the Law on Individual Labour Activity adopted in November 1986. This was to encourage production in the service sectors where the state was notoriously inefficient.

These measures were only the first in a long line of ministerial reorganisations and reforms that went on throughout the period of *perestroika*. Their purpose was not to remove the 'administrative command' system but to enable it to work more efficiently and flexibly. They failed in this aim because they did not address the real problem which was that central planning itself could not work. Instead they caused endless bureaucratic infighting, actually led in some cases to more bureaucracy and greater over-centralisation rather than less, and confused the old, well established chains of command and communication that had kept the system going. *Gosagroprom* was such an 'ungovernable bureaucratic mastodon' (Aslund, p. 118) that it had to be effectively abandoned in 1989. The result was that these changes disorganised the 'administrative command system' rather than reforming it, with rather serious economic results (see Chapter 10).

Campaigns

Campaigns were a time-honoured party method of trying to achieve change quickly in a priority area. They generally involved devoting vast amounts of time, energy, resources and propaganda to the attainment of a single goal, usually to the total neglect of the (generally disastrous) knock-on effects that such a campaign might have on the rest of the system. There were several such campaigns during the early Gorbachev years. All of them were eventually phased out or reduced in scale because of their terrible effects on economic performance.

1   *Quality control.* The solution to the problem of poor-quality goods was to initiate a campaign to improve quality, called *Gospriemka*. Nothing was done to change the working conditions that caused people to produce defective goods (often against their own better judgement). But quality controllers were placed in key industries with the power to reject goods that did not come up to scratch. These *Gospriemka* inspectors were well paid and good at their jobs. They had no difficulty whatsoever in rejecting a good 20 per cent of output as below quality from the word go. The

result inevitably was a dramatic decline in output, loss of bonuses for workers, unfulfilled plans and disrupted work patterns. This led to serious labour unrest and even protest strikes. This campaign was never formally abandoned but it petered out gradually from 1988 because it was realised that its consequences were potentially explosive.

2 *The anti-alcohol campaign* was another means of trying to force people to change their behaviour. Drunkenness and alcoholism had become social plagues by the 1970s. People regularly turned up drunk for work or got drunk on the job. Factory managers frequently used vodka as a means of bribing their workforce. They were a major cause of accidents at work, absenteeism, illness. They also contributed greatly to the growth of crime, divorce, suicide and mental illness (see Treml, p. 54). Yuri Andropov was the first party leader to make a serious effort to curb the problem, unsuccessfully. Gorbachev decided to seize the bull by the horns and stamp it out altogether. Unlike Andropov, Gorbachev did not simply want to reduce drinking he wanted to impose the Soviet equivalent of the American prohibition of the 1920s. However, Gorbachev's campaign, which began in May 1985, was so extreme, so punitive, and so lacking in planning that it was almost bound to fail. Its consequences were disastrous for the economy.

The failure of the campaign was officially admitted in 1988, although the campaign was not actually abandoned until early 1990. It did not result in the reduced consumption of alcohol. Although the volume of official sales had more or less been halved by 1987, the shortfall was rapidly made up by illegal distilling and black market sales of alcohol. It was, of course, naive to expect that people would suddenly stop drinking when the environment that encouraged them to drink in the first place had not changed at all. However, it did have the following effects.

(a) It resulted in the massive reduction of state revenues. In 1982 taxes on alcohol sales made up about 12 per cent of all state revenues or some 42 billion roubles. Halving alcohol consumption halved this return to the state exchequer. This worsened the Soviet budget deficit which was already running at about 35 billion roubles by 1985 (see Sakwa, p. 272), not that the Soviets admitted having a deficit before 1985. This problem was papered over (quite literally) by the simple expedient of printing more bank notes. This practice persisted throughout *perestroika* and contributed greatly to the collapse of the rouble and the high inflation rates in 1990 and 1991. It also made later attempts to reform the finance system almost impossible.

(b) By the same token, the disposable income of the Soviet population increased. They could no longer spend their money on alcohol to the same extent as they had done before (black market purchasing mopped up some of the difference but not all of it, because many people made their own using very cheap ingredients). However, there were no extra consumer goods in the shops to mop up this extra spending power. To make matters worse wages were increasing partly as a result of political promises to improve the standard of living especially for lower-paid groups and partly as a result of attempts to increase income differentials. This aggravated the general shortage of consumer goods; added to the inflationary pressures in the system and reduced people's general incentive to work even further.

(c) Those sectors of the economy concerned with alcohol production were devastated. For example, some 90 per cent of Soviet vineyards grew wine-producing grapes. Millions of acres were ruthlessly destroyed without any prior thought being given to the livelihoods of those who worked them. This had terrible effects in the wine-producing regions and republics: the North Caucasus, the Ukraine, Moldavia, Georgia and Azerbaijan. The output of the Georgian wine industry was cut by 50 per cent by October 1985 (and the campaign was only launched in May) resulting in immediate and correspondingly serious losses of income to the republic (see Treml, p. 67). It is not surprising that all these areas were to become political hot-spots after 1987.

(d) Needless to say, this campaign alienated large sectors of the population very quickly. Even people who did not drink and did not produce alcohol suffered from the knock-on effects of sugar and other shortages that were the direct result. For example, sugar (a vital ingredient in distilling) disappeared from the shelves almost completely and had to be rationed right across the country by 1988. This seriously damaged Gorbachev's reputation. He became disparagingly known as the 'mineral secretary' (*mineralny secretar* rhymes with *generalny secretar* in Russian) because he advocated the consumption of mineral water and fruit juices instead of alcohol.

3   *The campaign against 'unearned incomes'.* The purpose of this campaign as Gorbachev intended it was to eradicate the unearned income 'obtained through illegal activity, embezzlement, bribery, speculation' (Aslund, p. 158). In his speech to the Twenty-seventh Party Congress in 1986 Gorbachev focused on 'unearned income from public property' by which he meant direct theft from the state. He also touched on bribe taking (Aslund, p. 158). At the same time, however, he stressed that the campaign was not intended to affect those 'who obtain additional earnings through honest work' in the small private sector – the private plots, *kolkhoz* markets, and so on. This campaign was a key element of Gorbachev's drive for greater social justice since it was clearly intended to eliminate criminal activities which enabled officials in particular to exploit their positions to make money to the disadvantage of all those who earned their money through honest toil.

The campaign began in the summer of 1986 but petered out in late 1987. It not only failed in its objectives, it also resulted in considerable economic and psychological damage (see Aslund, pp. 158–63 for a good account). The main reason for its failure was that the party-state officials who were actually responsible for carrying it out used it to persecute everyone who obtained additional earnings 'through honest work' while leaving the real targets, the embezzlers, the bribe takers, the officials who were busy stealing state property, entirely alone. There were good reasons for this:

(a)   party-state officials were hostile to legal private sector activity because it was not 'socialist', but mostly because they had little control over it;

(b) no official had an interest in combatting the theft of state property because most party-state officials were themselves involved in it; and

(c) it was sometimes difficult to make a distinction between the two sectors. 'Honest' private traders often stole state property, or used public transport for private purposes, because it was the only way of getting their hands on scarce resources.

The results were deeply damaging to the economy.

To begin with, there was a great deal of outright lawlessness on the part of the local police and party-state authorities across the country who literally took matters into their own hands. Private agriculture (always the most successful sector of the agricultural economy) was a particular target. For example, perfectly legal deliveries to *kolkhoz* markets were stopped in many parts of the country, the produce confiscated and destroyed without compensation or legal recourse and the owners fined. Thousands of private greenhouses for growing tomatoes were wantonly destroyed by organised gangs of thugs in various parts of the country, often on the express orders of local party bosses, and their owners accused of being 'speculators' and of living a 'parasitic life-style'.

Secondly, this lawless clamp-down resulted in shortages and enormous price increases in the one sector of the economy – the *kolkhoz* markets – where food supplies, particularly of fresh meat, fruit and vegetables, had always been relatively plentiful and of good quality. *Kolkhoz* markets were especially important sources of supply in the big cities. This had long-term effects because, for example, greenhouses cannot be rebuilt overnight and because, crucially, this monstrous persecution put people off engaging in legal private activity. As one Soviet critic remarked in 1988:

We launched a campaign on a broad front to utilise all our frozen reserves and to develop independence, initiative, and enterprise, and suddenly, at the height of the march – we got the Decree on the Struggle against Unearned Incomes, which pulled society . . . back . . . in these tasks. The country was swamped by an avalanche of persecution against people who

tried not to sit down at the dominoes table after the plant whistle had
blown but to work a little more at their own responsibility and risk' (see
Aslund, p. 162).

The negative effects of this on Gorbachev's subsequent attempt in
1987 to encourage precisely this sort of private individual activity
were enormous. As Aslund remarks 'It was a big blow to the whole
reform endeavour' (p. 163). However, it ran so counter to the logic
of Gorbachev's statements that there is only one sensible explanation. The campaign against 'unearned incomes' that Gorbachev
initiated at the Twenty-seventh Party Congress in July 1986 was
hijacked, very successfully, by the party's conservatives for their
own purposes.

Political change

Although there was no talk of political reform during this early
period the 'activation of the human factor' also had its political
aspects.

Glasnost (or openness)

This policy was promoted from the beginning. Its central feature
was to improve the production and circulation of accurate information in the system through, for example, the relaxation of
censorship and political control over the media and the gradual
easing of political controls over the social sciences, culture and the
arts. However, it was not intended to create a free press or
freedom of information, but was supposed to serve a limited
number of interrelated purposes, most of which were concerned
with motivating people, changing their behaviour and therefore
improving the system's performance. Gorbachev anticipated that
it would:

1 Improve the decision-making and policy-making activities of
   party-state officials by giving them access to increased and
   more accurate information about the real state of affairs in the
   country and by subjecting at least some of their plans to public
   scrutiny in the media.

2 Make officials more accountable by acting as a form of public control over bureaucratic mismanagement and corruption. Ordinary people and subordinates were to be encouraged to blow the whistle on official misbehaviour so that it could be dealt with.

3 Help to create 'a more energetic and constructive atmosphere in the Soviet workplace' in Stephen White's words. 'Broad, up-to-date and honest information is a sign of trust in people, respect for their intelligence and feelings, and their ability to make sense of developments' as Gorbachev told a conference in December 1984 (White, pp. 70–1).

Gorbachev also seems to have assumed that *glasnost* in and of itself would renew people's enthusiasm and commitment to the ideals of the party, the cause of socialism and the tasks of *perestroika*. 'The better people are informed, the more consciously they act, the more actively they support the party, its plans and pro-grammatic objectives' he declared with total confidence in 1985 (see White, p. 71).

In practice, glasnost did lead quite rapidly to rather more accurate (and some investigative) reporting in the media, to a gradual thaw in the arts and (again gradually) to the investigation of social problems that had previously been taboo subjects (drug taking, prostitution, poverty).

However, as a means of enforcing official accountability, or of encouraging productivity, it could only fail dismally given the prevailing economic conditions in 1985 and 1986 and the lack of any protection for the individual in law. Some brave and honest (or naive) people did try to take Gorbachev at his word but they were almost invariably victimised for it by the very people they had complained about. As one young man, a worker in a local pro-cessing plant, told Gorbachev on one of his walkabouts in August 1986, 'They said at the Communist Party [Central Committee] Plenum that we should criticise all of them Lenin-style. I risked doing so, about the manager of the fisheries processing plant at a meeting of the trade union committee. Today I am out of a job' (see Goldman, p. 101). And, paradoxically, the media coverage that was given to these cases of victimisation under the banner of *glasnost* only served to frighten people off. In any case, there was little mileage to be gained out of telling the truth when the truth was that the party's policies (its ambitious plans, its campaigns) were actually creating more chaos. And when it was quite clear to everyone that the party leadership's own policies were definitely off-limits as a subject of public criticism.

Personnel policy (or cadre policy)

In line with his conviction that it was people not the system that was causing all the problems Gorbachev spearheaded a considerable (but civilised) purge of the party-state bureaucracies. This served the double function of enabling him to get rid of the old, the incompetent, or the corrupt and to replace them with his own appointees. He seems to have thought that this in itself would help to boost growth rates (presumably because he assumed that new, energetic and forward-looking leaders would bring a new dynamism and 'new thinking' to their jobs). For example, within a year of coming to power Gorbachev had managed to replace two-thirds of the top leaders. This included one-third of the government's ministers and one-third of the crucial republican and regional party leaders (see Sakwa, p. 13). And by the end of 1986 he had been able to achieve quite dramatic changes in the make-up of the party's top 'civil service' – the Central Committee Secretariat, the Central Committee itself, the Council of Ministers, the foreign policy-making establishment, at the top of the big industrial ministries as well as at lower levels in the party and state administrative hierarchies.

In the event, however, this massive turnover of personnel demonstrated the error of assuming that people mattered more than structures, because, in fact, a great many of Gorbachev's own appointees turned against him (for example, Prime Minister Ryzhkov) once his policies began to affect their institutional power-bases.

Political struggle

The first two years also saw the beginnings of the internal political struggle that was eventually to tear the party apart.

The spear-carrier of this struggle was Boris Yeltsin, a Gorbachev appointee, who became head of the Moscow City Party Committee in December 1985 (a very powerful position given that Moscow was the USSR's capital and largest city), and a member of the Politburo in February 1986.

Yeltsin took Gorbachev at his word and began to institute radical anti-corruption and clean-up policies in Moscow which upset almost every vested interest in the city, including, most importantly, the city's party organisation itself. He was extremely outspoken. He was the first to raise taboo subjects like party privileges in public. And he was highly critical (sometimes in public) of other, more conservative, members of the top leadership.

This transgressed the boundaries of what was permissible and Yeltsin was effectively forced to resign from both his party positions at the end of 1987 to the accompaniment of vicious attacks on his character even from close colleagues. However, Yeltsin had managed to up the stakes. By pointing the finger publicly at taboo subjects like party privileges he (1) began to gain himself a public following which was eventually to bring him back to power, and (2) managed to demonstrate that the new top party leadership was actually quite conservative. He was to remain the 'left-wing' thorn in Gorbachev's side from then on.

The economic and political record

The economic and political record of these two years was abysmal. All the worst characteristics of the Soviet economy were exacerbated.

1 The economy barely grew at all and the consumer market, in particular, suffered serious disruption and rapidly worsening shortages. Other factors made this worse. For example, declining world prices for key Soviet exports like oil, gas and coal led to reductions in foreign-exchange earnings. This resulted in cuts in imports of consumer goods to the tune of some 8 billion roubles.

This made it nigh-on impossible to reform the economic system at a later stage without causing further crises. For example, reform of the pricing system (a vital prerequisite for decentralising the economy) was endlessly postponed because in conditions of chronic shortages of just about everything any freeing of prices was certain to send them through the roof.

2   The Soviet budget deficit soared from about 3 per cent of national income in 1985 to about 14 per cent in 1989, swamping the economy with the increasingly worthless money that was printed to finance it. This reflected budgetary disasters like the anti-alcohol campaign as well as falling world commodity prices. It also reflected Gorbachev's commitments to increase wages and social benefits, massively increased investment in key industries like machine building (an old Soviet favourite), continued high levels of defence spending, and the cost of catastrophes like Chernobyl and the Armenian earthquake which happened at the end of 1988. The size of the deficit and the devaluation of the rouble made the subsequent reform of the finance and banking systems extremely difficult, if not impossible.

3   Gorbachev raised popular expectations enormously by his blunt talk and his trenchant criticisms of the system's deficiencies. His emphasis on the importance of *glasnost* and his recognition that the ordinary Soviet consumer had been very badly served raised people's hopes that some real change was finally on the way. However, his ham-fisted economic policies dashed these expectations very quickly. As a result, Gorbachev alienated a great deal of the public goodwill on which he might have been able to rely had he been willing to introduce more radical policies more quickly. Consequently, when Gorbachev executed a radical about-turn in 1987 and started calling for real economic and political change, it took a long time for people to believe that he meant what he said. And when they did their reactions were not at all what Gorbachev had anticipated.

Conclusion

What are we to make of these two years?

1   It is possible to argue that Gorbachev introduced the policies he did because of the strength of conservative opposition to change within the party-state bureaucracies. It is quite likely that Yegor Ligachev, a Gorbachev appointee but undoubtedly very conservative, was behind the worst excesses of the anti-alcohol campaign. And the campaign against unearned incomes was quite clearly hijacked by local party officials. There is certainly a lot of truth in this argument. But it does not explain all the facts.

(a)   Everyone agrees that Gorbachev was able to consolidate his hold on political power much more quickly than any of his predecessors. It took Stalin ten years to establish full control. And it took Khrushchev and Brezhnev five years to establish their positions within the Politburo and Central Committee. Gorbachev, by contrast, managed to bring his own people into the Politburo within a month of taking office. And as we saw above was able to make a fairly clean sweep of all the top positions in the system within two years of coming to power. This suggests that Gorbachev might have had sufficient authority to promote more substantial reforms in this early period than he chose to.

(b)   It was Gorbachev who presided over the ambitious revisions to the twelfth five-year plan.

(c)   Gorbachev himself admitted once he had gone into retirement at the end of 1991 that he was too slow to move towards radical economic reform and should have taken more advantage of these first two years than he did.

All this does suggest that Gorbachev introduced these policies because he genuinely thought they would work.

2   Gorbachev had very limited knowledge of how the system actually worked and of its grotesque deficiencies. Gorbachev himself confirmed that 'junior' members of the Politburo were only given limited access to sensitive budget information (see Goldman, pp. 97ff). And, in any case, the vicious circle of disinformation as well as the existence of informal networks described in Chapter 2 would have ensured that Politburo mem-

bers were quite ignorant of what was actually happening on the ground. Gorbachev only began to appreciate the real extent of the country's problems and their effects on the lives of ordinary people as he travelled round the country and saw them for himself.

3   Because of his conviction that it was people rather than institutions that mattered Gorbachev could not immediately grasp the fundamental structural problem which the aborted campaign against 'unearned incomes' demonstrated all too graphically. This was that the very institutions on which he was most reliant to get his reforms implemented, namely, the party, the *nomenklatura*, the big ministries, were the very institutions that were themselves most in need of reform, most resistant to reform and most difficult to control. It was this problem that was to animate much of the reform process after 1987.

In this respect, the period of *uskoreniye* did have one positive effect. It demonstrated that the old methods and the old ideas were bankrupt.

Further reading

Aslund, Anders, *Gorbachev's Struggle for Economic Reform*, Pinter Publishers, 1991 (expanded edition). Chapter 3.

Goldman, Marshall, *What Went Wrong with Perestroika*, W. W. Norton & Co., 1991

Sakwa, Richard, *Gorbachev and his Reforms, 1985–1990*, Philip Allan, 1990, Chapter 7

Treml, Vladimir, 'A Noble Experiment? Gorbachev's Antidrinking Campaign', in Maurice Friedberg and Heyward Isham (eds), *Soviet Society Under Gorbachev: Current Trends and the Prospects for Reform*, M. E. Sharpe, 1987

Walker, Martin, *The Waking Giant: the Soviet Union Under Gorbachev*, Michael Joseph, 1986

White, Stephen, *Gorbachev and After*, Cambridge University Press, 1991, Chapter 4

Questions

1 What, in your view, were the principal characteristics of the period of *uskoreniye*?

2 Is it useful or accurate to describe the policies undertaken between 1985 and 1987 as reforms?

7

Political reform

Political reform was central to the development of *perestroika*. But it was also political reform, and the processes to which it gave rise, that was most directly responsible for the failure of *perestroika* and for the ultimate collapse of the old Soviet system. It is therefore important to grasp what political reform was about. The issues involved are complex. This chapter will look at the principles (or lack of them) underlying political reform. The next chapter will look at its practical consequences, although it is not always easy to separate the two.

Understanding the problem

By the time of the Nineteenth Party Conference in June 1988, at which the detailed programme for political reform was finally adopted by the party, Gorbachev had come to realise that it was the 'administrative command system' and the country's 'ossified system of government' that was the major obstacle to the development of *perestroika* (see White, p. 26).

According to Gorbachev's analysis, the socialist system established in 1917, with its original emphasis on popular democratic rule and the gradual elimination of state controls, had been seriously 'deformed' by the repression and over-centralisation which had been imposed by Stalinism and reimposed to a lesser extent during the Brezhnev era of 'stagnation'. This had led to:

1 The massive over-bureaucratisation of Soviet life. The functions of the bureaucratic apparatus had increased out of all proportion to the needs of society. It had usurped the forms of democratic management (i.e. the soviets) established in 1917 and totally undermined the rule of law. Its officials were not accountable to anyone at all. Consequently, they were able to 'dictate their will' in a completely arbitrary fashion in both political and economic matters without any fear of opposition and regardless of the actual needs of the people, although it was in the name of the people that the revolution had been fought and won.

2 Political, economic and social life had been stifled and 'straitjacketed' by endless bureaucratic controls. Both party and government officials ruled 'by injunction'. They 'ordered', 'forbade', 'demanded', and expected unquestioning obedience, instead of enabling the 'self-government' of the people. The basic law of social behaviour had become 'everything is forbidden except what we (your superiors) allow you to do', which meant endless bureaucratic interference in people's everyday lives and in every aspect of the system. Whereas it should have been 'everything is allowed except what is expressly forbidden by law', which would give maximum room for the creative use of individual and local initiative, particularly in the economic field. As a result, Soviet citizens could not act on their own initiative because they were prevented from doing so by constant administrative regulation and interference. They had consequently become thoroughly alienated from the political system and from the management of public property over which they no longer had any control.

Gorbachev's solution

His solution was to try and reverse the balance between bureaucratic control and democracy so as to bring the managerial bureaucracy of the state under the democratic control of the people. As he saw it, this meant:

1 Returning to the Soviet Union's revolutionary socialist roots in order to restore Lenin's emphasis on 'people power'. This was

reflected in Gorbachev's emphasis on:

(a) Strengthening the power of the soviets as legislatures, as elected organs of popular self-government and as bodies for overseeing the activities of government executive bodies (i.e. the ministries).
(b) The introduction of industrial democracy which would enable workers and farmers to elect their managements and give them a say in the running of their enterprises. (This was written into the Law on State Enterprises which went into action at the beginning of 1988.)
(c) The reform of the CPSU to turn it from being the largely administrative and bureaucratic organisation that it had become into a genuinely popular representative of the 'people's will' (as Gorbachev naively assumed it had been in 1917).

2   Learning from the 'best practice' of other countries. In particular, the liberal democracies had demonstrated that:

(a) the absolute and impartial rule of law;
(b) the existence of a system of 'checks and balances' between the different institutions of the state: the body making the laws (the legislature), the bodies executing the laws (the government executive), and the bodies arbitrating the operation of the laws (the judiciary); and
(c) competitive elections; were indispensable mechanisms for securing official accountability and preventing the abuse of power. This was reflected above all, in the introduction of the idea of the 'socialist law-based state'.

As Gorbachev put it in his book *Perestroika*, 'There can be no observance of law without democracy. At the same time, democracy cannot exist and develop without the rule of law, because law is designed to protect society from abuses of power and guarantee citizens and their organisations . . . their rights and freedoms' (p. 105).

In short, Gorbachev's solution was to try to marry two different and rather incompatible political traditions, the Soviet and the liberal democratic (mostly the American system of which Gorbachev was a great admirer), in order to try to overcome the old conflicts between party control, bureaucracy and democracy. He wanted to keep the old revolutionary institutions – the party and its leading role, the soviets, planning, state ownership of property – but 'fill' them with new 'content' and make them work in new, more democratic, more constitutional, ways. After 1987 his dream seemed to become the creation of a new 'democratic socialism'.

On paper this solution looked plausible. As we saw in Chapter 2, the party, the soviets, the government ministerial structure and the federal structure had always existed as independent hierarchies formally speaking. Gorbachev therefore assumed that these institutions were sound in themselves but were failing to work properly because they had been overwhelmed by unnecessary bureaucracy and party interference. The answer therefore was to remove the interfering bureaucracy and restore each set of institutions to its proper place in society.

However, it was a rather utopian solution. It rested on the unrealistic assumption that it was possible to transform the ways in which the system worked without actually changing what the system was. It assumed that:

1 The bureaucratisation and repressive regulation of Soviet society were not the inevitable products of one-party rule and central planning but basically Stalin's and Brezhnev's fault for mismanaging the system.

2 One-party rule did not have to be repressive to be maintained. The CPSU could sustain its monopoly of political power not by suppressing any and all alternatives to it as it had always done, but by democratic and legal means.

3 The various organisations in society, the party, the soviets, the government ministries, were basically motivated by the same common goals and, given the right conditions (i.e. more democracy) would work harmoniously together to achieve those goals.

The problem was that Soviet society was not homogeneous, nor were its institutions motivated by common goals. As we saw in Chapter 2, the various parts of Soviet society were only held together by the sort of arbitrary bureaucratic interference and lawless party repression that Gorbachev wanted to remove. Once they were removed the system began to fly apart very rapidly.

The legal revolution

The legal revolution as Gorbachev rightly called it, got underway in late 1988. It had several aims.

1   *To lay the foundations for the rule of law.*

(a)   The judiciary and the legal system as a whole was to become independent of the party and the power system. The law was to become an impartial instrument of government. This would ensure that state officials particularly at the lower levels of administration, and local party officials, would be subject to the law and accountable to the public through the law.

(b)   Individuals were to be given legal protection and individual rights and freedoms were to be constitutionally and legally guaranteed.

(c)   A new constitution was to be written, which among other things, would create a system of checks and balances and establish a clearly defined separation of powers, functions and responsibilities between the key institutions in the political system: the CPSU, the soviets, the government bureaucracy and the judiciary.

2   *To transfer legislative power from the party to the soviets and to establish proper relations of accountability and oversight between legislative and executive bodies.*

(a)   An entirely new legislative body was established, in the form of the directly elected Congress of People's Deputies. This body was supposed to symbolise the new power of the people and the new supremacy of the constitution; and to establish the authority of the democratic process and of the new 'socialist law-based state'. It had the sole power to amend the constitution; to elect the USSR Supreme Court and a new Committee for Constitutional Review which had the crucial task of deciding on the constitutionality of all laws. It also had the power to elect the deputies to the new Supreme Soviet as well as to amend or ratify its laws.

(b) The institution of the Supreme Soviet was transformed. It was to become, and did become, a real working parliament. It was to be in session twice a year for three to four months at a time and its deputies were to become full-time paid MPs. It had the power to make all the detailed laws required for governing the country.

(c) All state bodies were to be strictly accountable to the soviets and all government appointees had to be ratified by the Supreme Soviet and not just by the party. Thus, for example, the new USSR Congress of People's Deputies had the power to elect and dismiss the President (formally speaking, the Chair of the new Supreme Soviet).

The new USSR Supreme Soviet was required to ratify the President's nominees for Prime Minister and other ministerial positions. It had the power to recall any elected or appointed official who failed in their duties. It also had the power to create a series of standing committees and commissions which had the right, among other things, to interrogate ministers and officials on their activities. Moreover, government ministers could no longer also serve as Supreme Soviet deputies. This was designed to ensure the independence of MPs.

It was originally intended that this new two-tier parliamentary structure, combining both a Congress of People's Deputies and a Supreme Soviet, would be adopted not only at the all-union level but also by all the Union-republics. In the event, however, it was only implemented at the all-union level ănd in the Russian republic. All the other Union-republics opted for a directly elected Supreme Soviet. However, all the republican Supreme

Soviets (Union and autonomous) were transformed into proper working parliaments following the central model. This meant that the Union-republican Supreme Soviets (with the exception of Russia) had direct control not only over detailed law making but over their republic's constitution as well as direct responsibility for the oversight of the executive (the republican presidents as well as the republican governments). These factors were to become of enormous significance after the republican elections of 1989–90. However, the powers and prerogatives of these new Supreme Soviets remained uncertain because of the continued dominance of the centre in both political and economic matters. In November 1988 Gorbachev made it clear that the reform of federal relations would not be discussed until after the reorganisation of the central and local soviets and the introduction of electoral reform had been successfully completed. This was a profound mistake. Federal relations were fundamental to the constitutional structure of the USSR. Consequently any redistribution of power was bound to affect the relationship between the centre and the republics. Gorbachev's failure to see this in time resulted in enormous and avoidable conflict (see Chapter 9).

At local levels, the soviets were also put on a new and more professional footing. Local elected deputies were given greater powers to control the soviet executive committees (the mini-cabinets, see Chapter 2) that ran local day-to-day affairs. They were also given enhanced powers over budgetary matters, over local economic affairs as well as over local legislation. However, as we will see in Chapter 8, this did not greatly strengthen their position.

Constitutional limitations

However, these new constitutional arrangements had serious weaknesses that reflected the very limited nature of Gorbachev's reforms. These weaknesses were to generate enormous political conflict.

Problem of the party
This was the most fundamental weakness. There was a clear

incompatibility between Gorbachev's desire, on the one hand, to create a democratic, law-based state in which there was a clear separation of powers and in which the constitution and the law were sovereign, and his determination, on the other hand, to maintain the leading role of the party.

To begin with, the CPSU could not retain its monopoly of power and at the same time subordinate itself to the law. At the very least, the top party leadership had to reserve the right to determine what the law should be (even if local party officials were obliged to be accountable before the law) otherwise it could not continue to 'lead and guide' society in what *it* thought was the correct direction of development. The idea of the 'law-based state' therefore directed everyone's attention to the fact that there would always be the possibility for a fundamental clash of interest between what the CPSU might think was right, i.e. the party's will, and what the people's elected legislative representatives might decide was right, i.e. the popular will as codified in the law. This was to become a fundamental source of conflict.

Secondly, the very idea of a 'law-based state' also served to demonstrate very clearly that the CPSU could serve no function in such a state. Try as they might, the party's politicians and the congressional committee charged with drafting a new constitution could not come up with a sensible division of powers that included the party and its 'leading role'. This was because the functions the party had fulfilled in the past: executive, legislative, administrative, managerial, all properly belonged to other bodies. Its 'leading role' therefore, quite literally, made no sense and could have no constitutional or legal foundation. Consequently, as long as the party insisted on maintaining its 'leading role' it retained an extra-legal and unconstitutional position in society which undermined the operation of the state institutions. Just as these newly empowered institutions undermined the position and role of the party. This problem greatly hindered the drafting of the new constitution which began in June 1989 and in the event was never completed. It also brought the party into direct and open conflict with the 'democratic forces' that the reform process unleashed (see Chapter 8).

Finally, competitive elections were a useful means of bringing party-state officials in the localities to account but they could not be allowed to threaten the party's monopoly position. Gorbachev was always very hostile to the idea of a multi-party system even after events had overtaken him, despite the fact that the development of a multi-party system was the logical outcome of a competitive electoral process, as almost everyone was very quick to point out.

Gorbachev's desire to secure and protect the position of the party within his new 'socialist law-based state', which was reinforced by trenchant opposition to his political reforms from the party's conservative *apparatchiks*, resulted in the presence of a number of profoundly anti-democratic restrictions within the new constitutional arrangements. These were built in at the time of the Nineteenth Party Conference in June 1988 to the considerable outrage of large sectors of the public (including pro-reformers within the party itself. See Urban, 1990, Ch. 2).

Anti-democratic filters

These 'anti-democratic filters', as the Russians called them, were as follows.

1   The elections to the new USSR Congress of People's Deputies which were held in March 1989 were heavily controlled by local electoral commissions in each constituency. These commissions were dominated by the local party apparatus which therefore acquired very considerable control over the nomination of candidates and the conduct of the elections. Consequently, these commissions were able to rig the elections in a large number of constituencies (although they were not always successful) to ensure that the candidates preferred by the party's apparatus got elected. The result was, unsurprisingly, that over 87 per cent of the new congressional deputies were members of the CPSU; while over 65 per cent were paid administrators of one sort or another.

These commissions attracted so much public criticism and hostility that they had to be dropped for the republican and local elections that were to follow in 1989–90.

2   Of the 2,250 seats on the new USSR Congress of People's Deputies, 750 seats were reserved for nomination and election by the membership of specific public organisations. This meant, that the CPSU itself, designated a 'public organisation' for this purpose (alongside e.g. the All-Union Society of Philatelists representing the country's stamp collectors), was awarded 100 seats on the new Congress to which it could elect its own candidates (the philatelists' society was awarded just one seat). This gave the CPSU Politburo direct control over 100 congressional seats. The internal party election for these seats was not at all democratic. In the end the Politburo presented exactly 100 candidates for these seats (one of whom was Gorbachev himself), all of whom were duly 'elected' by the CPSU Central Committee.

This arrangement of reserved seats also raised such a storm of criticism from within the party as well as outside it that republican and local authorities were given the choice of whether or not they wanted to retain the idea of fixed organisational representation when it came to making the arrangements for the local elections of 1989–90.

3   In the context of these highly compromised reform proposals, the creation of a two-tier parliamentary structure in the form of the Congress of People's Deputies *and* the Supreme Soviet was greeted with a great deal of public scepticism.

(a)   This arrangement was, and was popularly seen to be, undemocratic because only the Congress was directly elected by the Soviet population. The Congress then elected the Supreme Soviet which was to be the working parliament. This was rightly seen by many to be a way of ensuring that the membership of the much smaller Supreme Soviet could be rigged by the party's congressional majority (which it was).

(b)   It also confused the constitutional relationship between the two parliaments because they had to share legislative sovereignty. The Congress was only supposed to meet once a year (unless an extraordinary session was called, which happened frequently), yet it had the sole power to change the constitution, and could amend or annul any decision or law adopted by the Supreme Soviet. However, the Supreme Soviet had the power to make the laws and oversee the executive. This made life extremely difficult for both institutions. The Supreme Soviet was supposed to be a pioneering and reforming parliament. This meant that just about any law it passed was bound to affect the constitution. It was therefore under the constant threat of having its legislation annulled or amended by the Congress. The Congress itself, on the other hand, was confronted with an impossible choice. If it amended or annulled Supreme Soviet decisions at its annual meetings then everything that had been done on the basis of those decisions in the intervening period had to be cancelled and done again: a certain recipe for chaos. If, however, it simply approved everything that the Supreme Soviet did, then this made a nonsense of the fact that the Congress was the popularly elected body with the popular mandate.

These constitutional difficulties were never resolved. They led to an enormous amount of procedural wrangling within and between the two institutions and weakened them enormously both as legislative bodies and as bodies of government oversight. Their ability to control the government executive was weakened even further with the establishment of the executive Presidency in March 1990.

4   As a result of a proposal made at the Nineteenth Party Conference local party secretaries were also to be elected as the chairpersons of the republican and local soviets. In effect, this was to duplicate at lower levels Gorbachev's own occupancy of the top party position as General Secretary and the top state position as Chairperson of the Supreme Soviet. This generated enormous criticism because it ran counter to the constitutional aim of separating the party from the state. Nevertheless it was adopted and gradually put into operation during the spring of 1990, with enormous consequences for the new political leaders who took over the reigns of government after the collapse of the USSR in December 1991 (see Chapter 13).

However, despite these 'anti-democratic filters', the new constitutional arrangements were nevertheless a serious blow to the power of the party.

First of all, they undermined the mechanisms of the *nomenklatura* and overlapping membership that had been key means of party control over the soviets because the introduction of a genuine electoral process, no matter how constrained it was, and the fact that government appointments now had to be ratified by the Supreme Soviet at the appropriate level as well as by the party, meant that there was no longer any *guarantee* that party nominees would be elected as soviet deputies or appointed as government ministers.

Secondly, they established the new parliaments as separate centres of power that were independent of the party. The USSR Congress of People's Deputies and the new USSR Supreme Soviet may have been dominated by party members. But this did not make them compliant bodies. On the contrary, the deputies increasingly used their new powers and the new prerogatives of the Congress and the Supreme Soviet to challenge both the government and the party and to hold them to account.

Gorbachev had hoped that the new USSR Congress of People's Deputies would provide society with a living example of the new social consensus and the new 'socialist pluralism of opinions' that he wanted to forge in support of *perestroika*. In fact, what happened was that by the middle of 1989 the Congress of People's Deputies saw the appearance of the Soviet Union's first relatively formalised political opposition in the guise of the Interregional Group of Deputies which exploited every opportunity available to it to challenge the government, the party and the communist majority in the Supreme Soviet. The existence, and the radicalism, of this group in turn spurred on the organisation of informal movements and of new political parties in society at large. The creation of the Congress of People's Deputies and the introduction of semi-competitive elections therefore had precisely the opposite effects to the ones that Gorbachev had intended (see Chapter 8).

Reforming the CPSU

Reforming the CPSU successfully was obviously vital to the realisation of Gorbachev's conception of political reform. However, this was one of the areas in which he failed most completely. This was not just because there was conservative opposition to his reforms within the party. It was also because Gorbachev himself could not come up with a clear idea of what the party was supposed to do, how it was supposed to work, or what it was supposed to be achieving in the new conditions. Just like everyone else Gorbachev could not produce a new and workable definition of the 'leading role' even though he was insisting that it had to be retained.

Gorbachev was clear about what he did not want. He undermined or rejected everything that the party had previously used to justify and maintain its rule. He argued that the party did not and could not know everything as it had always claimed to. Its theories of society were seriously outdated. Its officials were seriously out of touch with ordinary peoples lives. Party officials had to learn how to listen and learn; how to discuss and negotiate policy options with other interest groups; how to engage in the free exchange of information and opinion. They had to stop interfering in matters – economic, social, cultural – that had nothing to do with them and that they knew next to nothing about. They had to stop coercing people and learn to persuade them. They also had to learn to obey the law.

Gorbachev was also clear that the party, like the society it was supposed to be leading, had to 'democratise' itself:

1   It had to introduce *glasnost* into its internal discussions and ordinary party members had to be given greater access to decision making.
2   Officials, at least up to regional (*oblast*) level, had to be competitively elected by the membership to their party positions. Delegates to the party's conferences and congresses also had to be competitively elected. This principle was patchily but increasingly implemented after 1988.
3   From 1988 no one could hold a party position for more than

two consecutive five-year terms.

The CPSU had to become a proper *political* party once more, concerned purely with political and ideological matters. The reform of the central party apparatus in September 1988 removed its control over economic policy. Reforms introduced in 1990 transformed the Politburo into a federal structure which was to be concerned purely with internal party affairs. They also eliminated the pattern of overlapping membership between party and state institutions at the top (although Gorbachev himself continued to combine party and state positions, thus breaking his own rules).

However, these changes left the party and its members in a profoundly ambiguous position.

Internal reforms
The internal reforms undermined the control that the top party leaders and the party apparatus were able to exert over party members and local party organisations. The gradual introduction of *glasnost* and elections undermined both the *nomenklatura* mechanism of appointments within the party and democratic centralism. Party officials were no longer able to demand unquestioning obedience, and party members were no longer willing to give it.

The CPSU and society
The reforms to the CPSU's relations with society also left many party members wondering what they were supposed to do. For example:

1   At the lowest levels party officials were still deeply involved in industry and agriculture where they continued to function in their old role as crisis-managers. A role that actually became more important as the economy deteriorated. After September 1988 these people were increasingly left without guidance as Gorbachev's reforms curtailed the powers of the central party apparatus and removed its ability to interfere in economic policy.

2   The elections to the soviets in 1989 and, even more

importantly, in 1990 presented soviet deputies who were also CPSU members with a real dilemma: were they supposed to be promoting the 'party line' and obeying Moscow or representing their electors' real and immediate interests? Gorbachev had always assumed that 'the party line' *was* what people wanted. However, the elections demonstrated that the very opposite was often the case.

3   It was difficult to know, above all, what it meant 'to be a political party' when there were no other political parties to struggle against and when 'the party' was still controlling many of the levers of power, such as the KGB and the armed forces, and was still dominant in many key institutions like the USSR Congress of People's Deputies and Supreme Soviet. What did it mean to be both a political party and the only ruling party?

This organisational and ideological confusion might not have been so bad had Gorbachev given the party a clear idea of where it was going and what it was supposed to be struggling for. Once the coercive controls that had kept the party together were removed what was needed was a new ideological consensus, a new conception of society and a completely new conception of the party, that could unite the party's members around common goals. However, Gorbachev did not provide this. He told everyone that they were struggling for:

1   *Perestroika*. But this was so contradictory that, as we saw in Chapter 5, no one really understood what it was supposed to be achieving or where it was going.
2   *A constitutional state*. However, anyone with the eyes to see it realised that such a state was not compatible with one-party rule.
3   *Democratic socialism*. But no one really understood what this meant in practical terms, not even Gorbachev himself. It was relatively easy to criticise the Stalinist 'deformations' of the system. But once Stalinism was removed it was not clear that anything was left. As the most radical critics of the Soviet system were already pointing out by 1988 the origins of

Stalinism actually lay in Leninism and the revolutionary origins of the system. Gorbachev himself acknowledged the problem when he declared in 1988 that the CPSU's most urgent task was to clarify 'what exactly socialism is and by what methods it can and must be built, renewed, perfected'.

The result was an ideological and organisational vacuum that left the party without an identity and with no proper ideological and political programme to unite around, to promote or to struggle for. It also left society as a whole without any sense of where it was supposed to be going.

The inevitable consequence was that the CPSU began to disintegrate from within from 1988 on. The top leaders lost control and the party itself began to split into factions over the question of what the party should become. This meant that the party could not withstand, let alone guide or control, the processes of fragmentation that also began to divide society as a whole (see Chapter 8).

The executive presidency

This was hurriedly established in March 1990 and was an acknowledgment on Gorbachev's part that his first set of constitutional reforms had failed to provide the country with a stable form of government. The constant wrangling between the USSR Congress of People's Deputies, the USSR Supreme Soviet and the government (in the form of the USSR Council of Ministers), and the accelerating disintegration of the CPSU had resulted in the fatal weakening of executive power. The creation of the executive presidency was Gorbachev's attempt to redress the balance. This altered the constitutional nature of the Soviet government considerably. Up until 1990 the Soviet Union had been evolving in the direction of a parliamentary political system. After 1990 it shifted direction towards the creation of a powerful and independent presidency.

1   According to the original proposals, the independence of the presidency was to be secured through direct election by the whole

Soviet population. This would have ensured that its incumbent was not beholden either to the party, or to the legislatures or the government for his (or her) position. It would also have enhanced the president's standing as the genuine representative of the people's will. In fact, Gorbachev was elected to the post by the Congress of People's Deputies on 15 March 1990 in an uncontested ballot (but not unanimously; not everyone took part and of those who did 71 per cent voted for Gorbachev, White, pp.60–1). As we have already noted, Gorbachev's failure to stand for popular election in accordance with his own rules undermined his credibility severely.

2   The constitutional powers of the new presidency were very considerable. They included the right:

(a)   to appoint the head of the Council of Ministers (the Prime Minister) and other key government officials, subject to Supreme Soviet confirmation;
(b)   to veto legislation (although the Supreme Soviet had the right to override these);
(c)   to issue decrees (as long as they were not unconstitutional);
(d)   to dissolve the government and suspend its directives;
(e)   to dissolve the USSR Supreme Soviet and to ask the USSR Congress of People's Deputies to elect a new one.

The president also had the constitutional right to declare a state of emergency and to introduce direct presidential rule on a temporary basis in specified parts of the country (see White, p. 61). This was to become highly significant in August 1991 (see Chapter 12).

New executive institutions were also established. The president became the head of a new Council of the Federation. This consisted of the heads of the fifteen Union-republics, and it had responsibility for inter-ethnic and inter-republican matters. The president also headed a new Presidential Council (whose members were presidential appointees) which had responsibility for determining the 'main directions of the USSR's foreign and domestic policy'.

In September 1990 these already considerable presidential

powers were further increased when Gorbachev was given the right to institute emergency measures to deal with potential crisis. Then in December 1990 the whole constitutional arrangement underwent a further shift, effectively completing the move to a presidential system:

(f) The Council of Ministers was abolished and replaced by a smaller Cabinet of Ministers, headed by a Prime Minister, whose members were nominated by, and accountable to the president.

(g) A new Security Council was established, headed and appointed by the president, with responsibility for defence and public order.

(h) The president was given the right to appoint a new vice-president (Gennadi Yanaev, later to head the Emergency Committee in August 1991, was eventually given congressional approval to take this position on 27 December).

(i) The Presidential Council was abolished and the Federation Council revamped. The latter, with President Gorbachev at its head, effectively became the supreme state decision-making body (White, p. 62).

These developments generated a great deal of concern among liberals and democrats who feared, rightly as it turned out, that the foundations were being laid for a new dictatorship. As Boris Yeltsin (then a member of the Congress and of the Interregional Group of Deputies) presciently remarked at the time, the centre was 'seeking to constitutionalise an absolutist and authoritarian regime that could ultimately be used to provide a legal pretext for any high-handed act' (White, p. 62).

However, they also generated further confusion within the institutions of government because the constitutional relationships between these new presidential structures and the two parliaments were never clarified.

On the one hand, the ability of both the Congress and the Supreme Soviet to exert control over this new presidential executive was extremely weak because the president could play one body off against the other. The Supreme Soviet, for example, had the right to override presidential vetoes and to approve presidential appointments. The president, however, could ask the Congress to overturn Supreme Soviet decisions (which it was constitutionally able to do) and even had the right to dissolve the Supreme Soviet altogether.

On the other hand, the president could not actually force the Congress to comply with his decisions since it was a popularly elected body with its own constitutional powers.

In addition, the relationships of accountability and responsibility between new executive bodies like the Presidential Council, the Council of the Federation, the Cabinet of Ministers, the old ministries and the two parliaments remained very unclear; and the constant changes confused matters even more.

The development of the executive presidency therefore had two important consequences:

1 It exacerbated the procedural and political wrangling that went on between the institutions of central government with deleterious results for the policy-making process as we will see.
2 President Gorbachev, with his enormously expanded powers, became the immediate focus for much of the political and ethnic conflict that was to ensue in 1990 and 1991. The creation of the executive presidency therefore weakened his position rather than strengthened it.

The cultural revolution

Glasnost was the final element of political reform. Even when its definition was broadened after 1987 this policy still did not mean unqualified freedom of information, unqualified freedom of the press or unqualified freedom of opinion. Gorbachev's attitude to *glasnost* remained very instrumental. He wanted to promote the circulation of information, public debate and the expansion of knowledge in all cultural and scientific fields in order to improve the functioning of the system as a whole. But he intended that the whole process should still remain within limits set by the party and, in particular, by himself.

For example, he was of the view that the media had a responsibility to society and the party to publish only 'healthy' news and views. And he grew increasingly angry with what he interpreted to be the media's excessive criticism of *perestroika* and its irresponsible sensationalism.

The new Law on Press Freedom, which was only adopted on 12 June 1990 (some five years after the first introduction of *glasnost*) although liberal in many respects, also contained criminal penalties for the 'abuse' of freedom of speech and for the dissemination of information that did 'not correspond to reality' (phrases which could be interpreted very widely).

In the end, no constraints could prevent *glasnost* from snowballing. Once it became clear to everyone that Gorbachev was serious about political reform and had genuinely abandoned coercion as an instrument of rule nothing could stop the rising tide of public demands for the 'whole truth and nothing but the truth' that *glasnost* generated.

The public and private worlds merged as people discovered that truths previously reserved for the kitchen could now be uttered in public without fear of retribution.

Culture, the arts, history became almost inexhaustible sources of new revelations. Hundreds of books and films were unbanned. Archives were re-opened. Special commissions were set up to rehabilitate millions of Stalin's victims, including leading revolutionary contemporaries of Lenin who had, quite literally, become 'non-persons' after their arrest and execution by Stalin. Soviet history had to undergo a complete re-write. One result was that all school textbooks on the history of the Soviet Union were destroyed in 1988 and the school exams in history cancelled across the country until a new, more honest version of Soviet history could be produced for school use. The gradual release of dissidents and political prisoners from labour camps or internal exile also provided the public with living testimony of the political persecution to which the system had routinely subjected many of its citizens.

The media – newspapers, television, journals – which had always painted a rosy picture of society, began to fill up with horror stories about crime, corruption, disasters, prostitution, drug taking, poverty, rape, murder, hooliganism, appalling environmental pollution, the irresponsibility of state officials. Subjects which had always been taboo because such things were not supposed to exist in socialist society. This often had the negative effect of suggesting that official policies were causing these problems rather than simply allowing them to be revealed.

In short, people discovered that there was a whole other side to Soviet society which they had only known about through their own immediate experience, their own family histories, hearsay, rumour and anecdote.

In this context, Gorbachev's continued attempts to impose constraints on *glasnost* and to keep it within the limits set by the party (i.e. himself) simply looked like a new attempt to impose old forms of censorship. This increasingly caused a great deal of public hostility and gradually lost Gorbachev the support of the intelligentsia, the group on which he had relied most to push through his reforms.

Conclusion

It is very easy, with hindsight, to criticise Gorbachev for not taking his reforms far enough. However, we have to remember that Gorbachev was asking the most powerful groups in Soviet society to give up some of their power voluntarily – a thoroughly thankless task that is highly unlikely to be successful in any society, communist or capitalist. Moreover, he was trying to achieve this without provoking a hostile backlash that might have risked the whole enterprise or resulted in a bloodbath. And in this respect at least he was remarkably successful.

Further reading

Gorbachev, Mikhail, *Perestroika: New Thinking for Our Country and the World*, Collins, 1987, Part I

Sakwa, Richard, *Gorbachev and his Reforms, 1985–1990*, Philip Allan, 1990, Chapters 3, 4

Urban, Michael, *More Power to the Soviets: the Democratic Revolution in Russia*, Edward Elgar, 1990

Walker, Rachel, 'The relevance of ideology', in R. J. Hill and J. Zielonka, (eds), *Restructuring Eastern Europe: Views from Western Europe*, Edward Elgar, 1991

White, Stephen, *Gorbachev and After*, Cambridge University Press, 1991, Chapters 2, 3

White, Stephen, Pravda, Alex and Gitelman, Zvi, (eds), *Developments in Soviet Politics*, Macmillan, 1990

Questions

1 What do you think is meant by 'the rule of law'? And why is the rule of law important?

2 Andrei Sakharov called Gorbachev's political reforms 'a campaign to achieve democratic change by undemocratic means'. What do you think he meant?

8

Collapse of the political system

This chapter will look at the practical consequences of the political cal reforms discussed in Chapter 7. We have already touched on some of them.

The revolution from below

Perestroika unleashed the pent-up social energies of Soviet society.

As a result of *glasnost* an identifiable *public opinion began to emerge*. For the first time people could voice their opinions relatively openly and could have their opinions shaped and changed by what was going on around them. They were exposed to increasingly sharp political debates about the nature of the system and the direction of reform. People got into fierce political discussions with neighbours, friends and strangers, particularly around the time of the elections. Many big cities began to develop their own versions of 'Speaker's Corner'. Expressing and defending their views in public forced people to think about them carefully for the first time. They began to develop political opinions and political preferences. And inevitably public opinion divided almost immediately.

Older generations who had spent a life-time 'building socialism' confronted a barrage of criticism which told them that their achievements were worthless and built on rivers of blood. This produced a deep sense of shame in some, particularly the more educated, that they had co-operated with this system; and a growing sense of anger in others who thought that the system's achievements outweighed the price that had been paid for them.

Younger generations, again especially among the educated, were increasingly confirmed in their conviction that socialism was meaningless and that the system could not be reformed but had to be fundamentally transformed. However, they disagreed, inevitably, about what it should be transformed into and how.

People's changing attitudes

People ceased to be obedient and submissive, and could no longer be relied on to behave in the ways that the party had always expected them to.

Thousands of party members became active in the informal movements and opposition politics, and opposed the conservative party apparatus as vigorously as non-party members of these new groups.

Soviet deputies at all levels became less willing to obey the dictates of the party and superior bodies and became increasingly vigorous defenders of local interests and local needs.

Ethnic groups, large and small, began to speak out against the repressiveness of central control and to demand more autonomy.

Ordinary people stopped being passive participants in party-organised pageants and public rituals. They began to protest, demonstrate, demand and in ever larger numbers. A vivid example of this was the public reaction to the official May Day demonstrations in 1990. In Moscow and many other cities these normally heavily controlled and carefully orchestrated celebrations of Soviet power turned into public expressions of opposition to the system. In Moscow, Gorbachev and the Politburo were driven from the reviewing stand on top of Lenin's tomb by the barracking of the crowd. People shouted 'Down with Gorbachev' and held up placards saying things like 'Seventy Years on the Road to Nowhere' (an ironic comment on the triumphant party-designed placards which were usually displayed).

Democratisation

Democratisation reinforced these processes by allowing people to organise themselves.

Thousands of groups sprang up across the country concerned with everything from the provision of social and cultural services to the combatting of alcoholism, crime and environmental pollution. These groups were known as 'informal movements', or the 'informals', both because of their uncertain legal status. There was no law either legalising them or banning them until October 1990 when the new Law on Public Associations finally legalised them. And because many of them were hostile to the formal, official politics of the party.

Many of these groups quickly acquired political overtones or were political from the beginning. Despite Gorbachev's hostility to the idea of a 'multi-party system', the early development of embryonic political parties was inevitable. The democratisation of society unavoidably introduced the idea of *political choice* into the system, even if Gorbachev himself was unwilling to recognise this. It was therefore only natural that at the very first opportunity people would begin to challenge party and state structures that had been coercively imposed upon them (some of which Gorbachev was himself criticising) as well as to discuss alternatives to them (which *glasnost* made possible). And to organise themselves to defend their political interests and to promote political alternatives to the *status quo*. This was especially so in many of the Union-republics where central domination of local affairs had been fiercely resented for years (see Chapter 9).

The year 1988 saw the emergence of the Popular Fronts in the Baltic republics and of the first small political parties some of which, like the Democratic Union, were extremely hostile to the CPSU and the socialist system and dedicated to their overthrow. By 1990, according to White, there were at least twenty parties operating at the federal level and at least five hundred more active at the republican level, although most of them were very small, poorly organised and had no clear political programme.

The year 1989 saw the emergence within the Congress of People's Deputies of the Soviet Union's first political opposition in the form of the Interregional Group of Deputies (see Chapter 7). This was a rather loose political coalition that united the minority of democratically oriented Congressional deputies (three hundred or so) who were opposed to the communist majority and who wanted much faster change. It included people like Boris Yeltsin and Andrei Sakharov amongst its leadership. It was ultimately not very effective in legislative terms (see below) but, for the duration of its existence, it had a profoundly radicalising effect on public opinion. People like Yeltsin and Sakharov spearheaded the radical attack on the old party-state and on the inadequacies of Gorbachev's reforms both within the Congress and outside it. This gave local activists courage and provided them with an example to follow. Sakharov, in particular, also became the symbol and the embodiment of the new democratic revolution. First of all, because he had never forsaken his democratic principles despite years of persecution, and continued to fight for them to the end of his life when he was already weakened and ill. Secondly, because the fact that a well-known and long-standing dissident could not only return from exile but stand for election and become a member of the country's supreme legislature had a simply stunning effect on public opinion. It revealed just how far democratic change in the Soviet Union had already gone by 1989 despite all the problems.

Contradiction and conflict

Unfortunately, however, although *perestroika* unleashed this revolution from below, it did nothing to channel it. On the contrary, people's demands, aspirations and expectations were constantly blocked, frustrated or ignored as a result of the contradictions and inadequacies of Gorbachev's institutional reforms.

The results, inevitably, were growing anger, frustration and cynicism on the part of party officials, political activists and nationalists of all political persuasions, and amongst ordinary people; and mounting social and political conflict.

The problem was that Gorbachev's attempts to marry incompatible principles: one-party rule, constitutionalism and popular sovereignty, meant that the country ended up with the worst of all possible worlds: a politically rejuvenated population and hopelessly inadequate and feeble political institutions.

Effects of continued party control

Gorbachev's obsession with the party and its 'leading role' and his desire to maintain the basic structures of the system intact, meant that hostile conservative party officials, local party organisations, the *nomenklatura*, state bureaucrats retained just enough control within the system to undermine the new democratic processes and fragment them.

Weaknesses of the new institutions

1 The elections of 1989 and the composition of the new USSR Congress of People's Deputies were blatantly rigged to protect the position of the party (see Chapter 7). This generated enormous hostility and conflict.

The elections and the Congress were supposed to be subjecting party-state officials to popular control and yet these officials retained their power to limit this process through the local electoral commissions and the system of reserved seats for public organisations (most of which were dominated by party members). This was so obviously contradictory that everyone could see it for what it was – a fix.

This had two consequences.

(a) In some places, particularly the big cities like Moscow and Leningrad (St Petersburg), the 1989 electoral campaign turned into a real political battle between the 'conservative forces' and the 'democratic forces' in which the party apparatus and the *nomenklatura*, at national and local levels, were readily identified as being the central obstacle to the reform process. The party and the people were brought into direct conflict with each other. An outcome that Gorbachev had wanted to avoid.

(b) The new Congress was dominated by Communist Party members or party-backed candidates and did not really reflect popular opinion. The three hundred or so radical deputies who did manage to get elected and who went on to form the Interregional Group of Deputies were overwhelmed by this 'aggressive obedient majority' as one radical called it. Consequently, although these radicals managed to dominate and influence the debates very effectively, they were unable to have any effect on the Congress's decisions because they were consistently outvoted by the much more conservative majority.

This weakened the authority and legitimacy of the Congress very considerably, especially when the going got very tough from late 1989 on, and frustrated radical opinion.

2   No one could understand why the country needed two elected legislatures at the all-union level in the form of the Congress of People's Deputies *and* the Supreme Soviet. As many critics argued, it made much more sense and was much more democratic to have one directly elected legislature which had the power to amend the constitution, make the laws and oversee the government. And this was the option that virtually all the Union-republics opted for. The fact that this two-tier parliamentary structure was nevertheless imposed at the all-union level was again seen by popular opinion to be an undemocratic means of protecting the party and the top leadership from the effects of popular sovereignty and people power.

The fact that it was the Congress (not the people) which elected the Supreme Soviet (the working parliament) ensured that the membership of the Supreme Soviet (which had only 542 seats compared with the 2,250 seats in the Congress) could be carefully controlled. It proved extremely difficult for the minority of radical MPs to get elected to it. This prevented them from having any influence on the legislative process.

In addition, any electoral link between the Supreme Soviet deputies and their constituencies was broken. The deputies on the Supreme Soviet owed their positions there not to the public but to their fellow deputies in the Congress. They were therefore accountable to, and dependent on, the Congress rather than the public.

Inevitably, this undermined their ability to represent popular interests and consequently greatly weakened their authority in the eyes of the public. According to public opinion polls published in

1990, 31 per cent of respondents thought society was managed by an 'elite that looks after its own interests', and only 14 per cent thought that state institutions took proper account of the needs of those that elected them (see White, p. 66).

3   Although the party's power and authority was progressively undermined after 1988 (see below), it still retained its ownership or control over vital resources like buildings, newspapers, information networks both at national and local levels. Local party organisations also retained considerable influence in local industries, local distribution networks, and so on. Party organisations used this influence and control to frustrate and hamper the activities of democratically elected soviets.

The republican and local soviets also found themselves powerless to do anything because of the continued existence of central planning institutions and the ministries, both of which continued to exert control over local industries, finance, supply and distribution networks.

Consequently, although the local soviets were vested with enhanced constitutional powers as a result of the reforms, and with considerable popular authority and legitimacy as a result of the local elections during 1990 (which, remember, were much more democratic than the 1989 Congress elections), they were quite unable to get anything done. The radical mayor of Moscow, Gavriil Popov, complained in November 1990, 'I essentially have no real power. I don't command anything. I cannot provide a building. I can't ensure protection for privately run shops. I can't do a lot of things' (see Morrison, p. 18). This caused a particularly acute crisis at the republican level (see Chapter 9).

This resulted in a great deal of local anger, frustration and public disenchantment with the democratic process. The competitive elections of 1990 had raised public expectations that life would improve once local government was genuinely representative. Instead, the new soviets proved to be almost as powerless as the old ones. Worse, the political and managerial inexperience of the newly elected deputies and their lack of any sort of common political programme (see below), resulted in even more inefficiency and incompetence, and endless political wrangling (which was certainly new but no less frustrating for the ordinary voter). Ordinary people were fed-up with the party bureaucracy. But they were also increasingly dismayed by the incompetence and divisiveness of the new democratic governments. For example, the approval rating for the Leningrad city soviet, where opposition candidates had won a majority, slumped from 74 per cent in June 1990 to just 20 per cent in January 1991 (see White, p. 65). Growing political apathy, cynicism and a certain nostalgia (particularly among older generations) for a return to 'strong leadership' which could impose a bit of law and order has been the result.

4   Finally, because Gorbachev assumed that the system would continue to be run on the basis of a more democratic version of democratic centralism, no thought was given to the links that were needed to hold all these democratically elected soviets together. The old links had been based on coercion and the presence of party members in all these bodies (overlapping membership, the *nomenklatura* mechanism, etc. see Chapter 2), who ensured that all the soviets adhered to the 'party line'. However, these links could not survive the new electoral processes intact. What was needed to replace them were a new set of relations based on the rule of law and clearly established lines of authority, accountability and responsibility between the soviets at different levels. However, these were not created (partly because such things take a long time). As a consequence the old hierarchy of soviets began to fragment and fly apart (and the political system with it). There was no way in which local soviets could properly communicate with, or be controlled by, the republican soviets. And the links between the USSR Congress and Supreme Soviet and the republican soviets were cut completely by the republican elections of 1990. The soviets began to fight each other for power and control. This added to the institutional confusion and made it even more difficult for the soviets to act as efficient and effective representative and government bodies.

Weaknesses of the new popular forces

The new 'democratic' or 'opposition' forces were bound to be weak and divided to begin with. They lacked political and organisational experience. They lacked resources. And there were bound to be enormous differences in political aspirations, goals, etc. between the different groups that emerged.

However, the environment in which they had to develop and operate made it infinitely more difficult for them to get themselves organised.

Gorbachev's hostility to the development and legalisation of a multi-party system (until late 1990) meant that the new social and political movements and parties developed in something of a vacuum. They were allowed to organise but were not always enabled to do so.

1 Political parties could be created, but they were barely tolerated and could not participate in the political process because they were illegal. Their electoral candidates (if they had them) therefore had to stand as independents.

2 As we have already noted, the legal status of the popular movements in many parts of the USSR remained uncertain until October 1990. In the Russian republic, for example, independent groups were neither legal nor illegal since there was no law either recognising them or banning them until 1990. Whereas in the Baltic republics, they were quickly legalised by sympathetic and progressive republican party leaderships.

3 The new movements and parties confronted the same problems that confronted the soviets. Namely, local party organisations continued to control access to resources – buildings, newspapers, paper, and so on. They also confronted the additional problem that vital pieces of equipment like typewriters, photocopiers, anything for producing and reproducing leaflets, posters, information sheets, were extraordinarily difficult to get hold of. And everyone suffered from a chronic lack of material and human resources.

These factors combined to produce the following consequences:

1   The lack of resources made it very difficult for all groups, but particularly for the newly born political parties, to acquire a large membership or a national identity.

2   The ability of the new popular movements and political parties to organise and operate depended heavily on whether the local party authorities were sympathetic to them or not and would give them access to the media and vital resources. Many local party officials were sympathetic. Many others were not and used all sorts of 'dirty tricks' to try to undermine the activities of the 'informals'.

3   The development of the 'informals' and consequently of local politics was therefore very patchy and followed no consistent pattern across the country. Most groups remained rather localised, even when they became quite large and successful.

4   Few groups were in any sort of position to fight the elections properly (either in 1989 or 1990). This meant that most of the non-CPSU candidates who stood and were elected were isolated independents who lacked any sort of organisational backing and did not share common purposes with other candidates. This made it almost impossible for them to be politically effective once elected because as isolated individuals they had no way of implementing the political programmes on which they had been elected (and these were often very vague and poorly formulated), or of doing anything about their electors' grievances. This weakened the electoral link between the public and its representatives even further, especially at the very local and the federal levels where nationalism was not so significant a unifying factor as it was at the republican level.

5   Even in those areas, like the big cities of Moscow and Leningrad, where the popular movements managed to organise themselves into electoral coalitions and 'popular fronts' (e.g. the Leningrad Popular Front), some of which were highly successful in getting their candidates elected, these coalitions tended to fall apart once the elections were over. This was because although everyone could unite against the CPSU in the struggle to get elected, once they were

elected, they thoroughly disagreed about the policies they wanted to implement and the best way forward.

As a result of all these difficulties the new political forces became increasingly fragmented and polarised. Hundreds of political parties emerged advocating everything from liberal democracy to a return of the monarchy. But none of them were able to acquire a mass popular following. Nor were they able to influence political decision making in any major way.

The only real exceptions were the republican Popular Fronts, particularly in the Baltic republics. These emerged in 1988 and rapidly became successful mass political movements at the level of republican government. This is because nationalism and the fight for republican autonomy were goals around which almost everyone could unite, regardless of their political views. However these Fronts only sought to organise popular opinion within their republics. They did not really seek to establish themselves as inter-republican organisations. Their very nationalism prevented them from doing so. As the CPSU disintegrated, therefore, nationalism, paradoxically, became the only force that could hold people together, just as it was also the key factor that drove them apart.

The effects of democratisation

The new democratic processes and political forces that Gorbachev's reforms unleashed were not strong enough or organised enough to provide the foundations for a new political system, but they were just democratic enough to undermine and destroy the structures of the old political system. This meant, essentially, that it was the power and control of the CPSU that was undermined. Because, as we saw in Chapter 2, the CPSU effectively *was* the political system before 1985.

The key to understanding what happened is to appreciate that:

1   The CPSU lost its identity and organisational integrity as an all-encompassing federal institution.
2   Gorbachev's reforms undermined or destroyed the links that

had held the political system together.

The CPSU, and KGB, lose their old power to coerce
Local party organisations could still wield considerable power over individual people's lives: harassing them, intimidating them, getting them sacked. But once *glasnost* began to set people free, the party lost its power to keep the whole population, and its own members, in a generalised state of repression and fear. People ceased to be automatically obedient and could no longer be relied on to toe the 'party line' and slavishly obey their superiors whatever the cost.

Moreover, the new emphasis on the rule of law meant that it was much more difficult for party officials to get away with the illegal and/or repressive practices they had used in the past. The public became much more aware of these practices because of *glasnost*, and party officials could themselves be brought to court for illegal behaviour.

Thus, although *glasnost* did not succeed in making party officials properly accountable, it did succeed in undermining their security and making it much more difficult for them to function in their old role as the system's crisis managers. They could no longer throw their weight about to the same extent as before and they no longer had any guarantee that their orders would be obeyed.

The CPSU loses its guaranteed control over the soviets and the legislative process
The elections of 1989 and 1990, the creation of the Congress of People's Deputies and the new emphasis on the rule of law established the soviets as alternative centres of power.

1   The emphasis on the rule of law and the idea of the 'law-based state' enhanced the status of the soviets as law-making bodies and, as we saw in Chapter 7, revealed quite clearly that the CPSU had no business interfering with the legislative process. This made it quite impossible for the party to justify its 'leading role'. It therefore had no choice but to agree to its removal from the constitution in February 1990.

2   The elections in 1989 and 1990:

(a) Gave the soviets a popular legitimacy that the party did not
     have and inflicted a fatal blow to the credibility of the CPSU
     as a nationwide institution that could represent all society's
     interests within its own ranks.

(b) Undermined the party's ability to plant its own personnel in
     the soviets through the mechanism of the *nomenklatura*. As
     Prime Minister Ryzhkov complained in 1989, there was a real
     risk that the elections would produce 'Soviets without Com-
     munists', and in some of the big cities, e.g. Leningrad, and
     some of the republics, e.g. the Baltic republics, they
     effectively did. Communist party deputies were forced into a
     minority in many soviets.

(c) Undermined democratic centralism. Multi-candidate elec-
     tions and, crucially, the introduction of the secret ballot, gave
     the public its only effective sanction against its elected repre-
     sentatives. This meant that in order to retain any control over
     republican and local soviets, party officials could no longer
     afford to ignore public opinion completely, as they had done
     in the past. This was particularly so at the republican level
     where the mounting fight for republican autonomy overrode
     almost everything else. Consequently, even where Commu-
     nist party candidates were elected in a majority there was no
     guarantee that they would follow the 'party line' coming from
     Moscow, especially where this conflicted with local demands.

None of these factors meant that the CPSU lost complete control
over all the soviets in the country. On the contrary, the number of
CPSU candidates for soviet deputy who were defeated in both the
1989 and 1990 elections were greatly outnumbered by the
number who succeeded in being elected. And in many parts of the
country, notably the central Asian republics, Communist Party
deputies continued to dominate the soviets. Sometimes their
victory at the polls actually enhanced their popular authority.
Although these victories often reflected the extreme weakness of
local 'democratic forces' rather than the genuine popularity of the
party's candidates.

However, taken together, these factors *did mean* that the CPSU as a nationwide institution, and its central leadership in particular, lost the power to control and integrate the activities of the soviets across the country. The soviets ceased to be obedient and compliant agents of central party-government policy because they also became the active representatives of popular interests. As Boris Yeltsin put it after the Russian elections in March 1990, the soviets 'could no longer play the role of passive conductors of the policy of Union organs; they could not, because there were millions of other voters behind them; they could not, because the policy of the centre diverges from people's basic interests' (see Morrison, p. 243). The central authorities therefore no longer had any guarantee that their policies would be implemented: they might be, they might not be. And, worse still, the centre had no means of making disobedient soviets implement these policies except through the use of very coercive measures. However, such measures would, of course, have undermined the whole purpose of democratisation and could only inflame public opinion (which is what happened in late 1990 when Gorbachev swung to the right). The result was that the system of soviets, and the party itself, began to fragment.

The CPSU loses its internal cohesion as a nationwide organisation

The party's ability to function as a tightly knit institution in which all local party organisations down to the lowest levels were closely bound to the centre and to each other (i.e. the party's organisational integrity) was fatally undermined by internal and external forces.

Note: the CPSU had a total of some 19 million members in 1985. As of 1 January 1986 these 19 million people were organised into 440,363 basic party cells (Primary Party Organisations or PPOs) across the country. These PPOs in turn supported a complex hierarchy of party committees (the full-time apparatus). These co-ordinated the day-to-day running of the party's affairs and required the services of some 5.3 million people (a quarter of the party's membership) in order to function properly. In short, the CPSU was a vast conglomeration of local party organisations and bureaucratic committees which required enormous resources and was difficult to manage even at the best of times.

Internal effects   Internally, as we saw in Chapter 7, this massive institution lost ideological and organisational direction.

1   Its members no longer knew what the party stood for or what they were supposed to be struggling for.

2   The introduction of more democratic practices into the party's internal affairs undermined all the old coercive practices that had held the party together.

(a)   Party members became less obedient. This undermined the 'feudal psychological complex' (see Chapter 4) that had kept everyone strictly subordinated to their superiors from bottom to top.
(b)   *Glasnost* and competitive elections, although only patchily implemented within the party, nevertheless undermined democratic centralism and the *nomenklatura* mechanism. And they certainly undermined the secrecy, the half-truths, the lies that had kept corrupt and incompetent officials, and indeed the whole system, in power for so long.
(c)   Reforms to the internal structures of the top party bodies undermined their power and authority. For example, the reorganisation in 1988 of the Central Committee Secretariat (the CPSU's top permanent 'civil service') disorganised the old lines of control and created considerable confusion.

The central leadership and the party apparatus therefore increasingly lost what power they had to co-ordinate and control the party's enormous number of component parts.

3   These factors combined led to the development of political struggles inside the party that in many ways reflected the political struggles that were going on in society.

(a)   The party's full-time officials and ordinary party members increasingly came into conflict. Ordinary party members were, on the whole, much more in favour of reform and of radicalising the reform process, than the party *apparatchiki*. This was because the reforms quite clearly involved the transfer of power from the apparatus to the ordinary member.

(b) The party's ranks were divided by enormous ideological disagreements into a number of irreconcilable factions. At one end of the spectrum the Democratic Platform (established in January 1990) wanted the creation of a proper multi-party system and for the CPSU to transform itself into a normal parliamentary party. At the other end of the spectrum the platform 'For the Re-creation of the Russian Communist Party' (established in April 1990) united Russian party conservatives around demands for the preservation of the old system. By 1991, according to party officials, there were at least a dozen currents of this sort within the party. These divisions eventually resulted in the first physical split, when leading members of the Democratic Platform finally resigned from the CPSU at the time of the Twenty-eighth Party Congress in July 1990.

In short, these political struggles quite literally tore the party apart.

External effects   Externally, the democratic processes unleashed by the reforms greatly exacerbated the CPSU's internal disintegration.

1   Thousands of ordinary party members became heavily involved in the new civic politics of the informal movements. This heightened their political awareness and made them even more determined to struggle for radical reform within the party. It also intensified their political disillusionment when it became clear by 1990 that the party was incapable of reforming itself and incapable of dealing with the new, more competitive, political conditions.

2   The republican and local elections of 1989–90 placed republican and local party organisations and officials in an impossible position and contributed enormously to the organisational

disintegration of the party. By forcing party candidates to the soviets to stand for competitive election Gorbachev brought the 'party's will' and the 'popular will' into direct conflict with each other. Party officials were therefore caught in a 'Catch-22' situation. On the one hand, Gorbachev insisted that they should remain loyal to Moscow. On the other hand, he was also insisting that if they wanted to retain their control over the soviets they would have to stand for, and win, a competitive election. However, winning competitive elections meant paying some attention to popular opinion. And this in turn meant reducing their obedience to the centre.

This conflict was most dramatically illustrated in December 1989 when the Lithuanian Communist Party formally split from the CPSU and set itself up as an independent social-democratic party. It did this in order to try to improve its plummeting popularity in time for the republican elections in early 1990. It did not work. The new party was too tainted by its communist past and lost the elections anyway. The same strategy was adopted by the Georgian Communist Party a year later.

3   For the first time in thirty years the party's membership began to decline. By 1 January 1990, according to Gorbachev, party membership had fallen to 18.8 million (from 19.3 million as of 1 October 1989). In 1990 3 million members left the party (or some 14 per cent of the total), most of them of 'their own volition'. In early 1991 another 12 per cent said that they were intending to resign (see White, p. 243). And even more of them stopped paying their party dues. As party officials themselves acknowledged this decline reflected a 'general crisis of confidence in the party'. People left (or failed to join) for many reasons, but foremost among them were:

(a)   The party's failure to democratise itself fully.
(b)   Its failure to admit responsibility for past crimes. The only party official who publicly accepted personal responsibility for the failures of the past was Boris Yeltsin and his personal popularity with the public began to soar as a result.
(c)   Its complete lack of direction.

One ex-CPSU member stated his reasons for leaving in the CPSU's official newspaper *Pravda* in May 1990: the party had committed 'unprecedented crimes' for which it had yet to show repentance; and it was still trying to dictate what kind of society future generations should live in, even though it had 'no idea what communism – or socialism, for that matter – really is' (see White, p. 244).

The accelerating disintegration of the CPSU deprived the country of its only unifying political (and economic) force. The party's ability to co-ordinate and crisis-manage the activities of all the different institutions in society: the soviets, the ministries, factories, farms, shops, etc., never very strong to begin with, began to collapse catastrophically after the elections in 1989 and 1990. And there was nothing to replace it. This helps to explain the mounting chaos that overtook the system after 1989 (see also Chapters 9 and 10).

The federal system also began to disintegrate. As we will see in Chapter 9, *glasnost*, democratisation, political reform unleashed the forces of nationalism and of republican separatism that were eventually to destroy the Soviet Union altogether.

Attempted re-centralisation of power

The creation of the new executive presidency in March 1990 was Gorbachev's attempt to halt the processes of fragmentation before they got beyond all control. It represented the return to 'strong government' that many people had been calling for. And it was justified on the basis that the crisis situation developing in the country could only be successfully overcome by a single leader who had the executive powers needed to make quick decisions and who also had the power to impose states of emergency and rule directly if necessary. Gorbachev also hoped that it would enable him to unite the Soviet population behind him in a renewed effort to create a new democratic Soviet socialism. Accordingly, he depicted himself as the non-partisan representative of all the people. At the same time, as we noted in Chapter 5, the new executive presidency also allowed Gorbachev to secure his personal position because it gave him a power base that was independent of the CPSU with its endless internal divisions as well as pre-empting any conservative party plots to oust him from the leadership: even if he had been removed as party General Secretary he would still have been able to rule as Soviet President. However, the enterprise was doomed from the start.

1   Gorbachev's failure to stand for popular, democratic election and his refusal to resign from the post of party General Secretary alienated everyone. The first demonstrated that he was actually unwilling to trust the very people that he presumed to represent and lead. He could hardly unite people behind him if he was not even willing to ask their opinion about his leadership. The second, compromised his position both as party leader and as a democratic reformer. On the one hand, party conservatives, profoundly mistrustful of his intentions and furious that the CPSU was being pushed out of government altogether began to organise against him in earnest. All sorts of conservative platforms and groups now began to emerge within the party, including, most importantly, the new Russian Communist Party that was finally founded in June 1990. On the other hand, the democratic forces, particularly in the Union-republics became convinced that Gorbachev had no intention of abandoning the party even though it was becoming patently obvious by this time that the party was a spent force. They therefore grew increasingly cynical about the possibility of further reform especially in the area of federal relations.

2   The enormous concentration of power in Gorbachev's hands drove the Union-republics who were by now intent on maximising their own autonomy (see Chapter 9) into an open struggle against him. This not only exacerbated the centre-republican struggle for power, it focused it directly on Gorbachev who, as executive President now became personally identified not only with 'the centre' but with the policies that were emanating from it. In this respect, Gorbachev's continued dithering and indecisiveness, despite all his new powers, particularly over the crucial question of economic reform which had reached crisis point by mid-1990, served to undermine him even more.

In effect, therefore, the new executive presidency simply made matters worse rather than better. By using his new powers to repress rather than facilitate the further development of the democratic process in a clear and unambiguous fashion Gorbachev directly undermined both his own position and that of the central government and drove the new democratically elected governments in the republics, the regions and the cities of the Soviet Union into defending themselves ever more vigorously against the centre and all the forces that represented it.

The fragmentation of power

The fragmentation of power at all levels in the system was the inevitable outcome.

The party retained physical control over a great many resources but lacked popular legitimacy, internal cohesion and could no longer function effectively. The new, popularly elected soviets had popular legitimacy but no power to control physical resources and lacked co-ordination. Consequently, they could not function effectively either. And the new executive presidency lacked all authority and had virtually no *effective* executive power. Some commentators have described this as a situation of 'dual power'. But in fact it was more a question of 'dual powerlessness'. As a leading Soviet journalist and social scientist described the situation in July 1990, a full year before the State Committee for the State of Emergency tried to take power in August 1991: 'I think we have a situation now that is even worse than the monopoly on power previously maintained by the party apparatus. The democrats don't have real power, but they can neutralise the power of the [party] apparatus. As a result, power in general simply doesn't exist' (Urban, 'The Soviet Multi-Party System', p. 6).

The new political system that emerged, particularly as a result of the republican and local elections, was therefore not really a *system* at all but rather a chaotic, vicious and localised 'guerrilla war' for resources and power that was fought out between:

1   the central institutions of the state (the party, the Congress of People's Deputies and the Supreme Soviet, the government in

the form of the Council of Ministers and the executive presidency);
2   the central authorities and the Union-republics;
3   the party and the different 'opposition forces' in cities and villages all over the country.

These struggles produced victory for the local party and *nomenklatura* establishment here, victory for the left-wing democratic forces there, stalemate somewhere else. By the time Gorbachev established the executive presidency in March 1990 in a bid to restore order the system was already spinning out of control.

In short, the political reforms undermined and overwhelmed the old political system but did nothing to enable the development of a viable alternative to it. As a result, society lost its cohesion, became thoroughly unpredictable, and, as a direct consequence, also became thoroughly ungovernable.

Conclusion

Again, with hindsight, it is easy to blame Gorbachev for everything that went wrong between 1987 and 1991. However, we should bear the following in mind.

No system can function without a heavy concentration of power in state institutions and without imposing considerable limits on the freedom of its citizens. And all systems find it difficult to balance the needs of government with the demands of citizen representation.

In liberal democracies the political system works largely because:

1   The majority of people are extremely apathetic towards national and local politics (many do not even bother to vote).
2   Two or three political parties (often supported by powerful vested interests) have managed, over time, to organise and monopolise political opinion concentrating it in the centre of the political spectrum. This makes it very difficult for minority interests or dissenting voices to get themselves heard (which is

why they sometimes resort to violence).

3   It is very difficult (although not impossible) to alter the distribution of power in such systems between state and society, rulers and ruled, elites and people to a significant extent because power is not completely concentrated in any one place. Thus elections give ordinary people the power to change the politicians in charge of government. But elections do not affect the economic elites who derive their power from the ownership and control of property, economic resources, private wealth, etc. Nor do they affect the professional elites whose power derives from their knowledge and expertise.

Gorbachev and the reformers who supported him therefore confronted two intractable problems.

1   In countries trying to make the transition to some sort of democracy (especially if they have no previous history of democracy) the fragmentation of the political spectrum into a myriad of parties and groups is almost inevitable because everyone *wants* to have their say, people are full of political energy and enthusiasm. However, it is extremely difficult to govern in such circumstances even when government institutions are relatively stable, well established and reasonably representative because government gets overwhelmed by a torrent of demands which it cannot deal with or satisfy (often known as the problem of 'government overload'). It is also extremely difficult to find ways of trying to reconcile all the newly emergent interests. People are much more unlikely to compromise when the political stakes are high as they generally are when a system is in the process of change.

2   In order to reform the Soviet system Gorbachev had to find a way of enabling the party-state to relinquish some power without losing power altogether. However, the concentration of political and economic power in the party was so complete, or rather, the powerlessness of ordinary people was so absolute, that any real change to the distribution of power, no matter how small, was bound to have profoundly destabilising knock-on effects. One-party rule was fundamentally based on coercion; party officials

controlled almost everything of any significance in their patch, usually through informal means, and the system had come to depend on this. Depriving party officials of even part of this control, therefore, inevitably threatened the cohesion of the system as a whole. The introduction of competitive elections did not just change the people in charge of government it inevitably challenged the whole nature of the system itself.

Further reading

Hosking, Geoffrey, *The Awakening of the Soviet Union*, Heinemann, 1990

Kagarlitsky, Boris, *Farewell Perestroika: a Soviet Chronicle*, Verso, 1990

Kornev, Nikolai, 'The Leningrad People's Front: the logic of hindsight', *Russia and the World*, No. 19, 1991

Lane, David, *Soviet Society under Perestroika*, Unwin Hyman, 1990, Chapters 3, 4

Morrison, John, *Boris Yeltsin: from Bolshevik to Democratic*, Penguin, 1991

Robinson, Neil, 'Gorbachev and the place of the party in Soviet reform, 1985–1991', *Soviet Studies*, Vol. 44, No. 3, 1992, pp. 423–43.

Sakwa, Richard, *Gorbachev and His Reforms 1985–1990*, Philip Allan, 1990, Chapter 4

Smith, Gordon, *Soviet Politics: Struggling with Change*, Macmillan, 1992, second edition, Chapters 5, 6

Urban, Michael, *More Power to the Soviets: the Democratic Revolution in the USSR*, Edward Elgar, 1990

Urban, Michael, 'Politics in an unsettled climate: popular fronts and informals', *Detente*, no. 14, 1989

Urban, Michael, 'The Soviet multi-party system', *Russia and the World*, No. 18, 1990

White, Stephen, *Gorbachev and After*, Cambridge University Press, 1991, Chapters 2, 7

Questions

1   In June 1988 a leading communist party official said, 'The question of power, that is the central question of *perestroika*'. Discuss.

2   Were Gorbachev's political reforms a success or a failure in your opinion?

3   In your view, which of Gorbachev's political reforms was most significant and why?

9

The fragile union

Militant nationalism and republican separatism contributed enormously to the mounting chaos described in Chapter 8. More importantly, it was nationalism and republican separatism that brought about the final dissolution of the Soviet Union and Gorbachev's removal from power at the end of 1991.

It is also nationalism that has been preventing the development of harmonious relations between the new sovereign states that emerged from the rubble of the old system; and that continues to threaten a great many of these new states, especially Russia, with the possibility of further internal disintegration (see Part III).

This chapter will examine why it was that, in a matter of about three years, nationalism and republican separatism became such powerful and destructive forces.

What is nationalism?

Nationalism is the collective political expression of ethnic identity. Generally, it only appears in response to oppression, deprivation and conflict of one sort or another. People who are leading tranquil lives and/or whose physical needs are largely being satisfied are not usually particularly conscious of their ethnic identity. They may celebrate their cultural traditions through ceremonies, public holidays, and so on, but in peaceful times these are usually inward-looking activities.

Conflict or oppression, on the other hand, force people to

defend themselves and their interests. Of course, conflicts particularly over scarce resources – jobs, housing, land, etc. – regularly go on between individuals and groups in most societies. But ethnic or national identity becomes the central organising principle, the central element to which people relate all their other grievances, if the people involved:

1 Become aware that they share certain traits in common: usually language, historical, cultural and/or religious traditions; sometimes skin colour; sometimes, but not always, the same geographic location.
2 Feel themselves or their interests to be collectively threatened by the actions of another group.

Nationalism, therefore, is a particular way of defining and defending group interests in a situation of conflict.

Nationalism has become a potent political force in the twentieth century, partly because of the development of the modern nation-state. Most of the states now in existence (and this included the Soviet Union) have their origins in imperial traditions (whether as colonisers or as the colonised) that resulted in the forceable incorporation of different ethnic groups into a single territory. This meant, on the one hand, that nationalism became an important instrument of state policy as a means of manipulating and changing people's identity. The dominant groups in the new nation-states sought to forge these disparate ethnic populations into new relatively homogeneous nations for administrative as well as political reasons. This usually meant imposing a common language, a common history, a common economic and political system and restricting or repressing those of the subjugated groups. On the other hand, nationalism also became a means of defence for these subjugated groups, a means for preserving their identity within these new states.

This process generated an enormous amount of conflict particularly in the early days of state building. However, in the modern industrial countries this conflict was eventually reduced to manageable levels or eliminated by the growth of state power and rapid economic development. The first ensured that any militant opposition that might emerge could be effectively crushed or controlled. The second ensured that everyone benefited from increased standards of living, better education, etc. and therefore:

1   had less reason to protest in the first place; and
2   had very good reasons to accept absorption into the dominant culture, particularly if they wanted to carve out a good career for themselves.

However, economic decline can, and is, threatening this process. As one Soviet observer put it in the context of *perestroika*, 'When the pie is large, all the people are happy. But when the pie is small, everyone fights for his own piece' (see Smith, *Soviet Politics*, p. 173).

Soviet federalism

For many years it looked as though the Soviet Union had been successful in following this general pattern. Modernisation increased standards of living, particularly in the big cities; created a literate and relatively well educated population and led to the development of indigenous political, social and cultural elites who benefited considerably from the system. According to the limited survey evidence available it also seemed as though the CPSU had been quite successful in getting people to identify themselves as 'Soviet' as well as identifying themselves with their ethnic group (see Goble). The level of visible conflict between national groups, or between national groups and the central authorities, was extremely low. There were occasional conflicts, especially over the use of language, but these proved to be easily contained by the central party-state authorities. And, on the whole, the federation's various republics and national territories seemed to be obedient to Moscow in all essential matters. In fact, the CPSU's management of inter-ethnic relations looked to be so successful, even by the mid-1980s, that there was enormous complacency both among the party's leaders who mostly insisted that the 'nationality question' as they called it had largely been 'solved'; and among outside observers of the Soviet scene, very few of whom considered that the 'nationality question' would ever become an unmanageable problem.

This complacency was fatal as it turned out. We can now see that the Soviet federal system generated the potential for enormous conflict, first of all, because its internal structure was extremely complex. And, secondly, because it was in the federal system that the old contradictions and tensions of the Soviet system were most precariously balanced. This was a legacy that went back to 1917. As long as the central party-state authorities retained their coercive control over society it proved possible to prevent these contradictions and tensions from becoming unmanageable. However, once the reform process began to undermine the power and authority of central institutions federal relations required much more careful and imaginative management than they actually received.

Unfortunately, Gorbachev's extraordinary complacency about, and insensitivity to, the 'nationality question', meant that he not only managed it very badly, he actually failed to manage it at all. Indeed, in crucial respects, his reforms almost seemed calculated to inflame inter-ethnic and centre-republican relations. The result was that *perestroika* exacerbated old problems, created new ones, and led to an escalation of (often interacting) conflicts that, in the end, no one could control.

This, in turn, left a legacy of problems for the new countries of the Commonwealth of Independent States (see Part III).

Historical legacy

The federal system that Gorbachev inherited both sustained and promoted national identity and simultaneously repressed it. This created fertile soil for the development of nationalism, once conditions allowed because, as we noted above, nationalism thrives on repression, conflict and discrimination.

The Bolsheviks inherited the old tsarist multi-national empire. The only way to hold it together after the 1917 revolution was to use a mixture of coercion and persuasion.

Coercion

The coercion consisted in:

1   Using force to incorporate countries, like Georgia, that did
    not want to become members of the new state.
2   Imposing unified political and economic control through the
    Communist Party and central planning in order to integrate
    the various parts of this huge empire.

Persuasion

The persuasion consisted in constructing a federal system that
recognised the aspirations of the various national groups to
liberation, self-determination, self-government and cultural
autonomy.

The result was the development of a complex federal structure
that combined democratic and decentralised political institutions
with repressive centralist control.

This paradoxical system *sustained ethnic identities* and
national consciousness in both positive and negative ways.

Positive

1   Almost every identifiable ethnic group was granted a territory
of its own and constitutional rights (in principle, at least) of local
self-government. This produced the fifteen Union-republics
(after 1940), the largest territorial units: five of which (Russia,
Azerbaijan, Georgia, Uzbekistan, Tadjikistan) contained twenty
autonomous republics, eight autonomous regions and ten
autonomous areas within their own territories (although Russia
contained by far the most of these and was actually a federation in
its own right).

2   The key institutions of the political and economic system
reflected this territorial structure in almost every respect.

(a) All the republics, Union and autonomous, had their own
    constitutions, Supreme Soviets, Councils of Ministers
    (smaller units only had soviets). Each of the Union-republics
    (with the exception of Russia until 1990) also had its 'own'
    communist party, with its own Party First Secretary,
    Politburo and Central Committee. Although the CPSU as a

whole remained a unitary organisation with a single programme and a single set of rules.
(b) Ethnic interests were the only sectional interests in society
that were allowed official representation within party and
government institutions:
● The old federal Supreme Soviet had two chambers. The
second chamber, called the Council of Nationalities, was
elected proportionally by all the nationalities in the Soviet
Union.
● The CPSU practiced a policy of appointing nationals to
key political positions at the Union-republican level and
below. This meant that republican party-state structures
were usually dominated by members of the titular
nationality (i.e. Georgians in Georgia, Ukrainians in
Ukraine and so on).

3 The central authorities promoted social and cultural policies
that nurtured and sustained the development of the different
languages and cultures within the overall framework of promoting
a 'Soviet' cultural identity. These included allowing local education in native languages and the celebration of local traditions.

Negative
1 Many of the USSR's internal borders were arbitrarily drawn
(mostly by Stalin), usually on the principle of 'divide and rule'.
And party leaders very often treated them as a matter of personal
whim. For example, Khrushchev donated the Crimea to the
Ukraine in 1954 for no very good reason, even though the Crimea
had been part of Russia for centuries (the Crimea has been a
considerable source of conflict between the new states of Russia
and the Ukraine since 1991). Consequently, many ethnic communities found themselves arbitrarily divided between different
republics, regions or territories; or arbitrarily shifted from the
jurisdiction of one republic to another. This perpetuated and
sometimes aggravated long-standing ethnic enmities that go back
centuries, or created simmering tensions.

2 Some small ethnic groups did not have territories of their own

but were dispersed and sometimes subject to local discrimination. Others were subject to systematic discrimination by the state, e.g. the Jews. Yet others, the 'punished peoples', such as the Crimean Tartars, the Volga Germans, had been exiled from their homelands by Stalin during the Second World War and wanted their homelands back, (even though these had been re-settled by other peoples).

3   As a result of industrialisation and economic integration some 60 million people (many of them Russians) lived permanently outside their 'own' territories. This meant that:

(a)   Most republics contained a mosaic of different peoples. This created considerable potential for discrimination and friction over access to resources, jobs, education, and so on.

(b)   In some republics the native population found itself in a minority. For example, in Kazakhstan, native Kazakhs constituted only 36 per cent of the total population of 17 million, compared with Russians at 41 per cent. In addition, Kazakhstan contained over 90 other nationalities. This created a sense of national vulnerability in the affected native populations (the Baltic republics were also considerably affected by this); and again created tensions over access to resources, and so on.

Consequences

Taken together these factors were guaranteed to ensure:

1   *that ethnic groups and cultures perpetuated themselves* rather than being assimilated over the long term as the CPSU hoped they would be. With some exceptions, even small ethnic groups had a patch of territory to protect and a vested interest in trying to maintain their language and culture not only against the central authorities but also against their neighbours. There was considerable inter-ethnic hostility within the various national territories (small minorities were often discriminated against by the dominant nationality), as well as tension between the central authorities and various national groups, particularly the large titular

nationalities (i.e. those after whom union and autonomous republics were named).

2 *the development of indigenous political, social and cultural elites* with a vested interest in trying to increase their local power and autonomy within the system. This was particularly so at the Union-republican level where, as the system degenerated and became more difficult to control, the party elites were able to carve out a considerable degree of bureaucratic autonomy for themselves. They had a great deal of latitude in deciding how central policies would be implemented and were able to wield enormous power over their populations. They sometimes used this power to practise discriminatory policies against minorities within their republic.

3 *the legitimisation of nationalism.* Grievances against the central authorities, demands for a fairer distribution of resources, and so on, were often expressed in (very weak) nationalist terms because this was the only way in which they could be legitimately advanced. Republican leaders in particular increasingly used the 'nationalist' card as a means of trying to increase their leverage over the central authorities and increase the resources flowing to their republic (see White, p. 151).

The extraordinary complexity of this system was also bound to mean that the system would be incredibly difficult to manage once *glasnost* enabled ethnic grievances to be voiced, and political reform raised the question of power and autonomy.

Unitary Federalism
To complicate matters, Soviet federalism also *repressed national identities* by enforcing political, cultural and economic integration through a cumbersome, bureaucratic and highly centralised political and economic 'command' system that, as we saw in Part I:

1 concentrated all power and control over national resources and the power to make all crucial political and economic decisions in the all-union party-state authorities. For instance, only some 6 per cent of industry was controlled at Union-republic level.

2   thoroughly undermined local autonomy and constitutional rights to self-government and self-determination.

3   therefore subjugated most local needs and local interests to the goals and plans of these central institutions.

4   tried to encourage cultural integration through the imposition of rather repressive policies such as 'Russification'. For example, the CPSU:

(a)   Promoted Russian as the official language and ensured that schools and universities teaching in Russian (as opposed to local languages) got the lion's share of available resources.
(b)   Promoted Russian culture as the 'best' and 'most advanced' culture and made it difficult for other ethnic groups to write about and publish works on their histories, literary traditions, etc.
(c)   Ensured that the top party-state positions in the system, and the central bureaucracies were dominated by Russians.

This policy reflected the party's desire to create a homogeneous and united 'Soviet people'. It created an enormous amount of friction, resentment and hostility among non-Russians. And a great many Russian citizens resented the way in which the party hijacked their culture for its own purposes.

Note. A word needs to be said about the peculiar status of Russia, or the Russian Soviet Federated Socialist Republic (RSFSR) as it was formally known. Russia was by far the largest republic in the Union, possessed the bulk of its natural resources and the bulk of its population and industry. (Look at an old map and you'll see how big it is). However, it always had a subordinate political status within the Union. It did not have its own republican party organisation, and although it did have its own government structure in the form of the Russian Supreme Soviet and the Russian Council of Ministers, most of its affairs were actually run and controlled largely by the all-union authorities in Moscow. The Russian government was therefore quite powerless even by comparison with the governments of the other Union-republics.

This came about because the all-union authorities used the wealth and culture of Russia in order to maintain their power over the Union as a whole. For example, they ruthlessly exploited its natural resources, exporting vast quantities of its gold, oil, diamonds and precious metals in order to finance the huge central bureaucracies and federal policies (e.g. defence) in which the Russian people had never had a say. This meant that Russia was frequently identified with 'the centre', with the result that Russians were often blamed by non-Russians for policies (like Russification) that actually had nothing to do with them and for which the central authorities were directly responsible.

This generated a great deal of Russian resentment which Boris Yeltsin was quick to articulate when he became Russia's elected president in June 1991.

It also meant that when Russia decided to demand its sovereignty, the 'centre' lost the reservoir of wealth that had kept it in power. President Gorbachev became a president without a country, and the Soviet government a set of institutions without a territory to govern or exploit. Russia's declaration of state sovereignty on 12 June 1991 therefore spelled the end of the old Union.

Centralised control did also have its positive aspects.

1 It ensured the redistribution of some wealth from the richer republics to the poorer ones in order to try to equalise levels of development and standards of living. Although, inevitably, this was resented by the richer republics, like Russia.
2 It was also the party's repressive control that prevented long-standing ethnic enmities from breaking out into open conflict. The inter-ethnic violence that broke out in February 1988 between the Union-republics of Armenia and Azerbaijan over 'ownership' of the autonomous territory of Nagorno-Karabakh was the most notorious example of what could happen once central control was weakened.

However, these were not experienced as benefits by ordinary people but as forms of oppression. The result was, in the words of a Georgian speaking in 1992, that 'many people regarded the oppression of the system as national oppression' (Kazutin).

The consequences for reform

This contradictory combination of ethno-federalism (i.e. in which territorial units are based on ethnic groups) and repressive centralism effectively ensured that the various nations and ethnic minorities were given just enough freedom to perpetuate themselves, but no freedom to govern themselves autonomously as was promised in the Soviet constitution. It therefore created an extremely volatile environment into which to introduce any reforms, let alone political and economic reforms whose success hinged on the *real but limited* redistribution and decentralisation of power.

Central mismanagement

Undoubtedly the biggest mistake of Gorbachev's career as Soviet leader was his failure to realise that any reform programme had to address the federal structure of the Soviet Union *first* if it was to be successful.

Republican and nationalist struggles for autonomy began in earnest in 1988 when it became clear that Gorbachev was really serious about introducing radical change, but that his detailed plans for political reform (as presented at the Nineteenth Party Conference in June) contained little on the question of reforming the federation and showed every sign of intending to retain the basic centralist structures of the Soviet system intact, like one-party rule. Worse, in November 1988, Gorbachev made it clear that he had no intention of even considering federal reform until the first stage of democratisation (elections, strengthening the soviets) had been successfully completed.

This was a fatal error. The fundamental difficulty that Gorbachev refused to confront, but that everybody else in the Soviet Union could see, was that every reform that was introduced, economic as well as political, carried clear and profound implications for the nature of the federation as a whole. This was because the federal structure was the bedrock on which the rest of the political system had been based. It underpinned the constitution, and all of society's key institutions reflected it. Any reform to those institutions therefore inevitably carried consequences for the federal relationships that they embodied. For example, strengthening and improving the representativeness of the soviets automatically raised questions about the division of powers between the USSR Supreme Soviet, the republican Supreme Soviets and all the local soviets. Federal reform therefore had to be a fundamental part of any new constitutional settlement – there could be no new constitution without a new Union Treaty to replace the one of 1922.

Gorbachev's failure to grasp this until 1990 (by which time it was far too late) meant that:

1   Right from the beginning his reforms were seen as inadequate half-measures that either ignored or infringed republican and local rights. This generated an enormous degree of frustration, anger and conflict.
2   Federal relations began to change anyway as a *practical consequence* of the reform process. The elections of 1989–90 and the catastrophic decline of the economy were absolutely crucial in this respect. However, instead of occurring in a relatively orderly way these changes increasingly took place in an unorganised, chaotic and conflictual fashion with each national group and each territory seizing its opportunities and fighting for its own rights irrespective of the rights and interests of others.

Crisis

To be fair to Gorbachev he was confronted with a number of intractable problems that were not of his making, that defied easy solutions, and which his reforms simply allowed to surface. For example,

The problem of internal borders

According to Gorbachev, speaking in early 1991, only 30 per cent of the USSR's internal borders were ever legally defined. By early 1990 about 35 were being disputed between different national groups. *Moscow News*, the radical Moscow weekly, estimated that by March 1991, there were seventy-six territorial claims being advanced by different groups against each other. The difficulty was that most of these claims were mutually incompatible. Consequently, even if Gorbachev had been willing to re-negotiate the federation from scratch it is certain that not everyone would have been happy with the result. Many of these problems continue to plague the new states of the CIS.

Inter-ethnic hostilities
These were mostly the consequence of long-standing historical enmities and/or of previous policies of divide and rule:

1   The bitter and violent Armenian-Azeri conflict over the 'ownership' of Nagorno-Karabakh. This autonomous territory was always largely populated by Armenians but was ceded to Azerbaijan by Stalin in 1921, and had been subject to a great deal of discrimination by the Azeri authorities ever since. The Armenians, not unnaturally, wanted it back and saw *glasnost* and democratisation as an opportunity to achieve this. The Azeris, on the other hand, refused to give it up. By mid-1992, this had turned into an all-out war between the two republics that threatened to spill over into neighbouring countries and in which national pride, revenge, and popular anger were all equally mixed. There is no solution to this conflict, unless one side is willing to give in. Even if the Armenians succeed in winning Nagorno-Karabakh back by force of arms the Azeris will never let them keep it (and vice versa).

2   In Uzbekistan in 1989 several hundred people were killed, and many thousands more turned into refugees, as the result of rioting between the Meskhetian minority (another one of Stalin's 'punished peoples', forceably relocated from Georgia to Central Asia in 1944) and native Uzbeks. Two of the main causes were poverty and discrimination.

These were intractable problems. However, there is no doubt that Gorbachev's singularly unimaginative approach to federal issues made them worse. In the absence of a willingness to renegotiate the federation, or to treat with all sides on the basis of equality, the only instruments that remained to Gorbachev were (1) to support the *status quo*, and (2) to use force to try and quell the unrest. For instance, Soviet troops were sent into Tbilisi, capital of Georgia in April 1989; Baku, capital of Azerbaijan, in January 1990; and into the Baltic republics in 1991 in unsuccessful attempts to quell nationalist disturbances. However, such measures simply served to inflame local hostilities, to radicalise the nationalist movements (especially, but not only, in the affected republics) and to destroy what remained of Gorbachev's credibility.

Still, these conflicts did not, on the whole, threaten the integrity of the Union because they were mostly localised. What did threaten the integrity of the Union was the conflict between the centre and the Union-republics. Here Gorbachev must take most of the blame.

Centre-republican conflict

To begin with none of the Union-republics, not even the radical Baltic republics, wanted to secede from the Union (such a thing was unthinkable in 1988).

Note: The Baltic republics of Lithuania, Latvia and Estonia were the most radical in their demands from the outset because they were only incorporated into the USSR in 1940 as a result of the Soviet–Nazi Pact signed in 1939. Prior to that they had been independent states from 1918 to 1939. They were also the most highly developed republics in the Union. However, even they were not demanding to leave the Union in 1988 or 1989.

What they all wanted was autonomy within the federation and federal relations that were based on mutual consent and an equal balance of power between the centre and the republics: in other words, the practical realisation of their status as 'sovereign socialist states' as promised in the 1977 constitution. This was the logical outcome of Gorbachev's own calls for 'profound demo-cratisation' and the creation of a 'law-based state'.

What radicalised them after 1988 was the inadequacy of Gorbachev's actual reform policies and his failure even to acknowledge the justice of their case. For instance:

1   *Economic reform* acknowledged the need for republican autonomy and gave considerable managerial control to the republics (in 1988 and 1989) but did not give them ownership or control over the natural resources and fixed assets (i.e. factories, power lines, railways, roads, etc.) on their territories. These remained firmly in the hands of the central, all-union authorities. Nor did it give them greater access to many of the administrative processes that governed economic activities on their territories. These also remained firmly in the hands of the central ministries and the central government.

At the end of March 1990 (just after the Russian republican elections), for example, Boris Yeltsin complained that Russia owned no more than 15 per cent of the fixed assets on its territory: 'Just imagine 15 per cent! The basic industries of fuel and power generation, iron and steel and engineering belong entirely to the Union . . . The Russian economy remains to this day, in essence, colonial and dependent' (Morrison, p. 243). And in mid-October the same year he was complaining that 70 per cent of industrial output in Russia still came from factories subordinated to the Union government. 'We have come up against a powerful and undisguised sabotage, by the Union government, Gosplan, Gosbank, and the Union ministries, of Russia's efforts to demarcate union and republican property' he declared (Morrison, p. 197).

2   Gorbachev's inadequate *political reforms* were an even greater cause of anger and frustration. Gorbachev's calls for the creation of a 'law-based state', the rule of law and a new constitution went to the heart of what the federation was all about. They raised fundamental questions about the division of powers and responsibilities, the composition of the Union, the political status of smaller territories, and about *who* had the right to dictate what powers to whom.

However, Gorbachev's refusal to acknowledge the need for a new Union Treaty for the two crucial years from 1988 to 1990 (during which period there were three new sets of elections, national, republican and local). His insistence that the new 'law-based state' was to retain key features of the old 'lawless state', notably central planning and the leading role of the CPSU (even if modified). And his insistence that the centre would continue to dictate terms to everyone else, meant that virtually all demands for change, however moderate and logical, were rejected out of hand.

This radicalised public opinion dramatically:

1   The struggle for democracy in the Union-republics (and smaller territories) became increasingly identified with nationalist struggles for autonomy and self-determination, the logical outcome of which was not autonomy within the Union but independence from it.

2   Popular support in virtually all the republics for politicians who promoted the democratic-nationalist cause, even if they were party officials, grew by leaps and bounds.

The first turning point

The republican and local elections of 1989–90

These consequently took place in an already volatile environment and were therefore guaranteed to exacerbate the situation. They enabled the ordinary voter to express an opinion. The result was victory for the nationalist Popular Fronts and their allies in, for example, the Baltic republics, Georgia, Armenia; and a string of successes for pro-democracy candidates in other republics like Russia and the Ukraine.

They also transformed the political environment by tipping the balance of authority away from the centre and in favour of the republics. The newly elected republican legislatures were much more genuinely representative than any of the federal institutions (either the Congress of People's Deputies elected on the basis of a rigged ballot in 1989; or the new presidency established in March 1990 which Gorbachev took over without standing for popular election). Consequently, the republics saw no reason why they should continue to be subordinate to the USSR constitution, all-union laws, and the demands of the centre, all of which they considered to be illegitimate.

The popular authority vested in them by the elections gave them the mandate they needed to try and take what the centre would not give them. Beginning with Lithuania and Estonia in March 1990, followed crucially by Russia in June, virtually every Union-republic and autonomous republic in the country had declared itself sovereign, or was moving towards such a declaration, by the end of 1990. These declarations were usually accompanied by amendments to the republican constitutions which gave precedence to republican laws over federal laws. This meant that no federal law would be implemented unless it was first approved by the republican Supreme Soviet.

Even at this stage none of the Union-republics, with the sole exception of Lithuania which voted for outright secession, were actually demanding the break-up of the Union. They were all too well aware of the potential costs of independence for their economies which were heavily integrated and unlikely to be strong enough to stand alone. The Union government continued to control the money supply, the banks, etc. And the 60-odd million people who lived outside their 'namesake' territories relied on the continued existence of the Union for their status as Soviet citizens.

However, republican demands became much more radical as a result of the elections.

1   The Union-republics now wanted the federation to be thoroughly transformed. They demanded the negotiation of a completely new Union Treaty. And they demanded a drastic reduction in the centre's powers. It was to have only the minimum powers necessary to serve as a co-ordinating centre. Speaking at a news conference in August 1990, Yeltsin held his hands apart almost as far as he could reach and said 'This is the sort of centre we have now.' Then held them about six inches apart and said 'This is the sort of centre we need.'

2   The Union-republics also wanted to ensure that they would have the dominant voice in deciding what the new Union would look like. As Ruslan Khasbulatov, the speaker of the Russian parliament put it in June 1990: under the old system 'The centre, with its authority, indisputably determines the extent of both its own powers and the powers of the republics. The proclamation of

sovereignty by the republics changes this procedure cardinally.' Any new deal had to be negotiated between the republics themselves 'without the participation of the currently empowered representation of the centre', i.e. without Gorbachev (Morrison, p. 190).

3   The Union-republics also used their new-found authority to challenge the policies and laws of the centre where they could. This became known as the 'war of laws':

(a)   They refused to implement Soviet laws unless they were first approved by republican Supreme Soviets. And there was nothing that the USSR Congress of People's Deputies, the Supreme Soviet, or Gorbachev as president could do to make the republics, or their citizens, obey Soviet law short of using force (and even this did not work). This conflict greatly undermined the status and authority of the central institutions. In September 1990 a USSR Supreme Soviet deputy asked Gorbachev: 'Why are your decrees not being fulfilled? When will they start to be fulfilled? That's one thing. And what measures will be adopted by you in the future, to prevent your decrees from not being fulfilled? I should like to hear this from you' (Morrison, p. 196). Gorbachev had no answer.

(b)   The republics could also refuse to co-operate with the centre in areas where the centre was most heavily dependent on them for the implementation of policy:
   •   The more radical republics encouraged their young men to resist the annual military draft (two years' military service was compulsory for all male eighteen-year-olds) with considerable success. By early 1991 this was beginning to have serious effects on the organisation of the armed forces.
   •   Many republics refused to implement price increases on retail and agricultural goods dictated by the centre during 1990. This added greatly to the galloping federal and republican budget deficits because it meant that state subsides on these goods had to remain very high.
   •   Most crucially of all, by the end of 1990 many of the

republics, led by Russia (which because of its enormous size and wealth made the biggest contribution), began to insist that their contributions to the Soviet budget should be drastically cut. This threatened to deprive the centre of the resources it needed to maintain its vast bureaucracies, the armed forces, etc.

The worsening economic situation in 1990 (partly the result of this 'war of laws') gave the republics (and smaller territorial units) additional incentives to become independent from the centre, as they sought to protect their economies from escalating economic collapse. Even relatively small regions, like the Crimea, the western Ukraine, and the cities of Moscow and Leningrad, began to push for greater independence so as to be able to implement their own plans for local economic management and reform (e.g. local rationing systems).

From this point on a final showdown was probably inevitable. The republics were no longer willing to make do with concessions handed down from on high. The three Baltic republics in particular were now determined on achieving complete independence. Pro-Soviet conservatives, especially in the central all-union institutions like the party, were becoming increasingly worried about the possibility that the Union might disintegrate altogether. The Union-republican drive for sovereignty not only threatened the enormous powers of the centre and therefore the power of many conservative officials, it was also causing all sorts of other problems:

1   Many autonomous republics were now demanding independent status as Union-republics. This sometimes caused considerable and occasionally bloody conflict at local levels. For example, the autonomous republic of Abkhazia in Georgia wanted Union-republic status while the Georgians wanted it to be fully assimilated. The result was armed and bloody conflict.
2   Minority groups and the smaller territories were waking up to the fact that they might not want to be part of sovereign republics that could well have even more power to

discriminate against them than they had possessed before. This was also the cause of considerable local conflict.

The second turning point

However, there was a point in the summer of 1990 when it looked as though things might have been different. As we noted in Chapter 5, the two presidents, Gorbachev and Yeltsin, co-operated in trying to produce a radical economic reform programme that would have turned the country towards the market and given genuine economic autonomy to the republics. And Gorbachev finally acknowledged the need for a new Union Treaty. Negotiations began in June, although the three Baltic republics refused to take part, and Armenia, Georgia and Moldavia (now Moldova) later dropped out. It was one of those crucial turning points, as the newspaper *Izvestiya* warned in October 1990: 'Today the moment of truth has arrived for Gorbachev and his team. Maneuvering between left and right is no longer possible. Any continuation of this line threatens to lead to a situation where the President will forever lag behind a departing train' (Morrison, p. 196).

Unfortunately, the 'left' was still extremely weak. The new political parties were poorly organised, lacked resources and were extremely divided amongst themselves about what they wanted to achieve. And radical politicians, like Boris Yeltsin, although enormously popular, could not actually do very much to help Gorbachev strengthen his position. Mass support among ordinary people did not translate into the sort of executive power that Gorbachev needed if he was to adopt and sustain radical, even revolutionary, policies against considerable right-wing opposition. As a result, Gorbachev blinked and swung to the right where what remained of the state's executive power still lay: in the hands of the conservative party apparatus, the KGB, the armed forces, the military industrial complex.

The third turning point

The result was a return to repressive measures and the publication of a draft Union Treaty in November 1990 which might have been deliberately calculated to inflame centre-republican tensions. This draft treaty:

1   failed to give the republics *complete* control over their economic and natural resources;
2   maintained the primacy of federal over republican laws;
3   decreed that Russian would be the official state language; and, above all,
4   failed to make any reference whatsoever to the right of secession. This was worse even than the by now wholly discredited 'Brezhnev' constitution of 1977 which had at least contained a reference to the right of the Union-republics to secede from the USSR even if it had not actually specified how they might go about it.

These proposals produced such uproar that Gorbachev and his conservative government were forced to retreat. The new draft Union Treaty that was proposed in early March 1991 restored the right of secession, although this was so hedged about with restrictions that critics dubbed it 'the right of non-secession'. It also promised a much looser federation in which the republics would have 'the right to independent action on all issues of their development' while the centre retained responsibility for defence, foreign policy, border security and the co-ordination of law enforcement. However, these concessions came too late.

Gorbachev also tried to outflank the Union-republics by holding the USSR's first ever national referendum on 17 March 1991. Voters were asked to express a view on the question: 'Do you consider it necessary to preserve the Union of Soviet Socialist Republics as a renewed federation of equal sovereign republics in which the human rights and freedoms of any nationality will be fully guaranteed?' A total of 76.4 per cent of the population voted 'yes' (on an 80 per cent turnout), but the question was so vague, and the whole issue of what such a 'renewed federation' should look like so contentious, that the referendum results were compromised. As a consequence only Gorbachev and the government took any notice of them. In any case, six republics, Latvia,

Lithuania, Estonia, Moldavia (Moldova), Georgia and Armenia, refused to participate at all, thus declaring themselves effectively independent of the Union and reducing the value of the referendum as a national exercise (see White, pp. 174–5).

The governments of the nine republics which did participate in the referendum remained seriously dissatisfied with the new draft treaty. Worse, they were furious that Gorbachev was still trying to dictate its terms. Gorbachev was seeking their approval but it was Gorbachev and his advisers who had drawn up the treaty's provisions, not the republics themselves.

The result was that the leaders of the nine republics, led by Yeltsin, forced Gorbachev into intense negotiations during April 1991 (the Nine-plus-One talks). They managed to convince him that no treaty would stick unless the republics had participated directly in negotiating its provisions. The joint statement that was issued as a result of these talks on 23 April 1991 effectively superseded Gorbachev's own Union Treaty proposals by calling on the participants 'to finalise work on a draft new union treaty'. The outcome promised, finally, to give the nine participating republics the autonomy and independence they had been demanding.

The final turning point

However, the process was cut short. On the day before this new treaty was to be signed (20 August 1991), the State Committee for the State of Emergency took power (19 August). The conservatives in the armed forces, the KGB, the CPSU apparatus, consistently outflanked and kept off balance by Gorbachev's manoeuvring, had been forced to swallow the loss of the East European 'empire' and the loss of the Communist Party's leading role. But they drew the line at the loss of the old Soviet Union. However, they were too late. As it turned out the processes of disintegration could no longer be stopped, let alone reversed. In the event the coup simply accelerated them.

Yeltsin's courageous public stand against the coup leaders earned him enormous public support not only within the RSFSR but beyond it. When Gorbachev returned to Moscow on 22

August, from the Crimea where he had been imprisoned, he had effectively lost power as had all the central institutions that he had created. Although Gorbachev continued as President of the USSR, it was Yeltsin who had become the pre-eminent leader in the country.

The Baltic republics moved swiftly to complete the process that they had begun in 1990. So did Georgia which had declared itself sovereign in April 1991. Moldova, Armenia and, crucially, Ukraine and Byelorussia (now Belarus) indicated their desire to follow suit.

The Russian government under the presidential leadership of Yeltsin began a creeping takeover of central Soviet institutions.

Union negotiations resumed, under the nominal leadership of USSR President Gorbachev, but they now had a completely different character. Instead of trying to create a new, democratic federal state, republican negotiations now concentrated on finding ways to prevent the immediate and catastrophic collapse of what remained of the unified Soviet economy. The agreement that was finally signed on 18 October 1991 committed its signatories (and only eight republics signed) to no more than the maintenance of what became known as the 'common economic space'. This meant that the republics, as independent member states, agreed to conduct common policies in transport, energy, banking, customs, taxes and prices, and undertook to honour the Soviet Union's foreign debts. At this point Gorbachev was still convinced that he could save the Soviet Union by creating a new form of confederal union (i.e. a voluntary association of independent sovereign states co-ordinated by a limited central authority). He was wrong.

Political union was no longer possible as each republican government established itself as a sovereign entity and basically ignored or bypassed the federal Supreme Soviet. In the event, the USSR Supreme Soviet could not even muster a quorum (the minimum number of deputies constitutionally required to vote on legislation) to agree to its own dissolution in December 1991. It simply petered out. And even the negotiations on the 'common economic space' were overtaken by events. The overwhelming vote for independence in Ukraine on 1 December 1991 marked the end of any attempts, by Gorbachev or anyone else, to keep some sort of federation or confederation together. Once Ukraine, the second most powerful republic in the Union decided to leave it, there was nothing left to preserve.

In what has become known as 'the second coup' the leaders of the powerful Slavic republics – Russia, Ukraine and Belarus – moved swiftly to pull the rug from under Gorbachev's feet completely. On Sunday 8 December the three leaders (President Yeltsin for Russia, President Kravchuk for Ukraine and parliamentary Chairman Shushkevich for Belarus) agreed to create the new Commonwealth of Independent States. This breathtaking piece of improvisation set the stage for a whole new set of problems to which we shall turn in Part III.

Gorbachev, even at this late stage, continued to resist these moves but was finally forced to bow to the inevitable and resigned on 25 December 1991.

Conclusion

An interesting question: why did Gorbachev's undoubted abilities in managing the Soviet Union's foreign policy where he brought about an end to the cold war, desert him when it came to managing domestic federal relations?

Gorbachev allowed the East European countries to go their own way in the momentous year of 1989 and subsequently agreed to German unification but completely failed to appreciate the extent to which these truly momentous acts of liberation would encourage the Soviet republics in their own quest for autonomy and independence (see Chapter 11).

Gorbachev was right to fear the consequences of federal disintegration. In the event republican separatism created even more problems than it solved. It is therefore even more astonishing that he failed to make any plans for federal reform.

The only explanations that make sense are:

1   As in so much else Gorbachev's approach to federal relations was contradictory and a product of the past. He wanted to give some real force to the potentially democratic aspects of the old system. But he also wanted to retain the federation in its old

form, with the central authorities continuing to dominate the republics. He assumed that this would be generally acceptable because:

2   The old Soviet system had been so successful in repressing national and republican aspirations that the central party leadership was completely ignorant of their potential once central control was weakened. As Richard Sakwa puts it, Gorbachev (and not only Gorbachev but many of his reformist advisers) fell victim to the party's 'propaganda of success' – its claim that the 'nationality question' had been largely solved.

It is an indication of just how out of touch top party-state officials were with what was actually going on in the country. This was to apply to the members of the State Emergency Committee as well (see Chapter 12).

Further reading

Akchurin, Marat, *Red Odyssey*, Secker & Warburg, 1992

Glebov, Oleg and Crowfoot,John, (eds), *The Soviet Empire: Its Nations Speak Out*, Harwood Academic Publishers, 1989

Goble, Paul, 'Gorbachev and the Soviet nationality problem', in Friedberg, Maurice, Isham, Heyward (eds), *Soviet Society under Gorbachev. Current Trends and the Prospects for Reform*, M. E. Sharpe, 1987

Kagarlitsky, Boris, *Farewell Perestroika: a Soviet Chronicle*, Verso, 1990, especially Chapter 4

Kazutin, D., 'What I have read, heard or seen', *Moscow News*, No. 8, 23 February–1 March 1992, p. 3

Lane, David, *Soviet Society under Perestroika*, Unwin Hyman, 1990, Chapter 6

Morrison, John, *Boris Yeltsin: from Bolshevik to Democrat*, Penguin, 1991, especially from Chapter 11.

Ogden, Dennis, 'A union of a new type?', in Bloomfield, Jon (ed.), *The Soviet Revolution. Perestroika and the remaking of socialism*, Lawrence & Wishart, 1989

Ra'anan, Uri, 'The end of the multinational Soviet Empire?' in Ra'anan, Uri; Mesner, Maria; Armes, Keith and Martin, Kate, (eds), *State and Nation in Multi-Ethnic Societies: the Breakup of Multinational States*, Manchester University Press, 1991

Sakwa, Richard, *Gorbachev and His Reforms 1985–1990*, Philip Allan, 1990, Chapter 6

Smith, Gordon, *Soviet Politics: Struggling with Change*, 2nd edn, Macmillan, 1992

Smith, Graham, (ed.), *The Nationalities Question in the Soviet Union*, Longman, 1990

White, Stephen, *Gorbachev and After*, Cambridge University Press, 1991, Chapter 5

Questions

1   How would you explain Gorbachev's inability to deal successfully with federal reform?

2   Were there any differences between the republican struggle for autonomy and the nationalist struggle for autonomy?

3   When, if at all, are you most conscious of having a specific nationality?

10

Collapse of the economy

Before we go on to examine foreign policy and the events of August 1991 we need to look briefly at what had happened to the economy by the end of *perestroika*. This will enable us to pull some of the strands from previous chapters together. It is also important because it was catastrophic economic decline that affected people most immediately in their every-day lives. And that was one of the basic reasons for the massive loss of popular confidence in Gorbachev, the government and the whole reform process by the middle of 1990.

The collapse of the Soviet economy also looks a bit mystifying on the face of it.

1 On the one hand, a great deal of the old 'administrative command system' was still in place by 1990–1. Almost all property was still owned by the state. The State Planning Committee (*Gosplan*), the state bank and other central institutions were still operating and they continued to issue plans and planning instructions. The big central ministries also continued to operate, although they were considerably reduced in number. And the key political and repressive institutions of the old system were still in existence: the CPSU, the KGB, the armed forces, etc.

2 On the other hand, the situation confronting consumers by 1990 was appalling. The general quality of life had declined drastically and levels of poverty had increased enormously. Hardly

any goods were freely available at state prices by the end of 1990. There was widespread rationing of basic consumer goods; for example, sugar rationing was virtually universal. Some shortages were so acute that even ration coupons could not be honoured. And factories couldn't get what they needed from the state system either. Producer goods (i.e. those needed to produce other goods) were mostly only available in exchange for other goods or needed resources through a primitive barter system between factories and farms.

By the autumn of 1990 the general outlook seemed to be so bad that there were widespread fears about the possibility of famine that winter. And as Ellman points out this was not just 'idle chatter'. There were people alive in 1990 who had lived through four famines, in 1921–2, 1931–4, 1941–3, 1946–7, all of which had been major catastrophes in which millions of people died, especially the first two. So people did not use the word lightly (Ellman and Kontorovich, p. 2).

Mercifully, these predictions did not in the end come true. This was partly because the situation was never quite as bad as people thought it was. Rumour, gossip and the awful political chaos and general uncertainty created the impression that the *physical* supply of goods was worse than it actually was. It was also partly because people proved to be enormously resourceful in hunting out and hoarding scarce goods. As Ellman puts it, people turned their flats into 'mini-warehouses', stocking them to the ceiling with supplies of e.g., soap, clothes, home-made pickled fruit and vegetables. Factories hoarded vast quantities of supplies too.

However, circumstances were awful enough for many people to look back with some nostalgia to the relative comfort and tranquillity of the Brezhnev years.

How the economic crisis happened

How then do we explain the economic crisis that overtook the Soviet Union from 1988? Domestic public opinion put most of the blame on black market operations, the 'mafia', the private co-operative sector all of whom seemed to be exploiting the shortages to their own profit. They also blamed various forms of 'sabotage',

for example, by the backward and conservative state administrative apparatus which, it was generally assumed, would stop at
nothing to abort *perestroika*. In 1990 and even more in 1991 the air
was full of rumour and conspiracy theory. Local party and
nomenklatura officials were siphoning off and blocking food supplies in order to starve democratic soviets into submission. Vast
fortunes were being made on the black market by party officials
and 'speculators' (i.e. crooks) who were diverting state supplies
and selling them on the black market at vastly inflated prices.

There was no doubt some truth in these rumours (although
there was very little hard evidence to support them), but they do
not explain the causes of the economic crisis. Black markets etc.,
may make things worse (or better), but they do not cause
economic crises. They are a reflection of a poorly functioning
economy. And official sabotage, which no doubt existed, could not
possibly account for such a rapid and massive deterioration in an
economy as large as the Soviet one was.

Effects of perestroika

The more sensible explanation is that the economic crisis was the
direct result of *perestroika* itself. The economy was not working
terribly well in 1985 (the existence of widespread black markets is
proof of that), but it was not in crisis. Its ability to deliver the goods
to the domestic consumer was very poor but not absolutely
hopeless. Most people, except for the very disadvantaged,
managed to get the basics of life and even some of the luxuries.
The wheels of the system turned slowly and had to be constantly
oiled with bribes, favours, backhanders and corrupt deals of all
sorts, but they turned all the same and people got by. *Perestroika*
fatally disrupted this system.

1   The economic reforms were poorly thought through, limited
in vision, haphazardly implemented and did not address the right
problems. Fundamentally, no one in a position of power knew
anything about economics, nor did they know much about how the
Soviet system *actually* worked. Gorbachev had a vague notion of
what he wanted to achieve – a modern, dynamic, innovative
high-tech, industrial economy – but he did not have any realistic

ideas whatsoever about how to achieve it. His dithering over the question of radical economic reform in the summer of 1990 was evidence of that.

2 Economic reform and economic change became inextricably intertwined with the political processes unleashed by *glasnost* and political reform.

The inevitable result, as in so much else, was that Gorbachev ended up with the worst of all possible worlds. Both economic and political reform disorganised and undermined the 'command' system sufficiently to prevent it from operating in the old ways, but just enough 'central planning' and state control remained in place to prevent the emergence of a viable market alternative. Consequently:

(a) All the worst aspects of the old system were exacerbated.
(b) The various parts of the system, from villages and farms, to individual factories, towns, cities, regions, and, of course, Union-republics were increasingly forced to try to become as self-sufficient as possible in order to protect their local economic interests. This reinforced the political fragmentation of the system and only added to the country's economic difficulties.

The end result was a spiralling crisis that simply accelerated with each additional factor.

Disorganising effects of reform

Economic reform
1 The constant reorganisations of the ministries at the federal and republican levels.
2 The drastic cuts in the staff of central institutions coupled with the sweeping personnel changes that took place as Gorbachev replaced old officials with his own appointees (see Chapter 6).
3 The decentralisation of some decision-making power to the

republican governments and to factories, farms, etc. at the level of production.

All these factors helped to disorganise the co-ordination between central institutions; and to confuse or even sever both the formal and informal chains of command and control between the central authorities, republican authorities, middle-level managers in the ministries and enterprises at the bottom.

Enterprises, in particular, (as a result of the Law on State Enterprises introduced in June 1987), acquired more control over the wages they could pay; the profits they could make and, most importantly *keep* for themselves, and the sorts of goods they could produce.

In addition, as the result of the element of industrial democracy that was contained in this law, enterprise managers became much more responsive to the demands of their workforce (and therefore less responsive to the demands of ministry officials and planners) because they had now to persuade their workforce to elect them as managers.

These factors combined meant that, as the economic and political situation deteriorated, enterprises used their new-found powers to ignore the demands of ministry and central officials when and where it *suited* them to (see below).

Political reform

1   The CPSU lost its functions as an 'all-purpose power struc-ture' (see Morrison, p. 195). It could therefore no longer hold the economic system together as it had always done.

(a)   Gorbachev insisted that the party should withdraw from economic management and become a *political* party con-cerned with purely political matters. 'Make the economy more economic' was the slogan. And he instituted reforms in 1988 and again in 1990 which effectively deprived top party organs of their influence over economic policy and management.

(b)   As a result of the elections the party could no longer use the *nomenklatura* or democratic centralism to integrate and control the system. Worse, the party could no longer even control the vast conglomeration of committees and organisations of which it was made up because these became far too interested in their own local political survival. And,

(c) *Glasnost* and democratisation meant that the party apparatus lost its old power to coerce.

As a consequence, although party members continued to retain a strong presence in workplaces all over the country, they could no longer exploit this fact to ensure that everything ran (relatively) smoothly. They lost the power to co-ordinate and crisis-manage the activities of the enterprises they worked in because the vast network of oppression, mutual fear and obligation, of bribery and corruption that had enabled them to wheel-and-deal, pull strings and exchange information right across the country began to disintegrate along with the system that had created and sustained it.

2   Ethnic assertiveness, nationalism and the republican struggle for autonomy, as we have seen, were animated in part by the desire for economic autonomy. By 1990, however, the Union-republics were no longer satisfied with the sort of limited autonomy that simply gave them a slightly greater say in centrally determined policies. What they wanted was full economic independence and the dismantling of the central 'command' structures. This was more or less what the Shatalin Plan of 1990 had promised the republics. But it was precisely what Gorbachev did not want because it threatened the destruction of the old system. The result was an intense power struggle in which the republics sought to thwart the central authorities at every opportunity by failing to implement or trying to countermand central policies (see Chapter 9).

3   There was a catastrophic loss of economic direction at the centre. This had a number of causes.

(a) Gorbachev's own incompetence and the incompetence of many of the government officials that he appointed.

(b) The institutional structures of central government underwent a bewildering number of changes between 1989 and 1991. This constant change created constitutional and institutional chaos. It prevented the establishment of clear lines of authority and accountability between the different government bodies. And it greatly hampered policy and decision making: even those who were supposed to be in the know because they worked in these bodies were not always sure who was responsible for what.

By the middle of 1990 there were at least three competing bodies with responsibility for economic policy: *Gosplan* under the control of the Council of Ministers. The 'State Commission on Economic Reform', which had been set up in July 1989, and the new presidential apparatus under Gorbachev. This contained a new Presidential Council on which prominent market reformers like Stanislav Shatalin (author of the Shatalin Plan) were represented; and a new socio-economic department, responsible to the president for co-ordinating economic policy. However, the powers of these new presidential bodies were so poorly defined that they could not co-ordinate economic policy. For example, Shatalin as a member of the Presidential Council wondered: 'May I ask, for instance, the Minister of Finance to do something or do I have the right to tell him that he must do it?' (Aslund, *Gorbachev's Struggle*, p. 205).

To these three competing centres we must add the USSR Supreme Soviet which had to approve economic legislation. And the group of reform economists surrounding President Yeltsin in the Russian government, who were coming up with their own plans.

All these different groups were competing to promote their own economic reform programmes and policies.

(c) As a consequence economic policy became the subject of an intense political struggle in which no institution, including the presidency, had the power to impose its will against the wishes of the others.

This became most evident during the summer of 1990 in the debate over the Shatalin Plan or '500-day' programme.

To begin with, Presidents Gorbachev and Yeltsin joined forces to support a combined team of economic advisers, led by Stanislav Shatalin, in an effort to come up with a radical new reform programme as quickly as possible. However, when the Shatalin Plan was produced the government under Prime Minister Nikolai Ryzhkov refused to accept it, partly because Yeltsin had had a hand in it, and partly because it advocated the radical devolution of economic power to the republics. In its turn, however, the Ryzhkov government could not persuade either Gorbachev or the USSR Supreme Soviet to accept its alternative, which was considered to be too conservative. The result, inevitably, was chaos and confusion.

Gorbachev attempted to get out of the stalemate by moving back towards the conservative right and removing the Ryzhkov government in November 1990 (see Chapter 12). The government tried to deal with the chaos through the arbitrary implementation of draconian economic measures that simply made the general situation worse. For example, in January 1991, the new Prime Minister Valentin Pavlov suddenly announced the withdrawal of all high-denomination bank notes from circulation. People were only given a week in which to surrender them and could only withdraw a fixed amount of money in exchange (regardless of how many such bank notes they had to surrender). Hundreds of thousands of people lost their life-savings almost over-night, especially people in the deep rural hinterlands who did not even hear about the measure until the deadline had passed. Then in April 1991 retail prices were increased on average by 70-90 per cent. Living standards were badly squeezed as a result of such measures.

Strategies for coping

In order to survive the disorganisation of the system, organisations and communities of every sort had to exploit every opportunity that was available to them. This had paradoxical results because the coping strategies that emerged both reinforced the old system and accelerated its disintegration.

Reinforcing the old

The terrible uncertainties of supply, the chronic and acute shortages, the mounting economic and political confusion, and the lack of any sort of *real* market, encouraged enterprises and ministries to try to hang on to the old 'command' relationships where they could. This was particularly so in the huge military–industrial complex where the big ministries were particularly powerful and 'command' relations particularly strong.

Many enterprises (factories, farms, retail outlets, mines, etc.) continued:

1   To look to the ministries and the central authorities for support in finding scarce but much needed resources.
2   To gear their production to the fulfilment of 'state orders' (which were really the old plan targets by another name) because this *guaranteed* them an income.

     Remember: even in 1990 the planning authorities, the ministries, and all state enterprises were still supposed to be fulfilling the highly ambitious twelfth five-year plan that had been imposed on them in 1986. Although this plan was more or less a dead letter by 1990.
3   To rely on state subsidies and handouts to keep going.

The central authorities – the government, the big all-union ministries, and to a certain extent central institutions like *Gosplan* – still continued to wield a great deal of naked power. For example:

1   They continued to 'own' and control the country's property and natural resources. Gorbachev exploited this power to impose an economic embargo on Lithuania in 1990 in an attempt to force it to withdraw its demand for secession. The embargo was unsuccessful because it made the Lithuanians even more determined.
2   The central government continued to control the main economic levers, most notably, the printing of money and the fixing of prices. Although this did not mean that the money

supply or prices were actually under control.

3 The central authorities continued to control people's access to jobs and services. It therefore made sense for enterprises, particularly those under the jurisdiction of the big all-union ministries, to hang on to their old ties where they could.

All these factors combined to reinforce the old and failing 'command' structures about which Yeltsin complained so bitterly (see Chapter 9). And they served to give the (mistaken) impression that the old system was still functioning as it had always done.

Disintegrating the old

However, the same forces of political and economic disintegration that encouraged ministries and enterprises to hang onto old relationships, also encouraged enterprises, organisations and communities of all sorts to adopt forms of behaviour that made the situation worse.

1 Enterprises still had every incentive to exaggerate what they needed and to lie about what they were doing, because of the hopeless irrelevance of the twelfth five-year plan and the stresses and strains of surviving in a chaotic and uncertain environment. The central authorities were therefore as ignorant as ever about what was *really* happening on the ground.

2 Worker unrest, strikes, go-slows from 1989 on brought factories and mines to a standstill with enormous knock-on effects for the whole economy in terms of the provision and distribution of vital products and resources.

3 Worker unrest also put pressure on enterprise managers to increase wages over and above what the workers' productivity actually merited. This was to keep wages up with price inflation and was therefore a means of trying to keep the workers quiet. It was for this reason that the element of industrial democracy contained in the 1987 State Enterprise Law was abolished in 1990 (by which time the damage was already done), because increased wages:

(a) Greatly added to the problem of excess purchasing power in the system and therefore to the problem of inflation (see below).

(b) Did not give the workers much incentive to increase production since there was so little to buy with their money.

So the effects of this were almost entirely negative.

4   Pressures to become more profitable and efficient encouraged enterprises to exploit their new powers:

(a) to change to more profitable lines of production, regardless of what the economy needed. This often had severe knock-on effects. An exotic example: when the only factory making parachutes in the USSR could no longer get hold of the right silk and decided to move into more profitable lines of production (in late 1990) the whole of the armed forces were left without parachutes; and/or

(b) to *reduce* the production and output of goods. This was because with inflation and increasing prices enterprises could actually make the same amount of money as they had always done by producing less. And since this made life easier for everyone this is what many enterprises tended to do. This greatly exacerbated the chronic shortages of goods in the system;

(c) to increase the prices of their goods by exploiting loopholes in the system. This of course aggravated (b) and encouraged inflation.

5   As the economic situation deteriorated and the vertical chains of command were undermined, enterprises of every sort relied more and more on the old informal networks developed under Brezhnev to barter directly for needed goods with other enterprises, bypassing the central authorities completely.

6   The galloping budget deficit coupled with the inflationary policy of printing money to finance it led to a collapse in the value of the rouble. Consequently, factories and farms would no longer

trade for money but only for other goods. This meant that they:

(a) often refused to honour old (planned) contractual arrangements unless they got something valuable in return (i.e. not money but a scarce and needed good or resource). This left their old customers stranded without supplies which in turn disrupted the chain of supply further down the line.

(b) hoarded goods in order to have them for barter rather than putting them on the market. This greatly aggravated the problem of shortages. The effects of this were particularly bad in agriculture. Farmers either reduced production and/or hoarded what they grew in order to strengthen their bargaining positions. This seriously affected the production and distribution of foodstuffs. It also put many regions at a disadvantage. For example, the oil-producing regions could not barter unprocessed crude oil in exchange for food or anything else because crude oil has to be refined before it can be used. By 1990 many Siberian cities were suffering very badly from acute shortages of food and other necessary goods. And as a result one of the main tasks of local soviet deputies was travelling the country in search of supplies.

Note: As the value of the rouble collapsed foreign currencies took over as the medium of exchange. This was especially so of the American dollar. Anyone with dollars, or 'greens' as they became known, could get more or less anything they wanted. This, of course, divided the population into the few 'haves' who could get access to foreign currency, and the many 'have nots' who had no such access.

7   The accelerating problem of shortages coupled with elections that made local soviets accountable to their electorates also encouraged republican, regional, even city governments to impose embargoes on the 'export' of locally produced goods in order to keep them (1) for local consumption, or (2) as bargaining chips in barter deals with other parts of the country. Thus, city soviets imposed local rationing systems that prevented anyone but registered citizens from buying goods. This had serious conse-

quences for everyone else, particularly for rural dwellers who could only get hold of certain goods by travelling into the big cities.

This 'bacchanalia of local protectionism' as one Soviet economist dubbed it in January 1990 (see Ellman and Kontorovich, p. 100) also acquired a nationalist tinge as republics put up customs barriers against each other and refused to allow the 'export' of scarce resources, very often on the principle of 'Russian resources for the Russians', 'Ukrainian resources for the Ukrainians' and so on. This created enormous problems given the integrated nature of the Soviet economy. For example, the Ukrainian coal-mining industry almost ground to a halt when the Russian timber enterprises on which the mines relied for pit-props refused to supply them.

This problem was to get considerably worse after 1991 and the collapse of the USSR.

8   The ordinary consumer also responded to the worsening situation by hoarding goods. A Soviet survey in early 1989 revealed that 90 per cent of families were hoarding goods as opposed to only 25 per cent a year earlier (Ellman and Kontorovich, p. 99). This further denuded the shops.

Supply side depression

These spontaneous and uncontrollable economic processes both reflected and contributed to what Goldman has called the USSR's 'supply side depression'. By which he means the Soviet economy's consistent inability to produce adequate supplies of goods to meet the ever-growing demands of the Soviet population (see Goldman, p. 28). This 'supply side depression' was really at the heart of the Soviet Union's economic problems and it continues to be fundamental to the economic difficulties of its successor states. It had a number of causes.

1   *Historical origins.* The ever-present fear of invasion by the capitalist countries which went back to the earliest days of 1917, and the post-Second World War demands of the superpower rivalry with the USA, resulted in very lop-sided investment

priorities. The Communist Party poured money and resources into the heavy industry and defence sectors, at the expense of light industry, manufacturing, agriculture and the service sectors. As a result the output of these sectors had never been able to keep up with the growth of the population or the increases in people's spending power. This was one of the principal reasons why Gorbachev launched the massive transformation of Soviet foreign policy (see Chapter 11) as well as the whole *perestroika* reform programme.

2   The Soviet economy was also *structurally vulnerable*.

(a)   The futile and hopelessly inefficient efforts to 'plan' such a huge economy often meant that the consumer and producer goods that were produced were defective and unwanted. TVs that burst into flames and hundreds of tons of size 16 left-hand shoes without a partner are no good to anybody.

(b)   The economy also lacked duplication. In capitalist economies there are almost always alternative sources of supply for any good because market competition ensures that more than one business will move into the production of profitable lines. Soviet planners had always despised this duplication as 'wasteful'. Consequently, they adopted the strategy of building huge single factories that were the sole producers of a given product for the whole country. However, the obvious difficulty with this strategy is that if anything goes wrong and the factory is forced to close; or its management decides to reduce production or move into the production of a more profitable good (as often happened under *perestroika*) then all its customers right across the country lose their supply of its product with serious consequences for the rest of the economy.

Note: This strategy of creating monopoly producers has also created enormous problems for:

(a)   The creation of a market economy and privatisation.
(b)   The independent states of the CIS who found that they were

dependent on each other for the provision of necessary products and services.

However, the processes set in train by government policies after
1985, made this situation infinitely worse by exacerbating the
economy's supply side weaknesses on the one hand, and inflating
individual purchasing power on the other, while doing absolutely
nothing to solve the underlying structural problems.

The demand side

Not only did money incomes increase, but the rate at which they
increased also rose. Between 1985 and 1987, the period of
uskoreniye, total money incomes increased by 11.2 per cent. In
1988 the rise in money incomes increased by 9.2 per cent, and in
1989 by about 14 per cent (Ellman and Kontorovich, p. 97;
Aslund, *Gorbachev's Struggle*, p. 187). This trend continued into
1990 and 1991.

These increases not only reflected greater enterprise freedom
in determining wages. They were also the product of a general
wage reform that started in 1987 and that was aimed at (1)
increasing low wages, and (2) increasing wage differentials.

Government social spending on things like pensions also
increased enormously, especially in 1990 (when they suddenly
increased by over 25 per cent as a result of decisions taken by the
USSR Congress of People's Deputies and Supreme Soviet.
Aslund, *Gorbachev's Struggle*, p. 187). This added greatly to the
government budget deficit and to the enormous circulation of
money in the economy. By 1991 the combined budget deficit at
the all-union and republican levels was standing at approximately
400 billion roubles. At the same time state revenues collapsed. In
the first quarter of 1991 the Union government only managed to
get 36 per cent of the revenues that it had planned for. And in
September 1991 this had fallen to 15 per cent of the planned level.
This was partly the result of drastic falls in production and
consequently in exports during 1990 and especially 1991. The
end result was that the government's printing presses went into
overdrive to try and cover the gap: in 1991 about 100 billion
roubles worth of money was printed and released, four times as

much as in 1990. This added greatly to the inflationary pressures in the system. In 1991 Soviet estimates reckoned that inflation was running at at least 150–200 per cent (Aslund, 'The Soviet economy', p. 46).

The government did make some efforts to stem the tide. The confiscation of high-denomination banks notes in January 1991, and massive retail price increases in April 1991 did curtail spending power a bit (at great cost to the population which therefore had to bear the brunt of years of CPSU economic mismanagement). But in the absence of reforms that dealt with the underlying problems of shortages, budget deficits and the irresponsible printing of money, these could do little even in the short term to change the situation.

The supply side

Not only did the provision of goods and services not keep up with the explosion in money incomes, it gradually collapsed.

Between 1985 and 1987 the pernicious effects of the campaigns against alcohol and unearned incomes, and the drive to reduce imports of consumer goods (see Chapter 6) meant that the total provision of goods and services increased by only 0.2 per cent in real terms (compared with an 11.2 per cent increase in money incomes).

The situation did improve slightly after 1987 because the government, alarmed by the accelerating crisis in the consumer market and the effect it was having on public opinion, took urgent and radical measures to try and improve the provision of consumer goods and services (see Ellman and Kontorovich, Chapter 5). The total supply of goods and services did increase very considerably as a result, by 7.9 per cent during 1988–9. However, even this was not enough to keep up with the accelerating increase in money incomes. Moreover, most of this growth was accounted for by a 36 per cent increase in the state production of alcohol and a rise in imported consumer goods (Ellman and Kontorovich, p. 98).

However, after 1989 and especially in 1990 and 1991 production and output began to collapse rapidly. According to official Soviet statistics (never very accurate), between January and June

1991 Soviet gross national product fell by 10 per cent, industrial output fell by 6.2 per cent and agricultural output by 11 per cent compared with the same period in 1990 (see Bush, p. 37). This resulted in a 23.4 per cent reduction in exports, which in turn resulted in the effective halving of the volume of imports (because the USSR had a 60 billion dollar foreign debt but no money to service it) (Aslund, 'The Soviet economy', p. 46). This further aggravated the problem of shortages.

The decline in production and output was the result of the vicious circles already touched on above:

1   The disorganisation of the old system and its inherent shortages meant that enterprises found it more and more difficult to get supplies and therefore to meet their plan targets. Moreover they hoarded what they did get hold of. This aggravated the shortages in the system.

2   As money flooded the system and the value of the rouble collapsed enterprises and workers had less and less incentive to increase their productivity. So productivity fell. Equally, enterprises had no incentive to trade goods for money. However, the barter systems that emerged were enormously inefficient because they involved a great deal of time and energy on the part of enterprises who had to search for contacts and trading partners across the country.

3   Increases in prices meant that enterprises had every incentive to reduce production further in order to make life marginally easier.

And so on. All of which aggravated the problem of shortages. The effect of economic collapse on public opinion was devastating unsurprisingly. For example, between May and June 1990 the proportion of people expressing full trust in the country's leadership fell from a low of 14 per cent to 7 per cent and continued to fall thereafter (Ellman and Kontorovich, p. 67). What is far more surprising is the stoic patience and relative lack of social unrest with which the population greeted the precipitate decline in its living standards that was the result.

Neither plan nor market

The end result of all this was that the economic system, just like the political system, began to disintegrate unevenly with a catastrophic loss of power on all sides. The old 'command' structures were still in place but increasingly their power was:

1 undermined by the disorganising effects of the reforms; and
2 blocked by the uncontrollable political and economic processes that were sweeping the country.

At the same time:

3 the new and more democratic governments in the Union-republics and other territorial units found themselves unable to implement their own economic policies because they did not control the crucial economic levers;
4 enterprises, organisations and communities of every sort were forced into a variety of *ad hoc* measures in order to survive since they did not have a proper plan, a proper market or even political commands to guide them in their activities. These in turn only served to undermine old economic relationships even more.

As Richard Sakwa put it, 'The economic system entered a state of endemic civil war in which no one any longer knew the rules: market forces were not allowed free play while central administrative mechanisms began to be dismantled' (p. 304). This mirrored the 'guerrilla war' in politics (see Chapter 8).

Problems of market reform

In these conditions the problems of market reform were insurmountable. By the summer of 1990 almost everyone in government and expert circles, and even many ordinary people, could see the need for a transition to some sort of market economy. But no one could agree on how to achieve it because the economic conditions simply were not there. Creating a market economy meant among other things:

1   privatising land and property;
2   eliminating the power of monopoly producers and introducing competition;
3   bringing the money supply, prices and wages under control and re-valuing the rouble;
4   eliminating acute shortages and improving the distribution system so as to prevent prices, once freed, from going through the roof;
5   eliminating rampant black markets and corruption;
6   introducing a system of law and regulation to underpin contracts and to enable new economic entities, like private companies, to operate.

In short, it required a genuine revolution in the way the Soviet economic system operated and the Shatalin Plan of 1990 came close to acknowledging as much. However, many of these measures could only be achieved in the long term.

At the same time the Soviet economy also needed drastic and immediate action to prevent it going into free-fall, often referred to as a 'stabilisation programme'.

Confronted by these enormously difficult choices, all of which entailed enormous social costs and enormous social upheavals, the political leadership under Gorbachev became paralysed by indecision and consequently suffered the almost complete loss of popular support. The inevitable result was that the economic crisis simply continued to spiral out of control both before and after the abortive coup of August 1991. It was left to the new states of the CIS to try to pick up the pieces.

Further reading

Aslund, Anders, 'The Soviet economy after the coup', *Problems of Communism*, November–December 1991

Aslund, Anders, *Gorbachev's Struggle for Economic Reform*, Pinter Publishers, 1991, 2nd ed

Bush, Keith, 'The economic problems remain', *Report on the USSR*, RFE/RL Research Institute, Vol. 3, No. 36, 6 September, 1991

Ellman, Michael and Kontorovich, Vladimir, *The Disintegration of the Soviet Economic System*, Routledge, 1992

Goldman, Marshall, *What Went Wrong with Perestroika*, W. W. Norton & Co., 1991

Morrison, John, *Boris Yeltsin: from Bolshevik to Democrat*, Penguin, 1991

Sakwa, Richard, *Gorbachev and His Reforms, 1985–1990*, Philip Allan, 1990

White, Stephen, *Gorbachev and After*, Cambridge University Press, 1991, Chapter 4

11

Foreign policy

The analysis of *perestroika* would not be complete without some discussion of Gorbachev's innovations in foreign policy. This was undoubtedly the area in which Gorbachev excelled and on which most of his international reputation as a radical reformer was based. His imaginative approach to old problems; his ability to outwit and out-manoeuvre the politicians of NATO and the West as well as the domestic opposition to his foreign policy changes; his evident sincerity and his astonishing willingness to compromise were startlingly revolutionary in an international environment where politicians, on the whole, whatever their nationality deliberately cultivate a grim narrow-mindedness and are obscenely ambitious and hungry for power regardless of the costs. In the international arena at least Gorbachev deserves the almost legendary status that he acquired.

However, Gorbachev's foreign policy innovations, or 'new thinking' as he called them, also had important domestic ramifications, some of which we have already touched on, which help to explain both the collapse of *perestroika* and the coup of August 1991.

Reasons for change

Mikhail Gorbachev was the first Soviet leader, and so far the only state leader in the world, to acknowledge that the cold war and the arms race that animated it, were crippling his country. The problem was not simply that the endless production of new weapons and the maintenance of a massive standing army was draining human and material resources away from the civilian economy and absorbing a large proportion of the state budget. It was also that the Soviet obsession with military security, the protection of Soviet interests overseas and the competition with the United States had resulted in:

1 The Soviet Union's failure to establish good bilateral working relationships with many other important parts of the world, like the European Community (which prior to Gorbachev the USSR had refused to recognise) as well as the individual countries of Europe; and with Asian countries like Japan, China, Hong Kong, Singapore.
2 The almost total neglect of what Gorbachev liked to think of as domestic security, i.e. ensuring that the Soviet population had enough goods and sufficient freedom to keep it happy and prevent it from rebelling against the power of the party.

Gorbachev was highly critical of the way in which previous Soviet leaders had subordinated the needs of the domestic economy to the demands of their foreign policy goals. For example, Brezhnev had achieved military parity with the USA in the 1970s and launched the war in Afghanistan at the end of 1979 without any thought for the long-term domestic costs these policies would entail.

Gorbachev therefore had several good reasons for wanting to change Soviet foreign policy. First and foremost he wanted to subordinate Soviet foreign policy to the more important goal of improving the Soviet domestic system. This meant:

1 Creating better diplomatic and military relations with the capitalist world in order to reduce the burden of the arms race on the domestic economy and, if possible, convert some of the military infrastructure back to civilian use so as to improve domestic economic performance.
2 Reducing the Soviet Union's overseas burdens in terms of military and other aid and assistance to Third World countries

and to the countries of Eastern Europe.

3   Improving diplomatic and trade relations with the capitalist
     countries in order to enhance the Soviet Union's chances of
     negotiating Western aid for its ailing economy and to
     strengthen its international trading position. Gorbachev
     wanted to be able to import more of the capitalist world's
     high-technology goods in order to help improve the Soviet
     economy's efficiency and productivity, as well as to export
     more Soviet goods and raw materials to pay for them.

Secondly, Gorbachev wanted to achieve a relaxation in international tensions in order to create a more stable environment in
which to engage in internal reform. He was aware that the cold
war did not just impose material pressures on the Soviet system, it
also imposed a psychological fear of war and fear of the 'enemy' on
the Soviet people as well as the populations of the Western
countries. This is not a good environment in which to promote
change. He also wanted to be sure that the United States and
NATO would not take advantage of any internal instability that
reform might temporarily create in order to destabilise the Soviet
system further. He therefore had to transform East–West relations: from being based on fear, mutual distrust, threat and
counter-threat, they had to be based on trust, mutual respect and
the sincerely held conviction on all sides that interference in
another country's affairs was profoundly undesirable.

Gorbachev's view that changes in international relations had to
be brought about before domestic reform could safely begin helps
to explain why new thinking on foreign policy was quicker to get
off the ground in the early years 1985–7 than new thinking on
domestic politics was.

In order to achieve his foreign policy goals Gorbachev had to do
a number of things, most of which had long-term destabilising
domestic implications.

Improving relations with the West

To begin with, Gorbachev clearly had to convince the capitalist
countries that the Soviet Union was not a military or a political

threat. He came to power at a time when Soviet–US relations were at an all-time low. The Soviet invasion of Afghanistan in December 1979 had put a final end to the reasonably co-operative period of detente between the two superpowers in the 1970s. And President Reagan had launched an ideological offensive against what he dubbed the 'evil empire' and endorsed a huge American military build-up that included the Strategic Defense Initiative (SDI) or 'Star Wars' as it became more popularly known. Gorbachev therefore had a great deal to overcome.

Gorbachev began by launching a whole series of arms control initiatives and reviving the idea of superpower 'summitry'.

For example, he imposed a unilateral ban on nuclear weapons testing in the USSR which lasted from 1985 to 1987. In January 1986 he announced a plan to rid the world completely of nuclear weapons by the year 2000. And nine months later at the second superpower summit held in Reykjavik, he managed to bounce President Reagan, first of all, into agreeing with the principle that all nuclear weapons could 'and should be completely liquidated by 1996'; and, secondly, into committing the USA to making some practical cuts. For example, both sides agreed to eliminate all medium-range nuclear missiles from Europe (otherwise known as Intermediate Nuclear Forces or INF), and to cut strategic missiles by 50 per cent over the following five years, eliminating the other 50 per cent in the five years after that. This eventually resulted in the signing of the INF Treaty in 1987 which in turn led to the physical destruction of a whole range of medium-range weapons that had been based in both the eastern and western halves of Europe. The INF Treaty actually involved considerable Soviet concessions since under its terms the Soviet Union was obliged to scrap 1,836 missiles carrying 3,136 warheads, while the United States only had to scrap 859 missiles carrying 859 warheads (see MccGwire, p. 272). It was the Reykjavik Summit that finally convinced the world at large that Gorbachev really was serious.

Other Soviet gestures followed. Most famously, in December 1988 in a speech to the United Nations, Gorbachev announced unilateral force cuts of 500,000 troops, 240,000 of them in Europe. In 1985–6 Gorbachev also began to negotiate the withdrawal of Soviet troops from Afghanistan, and the last troops were finally removed on 21 February 1989.

Arms control was also accompanied by a whole series of other measures.

Overtures were made to the USSR's old enemy China in the east, and to the European Community in the west. Gorbachev began to talk about a 'common European home' of which the Soviet Union was part. And he acknowledged that the post-war division of Europe into a Sovietised eastern half and a capitalist western half had been one of the causes of the cold war and continued to be an acute and dangerous source of tension. He therefore began to lay the ground work for the eventual re-unification of Europe and of Germany in particular (see below). He also argued that Soviet relations with South East Asian countries like Japan had to be put on a new more co-operative footing. As a result, Soviet relations with the countries both east and west of it slowly began to improve.

There was a radical re-think of Soviet military doctrine to make it less generally threatening and more concerned with defence than offence. In particular, Soviet policy-makers acknowledged the need for what were known as 'asymmetrical reductions' in arms control. This meant that the USSR would cut deeper than the USA where it had a preponderance of forces, as in, for example, intermediate nuclear forces or the number of conventional troops based in Europe. This was unprecedented.

There was also a radical re-think of the Soviet theory of international relations.

Beginning in late 1986 Gorbachev and his supporters gradually started to challenge and reverse all the old Stalinist concepts on which Soviet foreign policy had been based. For example:

1   The idea that the world was divided into two hostile camps – the socialist and the capitalist – and that the relationship between them was essentially a class struggle between the rich and poor of the world that would only end once socialism was victorious, was replaced by the concepts of 'universal human values' and 'interdependence'. These emphasised the need for global co-operation to eliminate the threat of nuclear weapons and to deal with common human problems such as environmental pollution and

famine.

2   The idea that capitalism was a permanently hostile and aggressive social system was modified considerably. Gorbachev argued that the nature of capitalism had changed enormously since Marx's day. It had become much more responsive to changes in the world. And it, too, had an interest in co-operating to prevent global catastrophe. In any case, Gorbachev insisted, that even where the interests of the capitalist countries and the socialist countries did diverge it was absolutely impermissible to try to resolve them by threatening war or going to war. All differences, no matter how large, had to be dealt with through negotiation and compromise.

3   The idea that there was only ever one 'right way' of doing things, and that only the Soviet Union (or the United States) knew it, was also rejected in favour of the argument that all nations had a legitimate right to their own opinions, which had to be respected. Gorbachev emphasised the principle of freedom of choice for all nations and the importance of negotiation and co-operation rather than coercion to resolve differences. It followed that any policy of intervention in another country's affairs was therefore unthinkable.

These principles had their counterparts in the domestic arena since Gorbachev also had to convince domestic opinion, particularly in the armed forces, that the capitalist world was not a threat to the Soviet Union or the Warsaw Pact.

1   From late 1986, and especially from 1987, debates about the more benign nature of capitalism, the importance of universal human values and the inevitability of global interdependence and so on, appeared in the Soviet press. Gorbachev also made these new principles quite explicit in his own book, *Perestroika: New Thinking for Our Country and the World*, which appeared in 1987. People could therefore read them and digest their implications for the domestic political system. For example, it followed that if, as Gorbachev stated in his 1988 speech to the United Nations, 'the

principle of freedom of choice' for all nations was 'a universal principle [that] knows no exceptions' then it must also apply to the nations of the Soviet Union itself (as well as those of Eastern Europe). It also followed that if capitalism was no longer threatening then Soviet society itself was no longer divided into two camps, those who supported the Soviet system and those 'bourgeois subversives' who supposedly did not and who had to be constantly guarded against, and that all points of view were equally valid, even those that promoted capitalism as the better system.

2   Gorbachev's insistence, from early 1987, on the need for the profound democratisation of society, the need for pluralism and greater *glasnost* also began to undermine the despotism of the CPSU from within and to challenge the old Stalinist definition of socialism that it had always promoted.

This all added up to a cumulative assault on the old divisive ideology and on the old 'mind set', as Russians described it, that had kept the CPSU in power but that had also helped to keep Soviet society divided against itself. The long-term effects of this assault on the fabric of Soviet society were bound to be destabilising as people began to take Gorbachev at his word.

The disintegration of Eastern Europe

Gorbachev's policies towards the Soviet satellite countries of Eastern Europe were part of this general trend. Gorbachev consistently undermined all the old coercive principles on which Soviet power in Eastern Europe had been based.

First, and most importantly of all, in late 1986 he privately informed the East European party leaders that they could no longer count on Soviet military intervention to keep them in power if things went wrong (MccGwire, p. 356). Soviet military intervention in Hungary in 1956, in Czechoslovakia in 1968; and the threat of it which hung over Germany in 1953 and over Poland in 1980, had shored up Soviet-style one-party rule against popular rebellion and/or against communist party reformers who (long before Gorbachev) had wanted to create a more democratic form of socialism. This deprived the communist parties in Eastern Europe of the one instrument that had been guaranteed to keep them in power.

This was followed, from 1987, by serious discussions within the Warsaw Pact alliance about how to achieve Soviet troop reductions in the countries of Eastern Europe.

Secondly, Gorbachev did not disguise his opinion that the Eastern European countries should follow the path of radical *perestroika* that was adopted in the Soviet Union after 1987. He did not actually tell the East European communist parties that they *had* to follow the Soviet route, since this would have conflicted with the principle of 'freedom of choice' that he was also advocating. But he made it clear that the Soviet Union would no longer support anyone who promoted the retention of the old party-dominated 'administrative command' system.

Finally, Gorbachev promoted the principle of freedom of choice for all nations within the arena of Europe itself. For example, in a speech to the Council of Europe in July 1989, Gorbachev asserted that 'respect for each people's sovereign right to choose a social system as it sees fit represents a most important precondition for a normal European process'. And he stressed that 'any interference in internal affairs of whatever kind, any attempts to limit the sovereignty of states, both of friends and allies, no matter whose it is, is impermissible' (MccGwire, p. 361).

The message to Eastern Europe was unmistakable and the consequences inevitable. From the summer of 1989 the peoples of Eastern Europe took to the streets in increasing numbers. The communist parties, demoralised by the Soviet reforms, bereft of Soviet support and without any new ideas of their own simply crumpled under the impact; except in hard-line Romania and Albania where they put up physical resistance. By December 1989 the communist party regimes had disintegrated. Shortly afterwards, the old cold war divisions of Europe began to follow them. By August 1991 the Warsaw Pact and the Council for Mutual Economic Assistance (the socialist equivalents of NATO and the EEC respectively) had been formally disbanded. Germany had been reunified and most of the countries of Eastern Europe, like Poland, Czechoslovakia and Hungary, were in the process of trying (not very successfully) to create market economies.

It is difficult to disagree with Michael MccGwire's assessment that 'The pattern of events in 1987–88 argues strongly that the Gorbachev leadership deliberately set in motion the process that would lead to the collapse of communist rule throughout Eastern Europe by the end of 1989' (MccGwire, p. 360).

The impact on the Soviet Union

The impact on the Soviet Union of these processes was considerable. Gorbachev's consistent advocacy of 'freedom of choice', 'self-determination' and the impermissibility of intervention; and his principled refusal to use force when the countries of Eastern Europe actually rebelled against communist party rule in 1989 were powerful precedents for the people back home. Soviet reform had initiated the process of liberation in Eastern Europe; the liberation of Eastern Europe in turn encouraged the nations of the Soviet Union, particularly in the Baltic, to demand their own freedom and their own right to self-determination. In this international environment Gorbachev's internal crackdown in late 1990 and early 1991 only served to enrage the independence movements in the Union-republics who could not understand why these new rules should only apply outside the USSR. Gorbachev's apparent blindness to the domestic implications of his foreign policies is one of the abiding mysteries of the period.

Gorbachev's international policies and their internal consequences also upset other domestic constituencies.

1   The arms reduction process that was intended, among other things, to relieve the pressure on the domestic economy was increasingly seen by conservatives within the party and the armed forces to be leading to the weakening of the Soviet Union's international bargaining power and to the ultimate destruction of the USSR's superpower status. By 1990 there was a conservative consensus that Gorbachev had conceded far too much to the West and had got virtually nothing in return. The United States was still continuing with its Star Wars programme and had scarcely

reduced either its military spending or the size of its armed forces. NATO continued to dispose of powerful military forces, even if it had become increasingly confused about what its purpose should be. Whereas the Soviet Union had lost control of Eastern Europe, withdrawn from the Third World, surrendered its military might and was itself disintegrating visibly. To the older generations of officials in particular, therefore, Gorbachev's reforms looked like the abject surrender and betrayal of everything that the Soviet Union had fought for and won during the Second World War.

2   Defence cuts and military reforms (not to mention the rapidly deteriorating economic situation) undermined the integrity of military structures and gave conservatives real cause to fear that the military security of the USSR could no longer be maintained.

They also threatened many officers and experienced troops with demobilisation and unemployment in what was already a profoundly uncertain economic environment.

The reforms also opened the armed forces up to public scrutiny. This had resulted in a great deal of public criticism of military inefficiency, bullying in the ranks, and so on leading to an even greater demoralisation.

3   The withdrawal of Soviet troops from Eastern Europe, which began in earnest in 1989 and accelerated in 1990 and 1991, resulted in the catastrophic collapse of living standards for the affected personnel. In particular, thousands of officers and their families who had become used to relatively luxurious standards of living in countries like East Germany or Czechoslovakia suddenly found themselves uprooted and dumped back home where nothing had been done to prepare for their return. They were forced to live in tents, converted bath houses and barns, and anything else that they could find, with no schooling for their children, on salaries that were no longer paid in foreign currency but in worthless roubles and with profoundly uncertain job prospects. The dismay, the confusion, the profound anger and deep humiliation were palpable. By November 1990 Gorbachev was being subjected to a barrage of criticism from almost all sectors of the armed forces and from conservatives within the party who feared

the worst.

This discontent was undoubtedly one of the factors that prompted Gorbachev's swing to the right at this point.

Some questions

Could Gorbachev have done things differently? The question is almost impossible to answer.

He could have moved much more slowly on the issues of arms and control and disarmament but then he would have lost the element of surprise that enabled him to bounce both his domestic opponents and the West into accepting his new strategic vision. It would undoubtedly have been much more difficult to extort concessions from either the United States or NATO, neither of whom have shown themselves willing to reduce their military power to any significant extent. All talk of a 'peace dividend' that hit the headlines in 1990–1 has now disappeared. Gorbachev would also have lost the opportunity to make the grand gestures that persuaded the world that the Soviet Union really was serious about wanting to transform international relations.

However, Gorbachev could certainly have planned better for the domestic consequences. His failure to ensure that proper contingency plans were made for the re-housing and re-deployment of returning Soviet troops, despite the awful economic situation, was a case of criminal negligence on a par with his failure to plan for the consequences of the anti-alcohol campaign in 1985–6 (see Chapter 6). And we have already remarked on his lack of foresight with respect to the whole question of Soviet federal relations. In all these cases, Gorbachev behaved in the classic fashion of the CPSU General Secretary: very good at grand gestures but utterly indifferent to the domestic problems of implementation and the *real* planning involved in their solution. He was to reap the consequences in August 1991.

Further reading

Gorbachev, Mikhail, *Perestroika: New Thinking for Our Country and the World*, Collins, 1987

MccGwire, Michael, *Perestroika and Soviet National Security*, The Brookings Institution, 1991.

Sakwa, Richard, *Gorbachev and his Reforms 1985–1990*, Philip Allan, 1990, chapter 8

Walker, Rachel, 'New Thinking' and Soviet foreign policy', in Pugh, Michael, Williams, Phil (eds), *Superpower Politics: Change in the United States and the Soviet Union*, Manchester University Press, 1990

12

August 1991

The coup began on 18 August when Gorbachev and his family suddenly found themselves under house arrest in their holiday home at Foros in the Crimea. It collapsed some sixty hours later, on 21 August, when its ring-leaders tried to flee from Moscow through the traffic jams caused by hundreds of retreating tanks.

The coup was an abject failure as an attempt to restore order in the country. Instead of halting the processes of disintegration that were tearing the USSR apart it only served to accelerate them. However, its failure was also a resounding demonstration of Gorbachev's ultimate success in revolutionising Soviet society.

The causes of the coup

There has inevitably been a lot of debate about whether the coup could have been avoided; whether it could have succeeded if circumstances had been slightly different; and the extent of Gorbachev's responsibility for it. We will probably never discover the full truth about what happened, but there is no doubt that developments in the months and weeks that preceded it gave the conservative opposition to Gorbachev plenty of grounds for thinking (1) that radical emergency action was necessary to preserve the Soviet state, and (2) that such action would succeed.

The new Union Treaty
The new Union Treaty was undoubtedly the main catalyst for the

coup. It promised to give the republics everything they had been demanding, and to destroy everything that the conservatives wanted to preserve: the old centralised Soviet federation and with it the central all-union institutions from which many of them derived their power.

1　It dropped the word 'socialist' from the country's title, which was to become the 'Union of Soviet Sovereign Republics'.
2　It deprived the all-union government of an independent tax base. It would therefore become dependent on the member republics for funding.
3　It called for the dissolution of the USSR Supreme Soviet; the devolution of the functions of all-union ministries to their republican counterparts; and declared that republican law would take precedence over all-union law. It also insisted that all-union institutions like the KGB and the armed forces would have to share decision-making power with the republics.
4　It was left to the republics to decide whether they would sign it or not, i.e. it was to be a completely voluntary Union.

The new Union Treaty therefore looked as though it would not actually create a new *Union* but simply exacerbate all the centrifugal tendencies that were already undermining federal relations.

1　Giving precedence to republican legislation over all-union legislation looked like a recipe for disaster because most republican legislation during 1990 and 1991 directly challenged the powers and integrity of central institutions.

2　The document that was to be signed on 20 August was extremely vague. It left the centre with no precise responsibilities or powers. It also left republican powers undefined. This meant that none of the crucial issues concerning the *actual* distribution of powers between the centre and the republics or between the republics themselves were properly resolved. It was therefore quite obvious that even if it had been adopted it would only have led to further conflict.

3   Allowing the Union to be voluntary appeared to threaten its physical destruction. Only five republics (the RSFSR, Kazakhstan, Uzbekistan, Tadjikistan and Byelorussia) intended to sign the new treaty on 20 August. Several republics, e.g. Lithuania, Latvia, Estonia, Georgia and Moldova had indicated that they definitely would not sign. And others, notably Ukraine, were undecided about whether to sign or not.

To conservative opinion this appeared to be a betrayal of the nationwide referendum held on 17 March 1991 in which the majority of the population had apparently voted to preserve the USSR as a 'renewed federation'. In short, in the words of 'Acting President' Gennadi Yanaev on the 19 August:

A real threat of disintegration has arisen, the breakup of a single economic space, a single space of civil rights, a single defence, and a single foreign policy. Normal life . . . is impossible. Under these circumstances, we have no other choice but to take decisive measures in order to stop the slide of the country towards catastrophe.

By acting to forestall the ratification of the new Union Treaty the coup leaders hoped to restore the powers of the centre before they could be signed away and to halt the republican rush to independence. However, it is not clear that they had any idea about how they were actually going to achieve this once in power.

The economic crisis

The economic crisis was the second reason for the coup. There was a torrent of bad news in the weeks leading up to the coup. For example, the economic data for the month of July published on 14 August revealed that the economy was not stabilising as had been hoped. The only things that were increasing were the country's money supply, prices, people's wages and unemployment. Everything else was in a state of decline or at a virtual standstill. This was creating a vicious circle of diminishing production, creating hardship, and driving the republics to take ever more radical protectionist measures.

It was also reported in early August, halfway through the harvest season, that the state had only received one-quarter of the deliveries it had planned for and that farmers were refusing to sell produce to the state at prices it could afford. Moreover, it looked as though the harvest overall was going to be much smaller than predicted. All this meant that state shops were going to remain empty of food for the foreseeable future.

And on 13 August, Prime Minister Pavlov predicted that electricity would be in short supply for the next five years with severe effects for industry and the population.

The country was rife with rumours of famine, chaos and economic collapse and it looked to many, and not just the conservatives, as though massive social unrest was a real possibility.

The Emergency Committee appealed directly to people's fears about the economic situation. It promised to end rationing, improve food supplies and halt the economic decline. However, it clearly had no idea how it was going to achieve this. When asked how they intended to improve the economic situation, Prime Minister Pavlov, a member of the Emergency Committee, lamely replied 'we will work better'.

Public opinion polls

These appeared to suggest that people were profoundly disillusioned with everything that Gorbachev had struggled for. This gave the coup leaders reason to believe (so they thought) that the majority of the population would support them if they took decisive action to stop the rot.

Gorbachev's popularity ratings had sunk from 80 or 90 per cent in the early years to 20 per cent in July 1990 and 'less than zero' by 1991. The coup leaders therefore took it for granted that no one would object to his removal. Anatoly Lukyanov, the Chairman of the USSR Supreme Soviet, and one of the men behind the coup, publicly said as much.

Asked in July 1991 whether they would have supported *perestroika* in 1985 if they had known what it would lead to, only 23 per cent of a representative sample said 'yes' and 52 per cent said 'no'. And when asked what Soviet rule had done for them, 65 per cent of another poll sample replied that it meant 'shortages, queques and poverty', and 28 per cent that it meant 'powerlessness, constant insults and humiliation' (see White, p. 250).

Moreover, many older people were frequently heard to say that life had been better under Brezhnev than it had been under Gorbachev. This gave conservatives reason to assume that ordinary people would not object to a return to centralised control.

Opinion within the armed forces

Opinion within the armed forces or the '16th Republic' as they became known (because of their enormous size and property holdings) was even more depressed and angry for all the reasons cited in Chapter 11. Gorbachev's reforms and their consequences had enormous effects on the status, security and standard of living of military personnel. The anger they directed at Gorbachev during 1990 and 1991 was again taken as evidence by the coup leaders that their assault on power would find ready support within the armed forces.

Gorbachev's contribution to the coup

Gorbachev himself laid the foundations for the coup despite all the warnings and protests from liberals and democrats to his political left about the anti-democratic implications of his actions.

1   Gorbachev insisted on greatly augmenting the powers of the presidency after March 1990. In particular, Gorbachev pushed through a new 'Law on the State of Emergency', adopted on 3 April 1990, which gave the president extraordinary powers to impose states of emergency in parts of the country and to impose direct presidential rule on a temporary basis.

As many of his critics pointed out, these extraordinary powers provided the legal basis for a new dictatorship should anyone usurp the position of president. In fact it was this 'Law on the State of Emergency' that Acting President Yanaev and the State Committee for the State of Emergency (the Emergency Committee for short) sought to exploit in August 1991.

2   Gorbachev massively increased the powers of the KGB and the Ministry of Internal Affairs (MVD). In Amy Knight's words (p. 39), 'Once he became President of the USSR in March 1990, Gorbachev issued decree after decree strengthening the powers of the KGB to maintain, with the help of the MVD, order and

stability in the increasingly chaotic political and social environment.' This greatly enhanced the power and influence of KGB
officials.

3   From September 1990 to April 1991, the months of his
famous 'turn to the right', Gorbachev 'cultivated the conservatives
and can even be said to have indulged them' (Mann, p. 3).

(a)   He countenanced the use of repressive measures against the
democratic and nationalist forces in society.
(b)   As Yeltsin, Shevardnadze and many others were to point out
after August, almost all the key people involved in the coup
had been handpicked by Gorbachev himself. For example,
six of the eight members of the Emergency Committee were
Gorbachev appointees – namely Vice President Gennadi
Yanaev (who was only elected to his position by the USSR
Congress of People's Deputies in December 1990 after two
votes and on the personal insistence of Gorbachev); Prime
Minister Valentin Pavlov; Defence Minister Dmitri Yazov;
KGB chief Vladimir Kryuchkov; Interior Minister Boris
Pugo; and Deputy Chairman of the Defence Council Oleg
Baklanov.

These people remained in office even after Gorbachev
renewed negotiations with Yeltsin and other republican leaders
over the new Union Treaty in April 1991. And there is every
reason to suppose that they felt thoroughly betrayed by his sudden
'defection' back into the 'rebel' camp.

4   Worst of all, perhaps, Gorbachev simply ignored the evidence
that was accumulating in 1991 that the conservatives were mar-
shalling their forces against him. For instance, from early 1991
leading military officials became more and more publicly outspoken about the possibility (even necessity) of military intervention.

The most notorious example was the short manifesto 'A Word
to the People' published on 23 July 1991. It was signed by twelve
prominent people, among them Army General V. Varennikov,

Commander in Chief of the Ground Forces, and Colonel B. Gromov, Afghan veteran and a deputy minister of the Ministry of Internal Affairs (who, incidentally, as of August 1992 was still in office). In the most lurid language it called for a popular uprising against *perestroika* and on the armed forces to do their duty and save 'the fatherland'. No disciplinary action was taken against any of the signatories despite the fact that the manifesto was treasonable.

What should have been even more worrying for Gorbachev was that there were at least two dress rehearsals for the August coup. In neither case did Gorbachev take any action.

(a) The Soviet military intervention in Lithuania and Latvia in January 1991 was accompanied by attempts to establish what were called 'National Salvation Committees'. These shadowy bodies were headed by conservative republican party and military officials who attempted to take power from the democratically elected governments. They failed because of overwhelming opposition to them and lack of support from the centre. But as a journalist in a leading newspaper subsequently noted in October 1991, 'The scenarios for the two [coups] – January and August – are surprisingly similar. The same methods; the same committees, only with different names; the same ambitions on the part of the . . . leaders as 'saviours of the nation'; and the same blood' (i.e. the blood of pro-democracy demonstrators in the streets).

Gorbachev's reaction to the January events was to wring his hands and deny responsibility (this upset the military who were left to carry the can). He subsequently made very little effort to track down and discipline the perpetrators. In the end the official report on these events was a whitewash. It exonerated the Soviet troops involved and blamed the deaths on local militants. The consequence was domestic and international outrage.

(b) In June 1991 Prime Minister Pavlov attempted to pull off a 'constitutional coup'. He tried to persuade the USSR Supreme Soviet to grant him extra powers to issue decrees having the force of law to enable him to deal with the economic crisis (so he said). He was supported in these demands by Pugo, Yazov and Kryuchkov. The Supreme Soviet debate on this request turned into a general attack on Gorbachev in which Kryuchkov even went so far as to suggest that developments in the country were following a CIA plan to make the Soviet Union collapse (see Morrison, p. 279). Gorbachev successfully fought off this attack, but he did nothing to discipline the leading government officials who had launched it. Pavlov, Pugo, Yazov and Kryuchkov all remained in power.

Taken together these developments must have persuaded the conservatives in the party apparatus, the central state institutions and the armed forces that:

(a) The Soviet state was threatened with destruction.
(b) Gorbachev was not acting decisively enough to prevent this.
(c) The general population would welcome a return to stability and normality.

To cap it all, Gorbachev was so complacent about the conservative opposition that he made things easy for the conspirators by going on holiday in the vital weeks before the signing of the new Union Treaty. This made it simple to isolate him.

The coup itself

This began on Sunday 18 August when five officials, among them close presidential aides, forced their way into Gorbachev's holiday home in the Crimea. They demanded either that Gorbachev issue a presidential decree declaring a state of emergency or that he should hand over his powers to the vice-president and resign (see Gorbachev, pp. 20–1). Gorbachev refused to comply with either demand. Thereafter, Gorbachev and his family were kept in complete isolation.

According to some accounts (see below) it was only after Gorbachev's refusal to co-operate that the Emergency Committee was formed on the evening of 18 August.

The first that the Soviet people (and the rest of the world) knew of the coup was at dawn on Monday 19 August when long columns of tanks began to rumble into Moscow past the crowds of commuters going to work and troops began to take over radio stations, occupy newspaper offices and to mobilise in different parts of the country.

Soviet radio and television announced the formation of the Emergency Committee and broadcast its first declarations:

1 That Vice-President Yanaev was taking over as Acting President because of Gorbachev's incapacitation through illness (which was not true).
2 The imposition of a six month state of emergency.
3 Decree No. 1 which outlined sixteen measures for the immediate restoration of order (most of them actually rather vague and sweeping).
4 A statement entitled 'Appeal to the Soviet People' which tried to justify the coup by claiming in vague terms that something had to be done to end the crisis in the country and which urged the people to support the Committee on the grounds that 'all true patriots and people of goodwill' should 'put an end to this time of troubles'.

Among the Emergency Committee's first moves were the reimposition of central control on radio and television networks and a blanket ban on the publication of all newspapers except for those approved by the Committee (almost all of them published by the CPSU). And the attempted mobilisation of the armed forces as the key instrument for the reimposition of order.

From the morning of the 19th until Gorbachev's return to Moscow on 22 August, the country was in a state of confusion.

It became clear almost immediately that the Emergency Committee did not have the power or the credibility to impose its will and that the whole affair had been bungled.

1 There were no mass arrests of opposition activists much to their own amazement. There were plans to arrest key figures like Boris Yeltsin and Anatoly Sobchak (the liberal mayor of

Leningrad) but these were mishandled. For example, Boris Yeltsin and leading officials of the Russian government managed to escape arrest by some ten minutes on the morning of the 19th and all of them (as well as many Russian Supreme Soviet deputies) made it safely across Moscow to the Russian parliament building (the White House) where the Russian parliament went into permanent session behind barricades (see Sobchak, Afterword).

This was a fatal mistake because Boris Yeltsin, the most popular leader in the country, was able to establish himself and the Russian government as the focus of democratic opposition to the coup with enormous consequences.

2   Even at the time there was clearly considerable confusion and deep divisions within the armed forces and the KGB. For example:

(a)   The long columns of tanks that moved into Moscow on the 19th had no idea what to do once they got there. They were simply told to 'enter and stay put', which is what they did.

(b)   Many officers either refused to obey orders or hesitated about implementing them long enough to render them ineffective. Many others who might have been expected to support the coup either refused to support it or lay low when it became clear that it would not succeed (Knight, p. 40). Consequently, the imposition of local military rule was very patchy and certainly not remotely adequate to the task of reimposing order across the country.

3   The immediate response of republican authorities around the country was decidedly lukewarm. Very few of the republican governments followed Russian President Yeltsin's example in condemning the Emergency Committee outright (the Baltic republics were the exception). But very few republican leaders came out and actively supported it either (with two or three exceptions). Most of the elected leaders adopted a 'wait and see' approach and appealed for calm. Above all, the republican authorities were extremely jealous of their new-found autonomy

and were not about to let the 'centre' in the form of the Emergency Committee dictate terms to them. The lack of prompt republican compliance weakened the credibility and effectiveness of the coup fatally.

4   Although controls were imposed on the media, other lines of communication – telephones, fax lines, computer networks, local radio stations in many parts of the country – remained open and provided the opposition (particularly President Yeltsin and the deputies barricaded in the White House) with invaluable access to the outside world. This lapse mystified everybody inside and outside the country.

5   Rumours began to circulate almost immediately that the Emergency Committee was internally divided and that some of its members, e.g. Defence Minister Yazov, were getting cold feet. Yeltsin exploited these rumours ruthlessly (he may even have helped to start some of them).

Why did the coup fail?

There are several explanations.

Incompetence

The most obvious explanation is that the members of the Emergency Committee were totally incompetent and that if they had not been the coup would probably have succeeded. This argument is based on the following:

1   The Emergency Committee was internally divided and lacked decisive leadership and this is what brought it down (see Brumberg). None of the 'Gang of Eight' (as they became known) proved willing to put their necks on the line and take ultimate responsibility for the coup or for the extreme coercive measures that were needed to impose emergency rule (see Sobchak, p. 175). According to inside accounts they bickered amongst themselves and mostly spent their time getting blind-drunk. They suffered a fatal loss of nerve and the coup therefore lacked direction and

purpose at the very top.

2   The members of the Emergency Committee were, and were seen to be, political nonentities, utterly lacking in popular authority and respect and completely out of touch with what had been happening in the country. They were all 'faceless' party-state functionaries of the old system. They therefore lacked the courage, the intelligence and the initiative to engage in the sort of strategic planning that was necessary both in the short term to restore order and in the long term to stabilise and restructure the country.

3   Preparations had apparently already been made for the possibility of a coup but the Emergency Committee did not exploit them. For example, according to information received by Anatoly Sobchak, the Mayor of Leningrad (St Petersburg), planning for a coup had been going on for at least a year before it happened (Sobchak, p. 180). And Yeltsin's people subsequently discovered, as they went through party and KGB documents after the coup, that considerable preparations for some sort of emergency had been made. Camps in the GULAG had been making ready to receive prisoners. Tribunals for summary trials had been organised. Extensive lists of people to be arrested had been compiled (see Odom p. 14). However, none of this was activated. If it had been then the coup would not have failed. As the Chinese pro-democracy demonstrators discovered in Tiananmen Square on the night of 3–4 June 1989, there is nothing that largely unarmed people can do against overwhelming and utterly ruthless military force.

The constitutional coup

A second explanation is that the coup failed because the Emergency Committee tried to create the illusion that it was engaged in a constitutional transfer of power (see Thorson, p. 21). This greatly limited the ruthlessness with which the coup was carried out. It also gave considerable ammunition to President Yeltsin and the popular opposition to the coup.

1   The coup was not a classic *coup d'état* in which power is wrested from the legitimate government by illegitimate military or other force.

(a)   Six of the eight members of the Emergency Committee were leading members of the government. The other two – Alexander Tizyakov, President of the Association of State Enterprises and Vasili Starodubtsev, Chair of the USSR Peasants Union, an organisation that represented the heads of collective and state farms not individual peasants – were leading party-state officials. In some ways therefore the coup was actually an attempt by members of the duly appointed government to take power from the president to whom they were responsible and who had appointed them. It was one arm of the state trying to take power from another arm of the state.

(b)   The Emergency Committee tried to claim that its acts were constitutional (see Carla Thorson for a full discussion). For example, Vice President Gennadi Yanaev assumed the responsibilities of the president citing Article 127(7) of the revised USSR constitution. This stated that in the event of presidential incapacity the powers of the presidency would temporarily be transferred to the vice-president pending new presidential elections. The imposition of a state of emergency for six months was also said to be based on the law concerning states of emergency (pushed through by Gorbachev in 1990) and the USSR constitution.

2   However, the Emergency Committee's appeal to the constitution weakened it fatally.

First of all, it made it very difficult to move decisively against the opposition. People like Yeltsin and Sobchak were not just popular leaders they were democratically elected government officials with an enormous amount of public support. No constitutional or legal reason could have been found for their arrest except a fabricated one. Moreover, it was difficult to know when to arrest them. Had they been arrested *before* the declaration of a state of emergency (which would have been the obvious thing to do) this would immediately have undermined the Committee's constitutional claims. However, leaving arrangements for their arrest until after the declaration of an emergency clearly gave them time to take evasive action.

Secondly, it also gave the opposition, and Yeltsin most of all, the opportunity to question the legal basis of the Committee's claims, to challenge its constitutional legitimacy and thereby to undermine its authority.

The whole constitutional claim hinged on whether Gorbachev really was incapacitated or not. The Emergency Committee could provide no proof, nor could it explain why Gorbachev who had seemed extremely healthy before he went on holiday should suddenly be taken ill just before the signing of the new Union Treaty. Even more importantly, several top officials, including Presidents Yeltsin of Russia and Nazarbaev of Kazakhstan, knew for a fact that Gorbachev was well because they had spoken to him on the phone on Saturday 17 August. Almost everyone was convinced that the Gang of Eight was lying and Yeltsin rejected the claim outright. Within hours of the first emergency broadcast on Monday morning Yeltsin had declared that the formation of the Emergency Committee was unconstitutional and illegal and that its measures were not enforceable in the RSFSR. And he demanded Gorbachev's immediate return. He was rapidly followed by the leaders of all three Baltic republics and numerous other regions.

The legality of the state of emergency was also questionable. According to the law only the USSR Supreme Soviet could declare a countrywide state of emergency. The president was empowered to declare states of emergency 'in particular localities', but such a presidential declaration had to be ratified by the USSR Supreme Soviet 'without delay' and by a two-thirds majority. The Emergency Committee could not therefore declare a countrywide emergency. However, it failed to specify 'the particular localities' to which the state of emergency was to apply. It also failed to make any reference to the question of ratification. These were fatal omissions. The first enabled republican and local governments to insist that the state of emergency did not apply on their territories. It also generated a great deal of genuine confusion since local authorities (whatever their attitude to the coup) had no way of knowing whether the state of emergency applied to them or not. The second enabled everyone to declare that the state of emergency had to be ratified by the USSR Supreme Soviet. This included the USSR Committee for Constitutional Review which insisted that the Emergency Committee consult the Supreme Soviet. As a result, an emergency session of the USSR Supreme Soviet was set for Monday 26 August, by which time, of course, it was all over.

In short, by appealing to the constitution and the law the Emergency Committee enabled the opposition to use both the constitution and the law against it. This automatically put it in a weak position because, as a result of *perestroika*, the republics (and for that matter local government) had developed as alternative sources of state power with far greater constitutional legitimacy than any institution at the centre. And consequently because the Emergency Committee found itself caught up in, and frustrated by, the same 'war of laws' that had defeated Gorbachev. The republics simply refused to implement its decisions.

Why the pretence?

One explanation might well be that the Emergency Committee was expecting Gorbachev to see things through. There are strong grounds for supposing (as we saw above) that Gorbachev led his government colleagues to believe that he would support a state of emergency but that he got cold feet once things were set in motion. This left them to carry the can.

This would help to explain the Emergency Committee's lack of forward planning and its internal disorganisation. The members of government involved would not have had any short-term plans to establish an Emergency Committee or long-term plans for running the country because they all assumed that Gorbachev would stay on as president. Had he done so the state of emergency would have been legitimate. As former prime minister, Pavlov, commented after the coup, 'extraordinary and emergency measures had been discussed before, in the spring for instance. The question of applying emergency measures to stabilise the situation came up all the time after all. So there was nothing new about that' (see Knight, p. 39).

It also helps to explain the Committee's lack of ruthlessness. It would have had no plans to mobilise the military for an over-whelming show of force. And it is quite possible that it would not have seen the need since its (vague) impression of public opinion was that almost everyone wanted the restoration of firm and decisive leadership, particularly in the economy, and would there-fore voluntarily support a state of emergency.

The second explanation is that Gorbachev's insistent demands for the rule of law and the general reform process had had a lasting impact on Soviet society. As Carla Thorson points out (p. 22), the fact that both the Emergency Committee and its opponents resorted to the legal weapon suggests that *perestroika* had successfully and permanently transformed Soviet society.

The final explanation is that the members of the Emergency Committee were moderate conservatives. They wanted to pre-serve the Soviet Union but as their public declarations made clear they also wanted to maintain the process of reform. They there-fore had a commitment to the constitution and the laws that they had helped to create. There were other, much more ruthless, hard-liners in the wings who failed to get their hands on the levers of power because the Emergency Committee pre-empted them.

Popular resistance and the 'counter-coup'

A third explanation is that the coup failed because of the popular opposition to it and, in particular, because of Yeltsin's decisive and courageous leadership. However, the evidence here is mixed.

Evidence for
1   *The counter-coup.* Yeltsin's extraordinary courage and pres-ence of mind were undoubtedly crucial in focusing opposition to the coup and in challenging its authority. In fact, it is possible to argue that the real coup in August was not the one conducted by the Emergency Committee, which at least tried to maintain a facade of legality, but the unconstitutional 'counter-coup' that was launched by President Yeltsin against it.

Starting with his declaration outlawing the Emergency Committee as unconstitutional on the 19 August, President Yeltsin issued a whole series of 'counter-decrees' on the 19th and in the days that followed. These decrees were designed to eliminate the old Soviet 'centre', and most of them were technically unconstitutional. For example, Yeltsin immediately assumed full control of all the armed forces on Russian territory. More controversially, on 20 August he placed *all* institutions located in the RSFSR under the jurisdiction of the Russian government. Since the seat of Soviet central government and virtually all the old party-state institutions were located in the capital of Russia, namely Moscow, this meant that the Russian President and the Russian government were technically taking over all the institutions and functions of the old Soviet 'centre'. This decidedly unconstitutional decree formed the basis for even more controversial decrees in the days that followed, almost all of which increased Yeltsin's powers (and the powers of the Russian government) at the expense of central institutions.

Yeltsin's actions were undoubtedly pivotal in destroying:

(a)   the shaky credibility of the Emergency Committee, since, having let him escape, there was nothing the Emergency Committee could do to stop him short of trying to kill him outright (with completely unpredictable consequences).

(b)   the old Soviet 'centre'. When USSR President Gorbachev returned to Moscow he effectively had no choice but to ratify almost all of Yeltsin's decrees (at an emergency session of the USSR Supreme Soviet on 23 August) because he had completely lost his political power-base as a result of the coup.

However, Yeltsin's actions, especially in the days after the collapse of the Emergency Committee, also generated a great deal of unease. Many democrats began to criticise him on the grounds that he was overstepping his powers and behaving in an anti-democratic and unconstitutional way. The non-Russian republics began to fear that the old dictatorial Soviet 'centre' was being replaced by a new dictatorial 'Russian centre'.

These tensions were to generate enormous problems both in the transition period between the collapse of the Emergency

Committee and the collapse of the USSR in December 1991 and for the new Commonwealth of Independent States that replaced it.

2   However, Soviet society also tried to resist the Emergency Committee in other ways.

(a)   Most commentators agree that the media was in the forefront of the opposition to the coup despite the Emergency Committee's attempts to muzzle it. For example, on 20 August several liberal pro-democracy publications managed to produce emergency issues despite the ban. Central television and even some of the newspapers approved by the Emergency Committee were able to convey information in such a way as to inform the public about Yeltsin's actions and about popular resistance to the coup.

(b)   There were massive demonstrations in Moscow and other cities across the country in opposition to the coup. In Moscow people built barricades around the Russian parliament building and stood permanent guard, prepared if necessary to defend it from attack with their bare hands (as happened in the capitals of the Baltic republics in January 1991 and again in August). This was particularly so of the young and of the new entrepreneurial classes, the private businessmen and women, who had everything to lose from any restoration of the old system and everything to gain from its destruction. These people manned the barricades in droves and contributed financial and organisational resources to the struggle against the Emergency Committee.

(c)   There was also a growing wave of strikes across the country in response to Yeltsin's call on 19 August for a general strike, with the miners leading the way.

(d)   Finally, there was considerable resistance within the armed forces and the KGB. In particular, many of the younger officers supported the new democratic processes and were opposed to the use of military force against the civilian population.

Evidence against

1   There was also a great deal of public passivity. For everyone
who took to the streets or went on strike there were a great many
more who did neither, afraid for their jobs and what would
happen to them if the coup did succeed. Yeltsin's call for a
general strike did not result in one. Although this was probably
due to the fact that it takes time to mobilise and organise people
and that the coup occurred without warning. The most
organised workers, like the miners, responded very quickly. It is
quite probable that if the coup had lasted strikes would have
increased.

2   Many of the republican leaders prevaricated, and only came
out against the coup once it was clear that it would fail. The same
was true of many local leaders. For example, a study conducted
by the chief State Inspector of the RSFSR in the autumn of 1991
indicated that 70.5 per cent of Russia's 73 regions did not
support President Yeltsin during the coup, and either sided with
the Emergency Committee or adopted a wait-and-see attitude.
While the remaining 29.5 per cent pledged formal loyalty to the
RSFSR President but did not actually give Yeltsin any active
support (there were only five exceptions, Moscow, Leningrad
and three other regions). Furthermore, not a single communist
party committee in the RSFSR supported Yeltsin. Instead, two-
thirds supported the coup, and one-third adopted a policy of
wait-and-see ('Weekly record of events', pp. 31–2). This local
bias was to present President Yeltsin with enormous problems
when he tried to introduce radical economic reform.

3   Public opinion polls conducted during the coup revealed that
there was a significant minority across the country who supported
it.

The evidence either way is inconclusive. Popular resistance was
undoubtedly crucial in undermining the Emergency Committee's
confidence and credibility. Having expected public docility, the
Gang of Eight were completely thrown to discover that so many
people were willing to resist them even if it meant risking their

lives. Soviet people had lost their fear of 'the authorities' and this was something that the Gang of Eight totally failed to appreciate. As Gorbachev warned the delegation who burst in on him on 18 August, 'The people are not a battalion of soldiers to whom you can issue the command 'right turn' or 'left turn, march' and they will all do as you tell them. It won't be like that. Just mark my words' (Gorbachev, p. 23). Society had changed too much. The Emergency Committee also did not bargain for the fact that the public's dissatisfaction with the chaotic state of affairs did *not* mean that they were in favour of preserving the old system. They wanted stability and order but they did not want them at the expense of their new-found freedom.

However, it is doubtful whether popular resistance and even Yeltsin's powerful leadership would have been enough on their own to have defeated the coup in the absence of the other factors discussed above. Had the Emergency Committee been more decisive and the armed forces more united in their support the coup would probably have succeeded, although undoubtedly at a great cost in lives. The experience of too many countries suggests that naked force ruthlessly applied almost always succeeds in crushing popular resistance at least in the short term and medium term.

The three explanations discussed above are therefore complementary and not alternatives to each other. Each one addresses a different aspect of the August events and we cannot fully understand what happened unless we take them all into account.

Immediate aftermath

The days after the coup's collapse saw the first steps in the physical destruction of the old Soviet state.

On 24 August Gorbachev finally resigned as General Secretary of the CPSU. He ordered the nationalisation of all party property, called for the dissolution of the CPSU Central Committee and banned party cells in the armed forces, the KGB and the police throughout the USSR, thus effectively ratifying Yeltsin's earlier moves in this direction. On 29 August the USSR Supreme Soviet passed a resolution suspending the CPSU's activities throughout

the USSR. Its financial assets were frozen, its archives and buildings sealed up, and an investigation ordered into its responsibility
for the coup. This did not mean, however, that the CPSU ceased
to exist entirely (see Part III).

The old symbols of Soviet power were removed amid
triumphant scenes of popular celebration. Giant statues of Lenin,
Dzerzhinsky and other revolutionary figures were torn down. So
were the giant red stars that adorned official buildings, and many
of the huge propaganda posters that substituted for advertising in
the old USSR.

The Baltic states finally achieved their independence and were
granted international diplomatic recognition by the European
Community, among others, on 27 August. The Ukraine proclaimed its independence on 24 August (subject to ratification by a
referendum on 1 December which won overwhelming support).
Other republics now began to speed up the process of breaking
away from the old federation. This was to become an enormous
source of conflict as inconclusive discussions on the new Union
Treaty continued.

President Yeltsin and the Russian government accelerated
their takeover of Soviet institutions. For example, a series of
decrees on 24 August brought all the all-union ministries directly
under RSFSR control. Another series of decrees on 28 August
brought the entire network of the USSR Ministry of Finance, the
USSR State Bank, and the Bank for Foreign Economic Relations
under RSFSR control.

With the pre-coup government sacked or arrested and many
officials forced to resign, all the key posts in the USSR government were filled by Russian officials who had the express approval
of Yeltsin. By the time he resigned on 25 December 1991 President Gorbachev had become no more than a figurehead.

Meantime the economic situation was continuing to deteriorate
and Russian officials began to make ever more urgent appeals for
international aid.

Gorbachev was right to describe the August events as a
'cleansing storm' which 'like floodwaters in spring . . . swept away
a great deal that was obstructing our forward advance'
(Gorbachev, pp. 46–7). However, the August coup did not solve

all the old problems and it created a great many new ones.

Conclusion

By August 1991 the Soviet Union was experiencing the multiple pre-revolutionary crises described in Chapter 1.

1   It was in the throes of a profound political crisis that affected everyone. The central institutions had almost completely lost all authority and power. The new political parties were too weak and fragmented to be able to represent popular interests, and the federation was disintegrating.
2   It was in the throes of a profound economic crisis. Collapsing production, spiralling inflation, the disintegration of the distribution system were leading to enormous inequalities in wealth and threatening the vast majority with complete impoverishment.
3   And it was in the throes of a profound crisis of legitimacy. Almost everyone had lost faith in the old system. Even the members of the Emergency Committee did not seek to turn the clock back completely. In their public statements they spoke of the need to continue the reform process once stability had been achieved.

In this context it is difficult to assess the significance of the August coup. It was clearly not the cause of the Soviet crisis but the consequence of it. And it did not in itself bring about the downfall of the Soviet state. Gorbachev must bear a lot of the responsibility for that. However, by utterly discrediting what remained of the old 'establishment' it hastened the anti-Soviet nationalist and democratic revolutions that did destroy the Soviet state and that are still underway. In so doing it helped to bring about the end of the world's last remaining old imperial empire. Will future historians consider it to have been a 'world-historical event' as some have recently argued (see Malia; Shub)? Or will it be forgotten, like its predecessor the failed Kornilov coup of August 1917 (see Chapter 1)? At this point no one can tell.

We cannot finish the story of *perestroika* and its self-destruction without returning to the paradoxical figure of Gorbachev. Gorbachev was both a resounding failure and a triumphant success.

On the one hand, Gorbachev must bear a lot of the responsibility for the chaotic disintegration of the Soviet system and a lot of indirect responsibility for the occurrence of the August coup. Some have even gone so far as to suggest (rather unconvincingly) that Gorbachev was one of the plotters (see Sixsmith).

On the other hand, Gorbachev also deserves to take an awful lot of the credit. Looked at positively the disintegration of the Soviet state meant the liberation of Soviet society. *Perestroika* may have failed to reform the system but its democratic achievements were enormous despite the flaws. The various nations and the citizens of the old Soviet Union got back their histories, their identities, and their right to make choices. Gorbachev cannot be blamed if they fail to use these opportunities wisely. Even more to his credit, Gorbachev managed to destroy the old system with a minimum of bloodshed. Very few empires have disintegrated so completely without causing wars and enormous international upheavals in the process.

William Odom summed up Gorbachev best when he wrote at the end of 1991 that Gorbachev 'turned out to be a skilled but inadvertent revolutionary and a wholly incompetent but dedicated reformer' (Odom, p. 15). This description is quite likely to become Gorbachev's epitaph.

Further reading

Problems of Communism, Vol. 40, November–December 1991. Almost the whole of this issue of the journal is devoted to a discussion of the August events, but see in particular:

Knight, Amy, 'The coup that never was: Gorbachev and the forces of reaction', pp. 36–43

Odom, William E., 'Alternative perspectives on the August coup', pp. 13–19.

Shub, Anatole, 'The fourth Russian revolution: historical perspectives', pp. 20–6.

Report on the USSR, RFE/RL (Radio Free Europe/Radio Liberty)

Research Institute (Munich), Vol. 3, No. 36, 6 September, 1991. The whole of this issue is devoted to analysis of the August events, but see in particular:

Mann, Dawn, 'The circumstances surrounding the conservative putsch', pp. 1–5.

McMichael, Scott R., 'Moscow prelude: warning signs ignored', pp. 8–11.

Thorson, Carla, 'Constitutional issues surrounding the coup', pp. 19–22.

Rahr, Alexander, 'Changes in the El'tsin–Gorbachev relationship', pp. 35–37.

Tolz, Vera, 'How the journalists responded', pp. 23–28.

Brumberg, Abraham, 'The road to Minsk', *New York Review of Books*, 30 January 1992

Gorbachev, Mikhail, *The August Coup: the Truth and the Lessons*, Harper Collins, 1991

Malia, Martin, 'The August revolution', *New York Review of Books*, 26 September 1991

Morrison, John, *Boris Yeltsin: from Bolshevik to Democrat*, Penguin, 1991

Sixsmith, Martin, *Moscow Coup: the Death of the Soviet System*, Simon & Shuster, 1991

Sobchak, Anatoly, *For A New Russia: The Mayor of St Petersburg's Own Story of the Struggle for Justice and Democracy*, Harper Collins, 1992

Teague, Elizabeth, Tolz, Vera, 'CPSU R.I.P.', *Report on the USSR*, RFE/RL Research Institute, Vol. 3, No. 47, 22 November 1991, pp. 1–8.

'Weekly record of events', *Report on the USSR*, RFE/RL Research Institute, Vol. 3, No. 44, 1 November 1991, pp. 31–2.

Questions

1 To what extent should Gorbachev be held responsible for the August events?

2 Was the failure of the August coup inevitable in your opinion?

3 What significance would you attach to President Yeltsin's role in the collapse of the coup?

Part III

The legacies of *perestroika*

13

The unfinished revolution

Introduction

The writing of Part III was finished in August 1992 on the first anniversary of the failed August coup of 1991 amidst considerable gloom about the prospects for the newly independent countries of the Commonwealth of Independent States.

An enormous amount had happened in the year that had passed since August 1991. The Union of Soviet Socialist Republics disintegrated and was formally dissolved transforming international politics in the process. The Communist Party of the Soviet Union was banned and its property expropriated. Fifteen newly independent states took their place, most with democratically elected governments at the helm and most of them embarked, at least rhetorically, on radical programmes to create privatised market economies.

At the same time, however, it is also clear that very little had actually changed. Although we should note that circumstances and conditions have varied enormously between these new countries. The CPSU may have been banned but many of its officials and most members of the old *nomenklatura* were still in power in the majority of the new states, both in central and local government. In at least one state in fact, Uzbekistan, the Communist Party changed its name (to the Popular Democratic Party) but retained all its old structures and most of its old influence virtually intact. Privatisation may have become everyone's goal but most property was still state-owned at least in a formal sense. Many of the old structures of government continued to operate within several of the new states, some of them under new names like the old KGB, some of them under the old, like the soviets. Above all, the processes of economic and political disintegration that were set in motion by *perestroika* and that ultimately destroyed it continued to confront each of the new governments with enormously difficult problems and some brutal dilemmas for which they have yet to find solutions and for which, indeed, they may never find solutions.

In short, the new governments found themselves betwixt and between the two stages of revolution discussed in Chapter 1. The disintegration of the old system still had some way to go and the task of managing the ensuing crises has been hindering the emergence of new institutions and new ways of doing things.

This chapter will look briefly at some of the internal dynamics of this process focusing in particular on Russia because of its size and geo-political importance. The final chapter will look at the external aspects, namely, the creation of the Commonwealth of Independent States (CIS).

Problems of disintegration

Inter-ethnic relations and nationalism

These issues have continued to present all the new states of the former Soviet Union with their most acute, most dangerous and potentially most unmanageable problem. As a result of the precedents established by the Union-republican struggle for autonomy in 1990–1 and its destructive outcome in December 1991, there is a real danger of further internal conflict and disintegration that could go on almost indefinitely.

As we saw in Chapter 9, all the former republics are composed of ethnically mixed populations. The situation in the Russian Federal Republic, as it is now formally called, is particularly difficult because of its sheer size and complexity. In many respects it is almost an exact copy of the old USSR. It has always been a federation in its own right (even while it was still part of the Soviet Union when it was known as the Russian Soviet Federated

Socialist Republic). As of August 1992 it contained twenty-one republics and an even larger number of provinces, regions and districts, most of them with ethnically mixed populations themselves. Several of its republics and regions are large enough and strong enough to be able to sustain independence at least as well as a small country like Estonia (e.g. Tatarstan). Others have an ethnic mix of phenomenal complexity. To take an extreme example, the republic of Daghestan contains fourteen distinct nations speaking twelve official languages and at least two dozen smaller ethnic groups (too small to have the status of nation), all living together in a mere 50,000 square kilometres of highly mountainous land (see Glezer).

The Union-republican struggle for autonomy created the following precedents.

1 It generated a nationalist desire for self-determination that has percolated down to the very smallest groups.

Many of the republics and regions within the Russian federation, for example, have expressed a desire for greater autonomy and independence from Moscow which, from their vantage point, has become the new 'centre'. Two of these republics, Tatarstan and Chechnya had already effectively declared themselves sovereign by March 1992 (only three months after Russia gained real sovereignty) and several others were threatening to follow suit.

Many of the 'landless' nations would like their own territories in order to acquire their own rights of local self-government. In 1991, for instance, five separate republics were declared on the territory of the Karachai-Cherkess Republic (a member of the Russian federation) although these have yet to receive any sort of recognition. Similar developments were taking place in Daghestan and elsewhere: e.g. the Kurdish minority in Azerbaijan have been demanding their own autonomous territory (probably a forlorn hope given the on-going war over Nagorno-Karabakh).

2 The contempt shown by the governments of the Union-republics towards the Soviet constitution, the success of their 'war

of laws' against the Soviet government, and the extent to which the Soviet government was shown to be powerless to do anything about it, also provided all the other national groups with a ready-made and proven strategy for getting their own way. By late 1991 President Yeltsin and the Russian government were already embroiled in a 'war of laws' with Russia's constituent republics. A situation that economic collapse aggravated because the 'autonomies' have had to take local measures to protect themselves. And both Tatarstan and Chechnya (or Checheno-Ingushetia as it was then known) were successfully managing to defy the Russian constitution and the duly-elected Russian government. Similar processes were occurring in other CIS states, e.g. Tadjikistan and Ukraine.

3 Secession, or the threat of it, rather than negotiation and compromise, have increasingly come to be seen as the only solution to political and economic disagreement and conflict. In Tadjikistan, for instance, the northern region of Leninabad (where almost one-third of the population is Uzbek) has been in conflict with the southern regions (dominated by Tadjiks) where the capital, Dushanbe, is situated. It has been engaged in something of a 'war of laws' with Dushanbe and has threatened to secede and join Uzbekistan if its demands are not met.

However, the particular way in which the USSR collapsed, with the Union-republics playing the dominant role, also generated some potentially dangerous counter-tendencies to these centrifugal processes.

Statehood was understood as applying only to the old Union-republics. The 'big presidents' of the former Union-republics would therefore like to prevent disintegration from going any further. They did not seek power and struggle for national independence in order to preside over the destruction of their countries or to lose their positions as state presidents. On the contrary, the ultimate goal for many of them has been to forge new nation-states with all the trappings of modern statehood, and to see their names go into the history books as a result. This applied as much to Boris Yeltsin as it did to Leonid Kravchuk in Ukraine or Vitautis Landsbergis in Lithuania. By the same token, the titular nationalities of the old Union-republics want to keep their new states territorially intact and to preserve or to promote their own cultural dominance. There has therefore been considerable resistance to the demands of the 'autonomies' and of minority groups within many of the new states which, of course, is only likely to exacerbate inter-ethnic conflict.

This has manifested itself in a variety of ways. For example, the threat of territorial disintegration in Russia and the growing sense that Russia as a great power has been humiliated has generated an increasingly powerful Russian nationalist backlash that has united all sides of the political spectrum behind the determination to hold the country together, although there has been enormous disagreement about how this is to be done (see below). This, in turn of course, may simply encourage local nationalisms to fight back.

In the much smaller Baltic states the fear of cultural submergence and hostility to the Russian minorities (which in Latvia and Estonia constitute 30 per cent or more of the population) have resulted in fiercely restrictive citizenship laws that have basically turned even second-generation Russians into foreigners. These, it is hoped, will either force Russians to assimilate completely or drive them out altogether. Needless to say, these laws have greatly exacerbated inter-ethnic tensions in the Baltic states and in Russia where concern about the fate of the Russian minorities still resident in the other states has been growing.

The difficulty with creating nation-states is that, inevitably, it raises the thorny question of what nation the state should represent and how. No one can avoid this question because in a tense multi-ethnic environment everything can become the object of nationalist grievance, including the ethnic origins of politicians and government officials. However, if the history of Europe is anything to go by, the answers generally cause enormous conflict.

Prospects

It is difficult not to be gloomy about the future whichever way one looks at it.

There have been some oases of relative calm. In Kazakhstan, for example, President Nazarbaev has thus far been successful in promoting ethnic harmony, particularly between Kazakhs and Russians who dominate the population and are almost evenly balanced (there are 6.5 million Kazakhs and 6.2 million Russians). Kyrgyzstan has also managed, thus far, to establish a reasonably democratic balance.

In general, however, *the potential for conflict* is enormous. The collapse of the Soviet Union established nationalism as a powerful and extremely effective weapon of political and economic struggle. It is an instrument that local politicians are quite likely to exploit in order to maximise their own popularity and power and/or to oppose unpopular reforms. It is also an extremely potent and dangerous force in conditions of:

1   General economic collapse when the struggle for scarce resources between groups becomes a war for survival, and people begin to look for scapegoats and enemies to blame for their misfortunes.
2   Acute political uncertainty when the old laws and the old rules have lost their meaning, government institutions are weak and the whole question of the identity of the state in each of these new countries is completely unsettled and, often quite literally, 'up for grabs'.

To make matters even worse, according to a report in *Moscow News* there were some 30 million firearms in private hands across the old Soviet sub-continent in July 1992. This number has undoubtedly increased since then. The slow disintegration of the Soviet army and the hasty and disorganised withdrawal of Soviet troops and weapons from Eastern Europe has flooded the black market with illegal weapons – everything from Kalashnikovs to tanks – at rock-bottom prices. The easy availability of weapons has helped to fuel the local wars in Nagorno-Karabakh, Moldova, Georgia. Many national groups have been deliberately arming themselves. The breakdown of law and order has also encouraged the development of local vigilante groups and informal 'law enforcement' agencies (see Gubarev), many of them created on an ethnic basis.

Dilemmas

The general situation has confronted the more far-sighted politicians with some horrible dilemmas to which there are no obvious solutions.

1   Once the fuse is lit, nationalism is rarely amenable either to negotiation or coercion. On the one hand, negotiation takes a great deal of time, something that no one has got much of; and requires a great deal of willingness to compromise on *all* sides, something that is rarely forthcoming in times of acute crisis. Very often warring factions tend to increase their demands rather than reduce them. On the other hand, coercion, particularly if it involves the outright use of force, simply makes its victims more determined (as Gorbachev discovered) especially if they are already armed.

2   Developments in the individual states are heavily dependent on what happens in other states. For example, the treatment of Uzbeks in Tadjikistan will influence the treatment of Tadjiks in Uzbekistan. The fate of the Russian minorities in the Baltic republics or Moldova, and how Russia itself decides to handle these problems, could well destabilise the situation in e.g. Kazakhstan, and so on. Politicians therefore have to be conscious not just of the domestic but of the external consequences of their policies (although the fact that they ought to be does not mean that they will be).

3   It is not just nationalism that has been driving groups apart, but spontaneous processes of economic and political disintegration over which no one has much control. Political and economic chaos have forced (or encouraged) local authorities to take matters into their own hands and nationalist demands for greater local autonomy have both exacerbated this process and been stimulated by it (see below). However, bringing these spontaneous processes under control so that people do not starve or riot requires the heavy concentration of power and the use of extraordinary measures in order to try to re-establish order and effect change. The trouble is that such measures could actually

make the nationalist problem worse by appearing to infringe local autonomy, which in turn makes it more difficult to do anything about the economic crisis at a national level (see below). It becomes a vicious circle that is increasingly difficult to get out of.

The situation in Russia provided a graphic illustration of these dilemmas.

The Russian government has become increasingly divided over the issue of how to manage federal relations. Vice President Rutskoi has been a powerful advocate of the use of force to hold the federation together within its old borders and to protect Russian minorities in the former Soviet republics. Foreign Minister Kozyrev, on the other hand, has insisted on the need for peaceful negotiation and diplomacy in *all* circumstances. Neither approach prevented either Checheno-Ingushetia (where force was attempted in November 1991) or Tatarstan (which was treated more gently) from going their own way. And President Yeltsin himself (like Gorbachev before him) has come under increasing criticism from all sides (including his closest supporters). When he has opted for patient negotiation he has been accused of not protecting ethnic Russian interests vigorously enough. When he has sought to concentrate power and to impose solutions he has been accused of infringing national rights and of undermining the development of democracy.

As of August 1992, the moderate approach, represented by Kozyrev, had managed to retain the upper-hand with Yeltsin's support, and the Russian government had been reasonably successful in stabilising the situation at least in the short term. A new federal treaty was signed at the end of March 1992 by everyone except Tatarstan and Chechnya, and the government had managed to pre-empt some protests by entering into bi-lateral deals with the various republics and regions over such things as local control over natural resources and economic affairs. It also initiated separate negotiations with the two rebel republics on mutual relations.

However, it is impossible to say whether these developments will be sufficient to hold the federation together.

1   The federal treaty is rather vague on crucial issues like the distribution of powers and, in any case, can do little on its own to halt the destructive effects of economic and political disintegration (see below).

2   President Yeltsin himself has been rather badly compromised by his behaviour during the fateful years of 1990–1 when he did everything he could to promote the struggle for autonomy at all levels in order to undermine Gorbachev. A lot of people, on the liberal as well as the pro-communist and nationalist wings have been blaming this for many of Russia's subsequent problems. Equally, his sudden turn-about after December 1991 when he began to insist that Russia had to remain whole and indivisible, also upset a lot of people in the localities.

3   Nor is it clear whether people like Kozyrev will continue to win the argument. By mid-1992 political and social pressures on Yeltsin had already forced him to compromise on economic policy and make changes in the government, and Russian nationalist opinion was becoming more strident. The deteriorating situation plus the rumours about coups that have periodically circulated in Moscow since the beginning of 1992 will probably force Yeltsin to compromise further if he is not removed from power altogether before his presidential term is due to end in 1996.

The future is therefore profoundly uncertain but it is difficult not to come to the conclusion that the Russian federation will disintegrate very rapidly just like the Soviet one did. Much will depend on how the country's economic problems are dealt with and how quickly, and on whether reasonable people like Foreign Minister Andrei Kozyrev can continue to hold on to power. As of August 1992 the signs were not good (see below).

Economic crisis and the market

Economic disintegration has also continued to present all the new states with acute and dangerous problems. The processes described in Chapter 10 simply got worse with the collapse of the USSR.

In principle, all the new governments came to the conclusion that the only way out of the crisis was to create market economies. This applied as much to the highly conservative government in Uzbekistan as it did to the radical governments that came to power in Russia or the Baltic states. The old central planning system had been so massively discredited that no other alternative seemed possible. In addition to which, there was also a strong belief amongst leading politicians at any rate that the creation of a competitive market economy in their countries would not only solve the accumulated problems of seventy years of Soviet mismanagement but would eventually result in a standard of living and a level of productivity that would approximate to those enjoyed in the developed capitalist countries. This belief has been much encouraged by Western governments and Western institutions like the International Monetary Fund.

However, as Boris Yeltsin and others were beginning to discover in the course of 1992, the practical problems involved in implementing such a goal are breathtakingly difficult and entail social costs and the potential for social conflict that are incalculable. By mid-1992 therefore none of the privatisation or marketisation programmes were proceeding very fast, not even in Russia where a radical pro-market government was appointed in November 1991.

The main problems and dilemmas are as follows:

1   Economic and industrial restructuring inevitably have social consequences.

(a)   Closing down obsolete factories; forcing others to become profitable; breaking up large monopolies in order to introduce competition; and removing all the unnecessary bureaucrats who were previously engaged in interfering in the economy unavoidably means large-scale unemployment and labour re-location.

(b)   Bringing huge government budget deficits and the runaway money supply under control means cutting state spending to a minimum by removing all subsidies, slashing social welfare and defence spending, imposing strict controls on the credit available to agriculture and industry, and imposing even stricter controls on the amount of money that can be printed. Such measures inevitably entail severe social hardship because, for example, removing all subsidies means allowing all prices to rise as high as is necessary to balance supply and demand, even if this means pricing a lot of people out of the market altogether. It means allowing unprofitable factories and farms to go to the wall, causing unemployment; or forcing them to shed labour in order to become more profitable. At the same time, slashing social spending means, in principle, providing no social safety net to protect people from the worst consequences of economic restructuring.

2   Privatisation is politically and technically difficult. It requires enormous amounts of legislation which is time-consuming and also requires the existence of a consensus between government and parliament about what has to be achieved. This has not always been forthcoming in any of the new states. It directly challenges powerful vested interests, notably those of the old *nomenklatura* which still runs the big state-owned factories. It also raises difficult technical questions. For example, how does one even begin to privatise land and property when neither land nor property has a value because there is no market, money is virtually worthless, and very few people have the resources to buy anything anyway? And even if one solves the problem for things like housing, where there are obvious purchasers, and small-scale enterprises like shops, where there is the possibility of competition, what does one do about the mammoth state-owned factories that employ thousands of people under one roof and that dominate the 'market' as monopoly suppliers? Who does one sell them to and how? It will be almost impossible to break them up into smaller companies without massively interrupting the process of production thereby making the general 'supply side depression' even worse than it already is. On the other hand, if they are sold off intact it will be almost impossible to introduce market competition at least in the short to medium term (i.e. until other, more modern factories are built to compete with them).

3   Privatisation and the creation of a market economy inevitably

involve enormous conflicts of interest. As we have already noted privatisation is a direct challenge to the interests of the old *nomenklatura* unless they can exploit the lack of legislation to ensure that they become the new owners of property. This has been happening on a large scale in Russia. Privatisation and marketisation also constitute obvious threats to populations that have grown up with the idea that the state should bear considerable responsibility for the provision of social welfare; and to skilled and educated labour forces that have:

(a)   learned about trade unionism and workers rights from seventy years of party rule in what was supposed to be a 'workers state'; and

(b)   discovered the efficacy of self-organisation and of industrial action during the Gorbachev years of protest and opposition.

These people are not necessarily going to be opposed to all aspects of marketisation, but they will oppose and have already opposed the brutal impoverishment that would be the consequence of swift and complete de-regulation.

As a result of all these problems, although almost everyone had more or less agreed in principle that a transition to the market is ultimately inevitable, there has been intense disagreement about how this is to be achieved and how quickly.

At one end of the extreme, Western institutions like the International Monetary Fund, have been advocating what is euphemistically known as 'economic shock therapy'. In practice, this would mean an immediate end to almost all government regulation and intervention in order to bring the budget deficit and the money supply swiftly under control and to create the conditions for 'free' market activity. This means the rapid implementation of everything listed under 1(b) above: the immediate liberalisation of all prices; the rapid withdrawal of all state subsidies and rapid reductions in social spending; strict controls on credit and the printing of money.

At the other extreme, representatives of the old *nomenklatura*, appalled both by the threat to their interests and by the potential for social deprivation and conflict that might result if such a radical 'shock therapy' programme were fully implemented, have advocated a much slower and more managed transition to the market.

The implementation of privatisation and marketisation programmes has therefore varied enormously from state to state but in every case it has been proceeding slowly. In neo-communist Uzbekistan which has a poor, predominantly agricultural economy dominated by a cotton monoculture, hardly any progress had been made in either direction by mid-1992 and most of the old planning structures remained in place. In Estonia and Latvia, by contrast, despite severe economic crises brought on, among other things, by their loss of access to cheap Russian energy supplies, the legislative foundation for privatisation had at least been laid.

However, although most of the new states have managed to begin the privatisation of housing and small-scale enterprises relatively successfully, and even in some cases of land, no one had come up with solutions to the problem of privatising and de-monopolising big industry. Even foreign buyers have not been particularly interested because so much of what was once Soviet industry is so horribly out of date.

Russia

In Russia the conflict over both privatisation and marketisation has been intense. Russia has been one of the few former Soviet republics (Ukraine has been another) to attract the promise of significant IMF and international support for its restructuring programme. It has therefore been under considerable pressure to implement the radical economic 'shock therapy' programme advocated by the IMF.

The first radical restructuring programme promoted by Yeltsin's economic reform supremo Yegor Gaidar in November 1991, tried to implement a version of shock therapy. Most prices were liberalised in January 1992 (but upper limits were placed on the prices of many products including energy, precious metals, dairy products, sugar and vodka), with the result that many of them shot through the roof. This did have the virtue of bringing more goods into the shops but at prices that hardly anyone could afford. Social spending was slashed by some 70 per cent. Military spending was reduced from anywhere between 15 and 25 per cent of GNP to 8 per cent (depending whose figures one uses). The money supply and credit were placed under relatively tight control which effectively resulted in an unofficial incomes freeze in 1992 because there was not enough physical money in circulation to pay everyone's wages, pensions or grants (this effectively cancelled out the income increases that had been granted to the population in order to compensate for the liberalisation of prices). And a start was made on the privatisation of small-scale enterprises, shops, housing and some land.

This programme almost immediately began to run into intense political and social opposition from parliamentarians in the Russian Supreme Soviet and Congress of People's Deputies; from industrialists in the state-owned sector and to a certain extent from the trade unions. This was partly because it threatened vested interests but largely because people began to fear the economic and social consequences if this economic shock therapy continued.

In fact, as of mid-1992 the Russian population had been extraordinarily patient and stoic in the face of circumstances that, for example, had pushed over 60 per cent of Moscow's population below the poverty line by the end of 1991 (see Robinson). None of the worst fears about mass social unrest had actually materialised. There are several explanations for this.

1   People's domestic hoards of food supplies and money savings had not quite run out, and the majority were still able to generate supplementary incomes on the black market or by selling-off personal belongings (and anything else they could get hold of) in the huge street markets that had sprung up in most cities.

2   Most people appreciate, at least in general, that radical economic reform is necessary and is going to hurt.

3   Yeltsin was still sufficiently popular to carry most people with him.

4   Yeltsin, acutely conscious of the opposition that his economic reform policies might generate from the trade unions and the

big employers, initiated a policy of 'social partnership' in late 1991. This combined representatives of government, employers and trade unions in a 'tripartite' mechanism that was intended to provide a forum both for the discussion of economic policy and for the resolution of industrial conflict. Up until mid-1992 this mechanism had been quite successful at keeping industrial unrest to a minimum, largely because the government consistently caved in to trade union demands for higher wages.

However, none of these factors can be counted on to keep the peace indefinitely.

As a consequence of the intense criticism to which the government was subjected in April 1992, President Yeltsin and his Acting Prime Minister Yegor Gaidar, watered down the shock therapy programme even further: increasing wages and pensions; easing restrictions on credit especially to the big industrial enterprises (which would quickly go bankrupt otherwise); and easing the restrictions on the printing of money (which was actually only limited by the physical capacity of Russia's four printing presses to keep up with demand). By August 1992 the government was planning for a budget deficit of almost a trillion roubles as a result. So the financial stabilisation and shock therapy programmes were in tatters, despite the significant social costs already borne by the population. In fact, the Russian debate over economic reform in the early summer of 1992 was rather similar to the arguments over the '500-day programme' in the summer of 1991. Numerous economic reform programmes were being put forward by economists from all sides of the political spectrum while government policy making lacked direction.

Yeltsin also modified the make-up of the government to include some representatives of the big state-run industries. These people were not opposed to market-oriented reform, but they were opposed to radical shock therapy. And some of his leading advisors began to criticise the IMF programme publicly, causing consternation in IMF and Western circles. This threatened the release of the 24 billion dollars promised by the IMF (by August 1992, in fact, only one-and-a-half billion dollars had been released, so the IMF had actually given very little to help Russia through its first crisis).

By August 1992, therefore, Yeltsin was in the process of constructing a centre-liberal coalition government combining radical academic economists like Yegor Gaidar, top industrialists, and members of the old Soviet government elite, people like Vice-Premier Chernomyrdin, the old Soviet Minister of the Gas Industry and Vasily Barchuk, the key budget advisor to ex-Soviet Finance Minister and Prime Minister Valentin Pavlov. This coalition has in turn been based on tripartite (or 'neo-corporatist') negotiations between government, employers and labour.

The supporters of radical 'economic shock therapy' had therefore lost the argument to the moderates who propose a longer-term managed transition to the market. As Sergei Stankevich, a well-known democrat and a political adviser to President Yeltsin, remarked in August, there had been a 'choice in favour of gradual evolutionary reforms on the basis of strong authority' (see Leontyev). The only difficulty with this statement is that there has been no strong authority in Russia since at least 1990, which is why the economic shock therapy failed in the first place. However, as Mikhail Leontyev, the Deputy Chief Business Editor for *Moscow News* remarked, the return to Russian government circles of old faces from the *perestroika* period and this new emphasis on strong authority, 'amounts to a justification for the motives of the putsch [in August 1991] from at least an economic side' (ibid, p. 10). What the Russian government is now engaged in, in his view, is the continuation of the 'same nomenklatura-based market evolution' that was occurring before August 1991, 'until the stage has been set for the rise of a truly liberal, postcommunist regime' and for a new set of reforms.

In the meantime, the severe economic problems confronting the country continued almost unchecked.

1   Production continued to decline – industrial output fell by another 13 per cent in the first quarter of 1992 and the output of foodstuffs by some 28 per cent. This downward trend showed no signs of being reversed during 1992. Inflation continued to soar, and large sectors of the population found themselves without cash

money. The combined effects of increased prices and increased incomes means that every transaction now required two or three times as much money as it had done before. By mid-1992 most of the districts, regions and republics of Russia simply did not have enough cash money to pay wages, pensions, grants or to support services, and factories were either making their own money or paying their workers in kind if they could. By April 1992, for example, the region of Chelyabinsk alone was running a 3 billion rouble deficit on wages and pensions payments and many workers were staying away from work in protest because they had not been paid, with the inevitable knock-on effects for production.

2   A process of chaotic, spontaneous and semi-controlled privatisation and marketisation has been going on anyway as a result of the processes unleashed by *perestroika*. In the absence of adequate government control it might almost be called anarchocapitalism.

(a)   A small but growing private sector has developed in the form of co-operatives running everything from restaurants to private police forces, joint enterprises (combining domestic and foreign capital and know-how); a primitive commercial banking system and primitive stock-exchanges which have sprung up in all the major cities.

(b)   On the basis of the very limited legislation already in place, local authorities, for example, have been able to develop local schemes for the privatisation of housing, small-scale shops and industry, and the creation of private farms. However, the reverse has also been true – local authorities have been able to hinder the legal processes of privatisation. Or to exploit these processes to their own advantage: unfortunately, even the new 'democrats in power' like the ex-mayor of Moscow Gavriil Popov have not been averse to engaging in illegal property deals to make money.

(c)   There has been an explosion in black market dealings and the exploitation of 'old boy networks' by the old *nomenklatura*. In particular, members of the old Communist Party and managerial elites have been able to exploit the absence of law and their remaining 'positional power' as industrial managers to hive-off the profitable parts of their state enterprises into private companies of which they are also the directors. The local authorities which have to register these companies have generally been open to bribery and have turned a blind eye. This '*nomenklatura* privatisation' has caused some enormous scandals (see Steele).

(d) Poverty and lack of resources have also prompted extreme measures. A primary source of income for individuals has been street trading in personal and black-market goods. A primary source of income for state institutions deprived of resources has been the piecemeal, and illegal, selling off of their assets to the highest bidder. For example, the armed forces have been selling weapons, tanks, even ships, to anyone that will buy them. State archives have been selling off access rights to their documents mostly to American universities and companies. Even the KGB (now called the Ministry of Security) has jumped on this particular bandwagon by selling off secret documents for hard currency.

3   One result of these cumulative processes has been the gradual but accelerating economic disintegration of the Russian federation. For example, by July 1992 according to a report in *Moscow News* by a Russian business analyst (see Neshchadin):

(a) Several republics and regions of Russia including the region of Chelyabinsk and the enormous and resource-rich republic of Yakutia (now Sakha) and the Siberian regions, as well as Tatarstan, had adopted resolutions to stop paying federal taxes. If this catches on, and given the general lack of money and resources, there is every reason to suppose that it will, then the federal budget will cease to exist and so effectively will the central government. This threatens Russian President Yeltsin with the same fate that ended Gorbachev's career as President of the USSR. He would become a President without a country and head of a bankrupt government.

(b) All of Russia's republics and regions had established their own banking systems which gives them the possibility of adopting their own credit policies. This would make central control of the Russian budget impossible.

(c) Several republics, regions and territories had begun to issue their own 'currencies'. One territory had printed its own regional banknotes (looking a little like dollars). Another region was using lottery tickets with a value of 250 roubles each. The republic of Yakutia was issuing its own cheques worth millions of roubles. And the Urals region and the Far East were talking about issuing their own currencies.

(d) Numerous republics and regions had established their own customs posts and were controlling the 'export' and 'import' of goods over their borders.

(e) Everyone was trying to privatise the army property on their territory.

In fact, by July 1992 the logic of decentralisation had gone so far that one of the districts of Moscow had declared itself sovereign in order to demand overflight payments from the Aeroflot Airline (see Olshansky).

As the analyst in *Moscow News* commented, neither 'totalitarian terror' nor Yeltsin's economic reforms can any longer stop these processes of disintegration. Totalitarian dictatorship either from the right or the left would simply hasten them, in the same way that the abortive August coup of 1991 hastened the disintegration of the USSR. And economic reform will not be able to produce results quickly enough. In his view, therefore there is only one possible alternative: 'It is impossible to reform Russia as one entity. The only possibility is a combination of reforms in most autonomies and regions forming the Russian Federation.' In other words, combinations of centrally directed and individually tailored reforms designed to suit local needs. The result would probably be an economic confederation rather than a federation (which is what republics like Tatarstan have wanted anyway). However, whether the Russian government can acknowledge this or could handle the Russian nationalist backlash that might result remains to be seen. Whatever happens, the Russian federation, like the Soviet federation before it, is transforming itself anyway as a practical result of spontaneous processes over which no one has much control. This time round however, Yeltsin, unlike Gorbachev, has had *no* excuse for not foreseeing the problem.

4   The other consequences of this anarchic process of change have been a massive growth in inequality, corruption and economic banditry of all sorts that the central government has been powerless to regulate or control and that has been causing a great deal of cynicism, disillusion and suffering amongst ordinary people. And a continuation of the 'endemic economic civil war' (see Chapter 10) that began under *perestroika* in which the only intelligible rules are 'I'm alright Jack' and 'devil take the hindmost'.

No one can say when, if or how this situation will be brought under control let alone transformed into a 'civilised market'.

Dilemmas

The new states of the former USSR, large and small, are confronted with some brutal dilemmas.

Their economies are technically bankrupt. They are saddled with enormous internal and external debts and their economies are uncompetitive. They cannot afford the huge sums required for the maintenance of extensive social welfare as well as for investment in new industry, new infrastructure, and so on. At the same time, they cannot afford not to maintain some sort of social safety-net if they want to avoid massive social unrest.

All of them also have appalling environmental problems to cope with that will require enormous resources and government intervention to be put right (assuming they can be). In one region of Kazakhstan, for example, 40 per cent of babies are born deformed because of polluted water supplies (see Critchlow).

The new governments have had to do something to bring the money supply under control; to reduce crippling levels of subsidy and their huge budget deficits; and to revalue their currencies (or introduce new ones). They also have to do something to improve the productivity and competitiveness of industry and agriculture. However, at the same time, they cannot afford to destroy what industry and agricultural production they do have. Especially since none of them have had enough foreign currency to import anything other than foodstuffs and essential goods since the beginning of 1992.

Above all, however, even the governments of Russia and the Baltic states will have to recognise that they cannot create the equivalent of a modern capitalist market overnight and that the model of development which is being urged on them by the United States and the West European countries is profoundly inappropriate for the circumstances in which they find themselves.

The modern capitalist economies of Europe and the USA have taken nearly two centuries to reach their current stage of development. That development was extremely brutal and enormously conflictual, particularly in the early stages, but it was also relatively gradual. The institutions of private property and the free market were already established by the time the first real attempts were made to regulate them (beginning in the early nineteenth century); and fully established by the time meaningful democratic reforms began to take place (from about the 1870s on). And the idea that extensive social provision had to be made for the general population, in the form of, for example, universal education and health provision, and the popular expectations that this gave rise to, did not fully take root until after the Second World War. This meant that the market was already generating considerable wealth before serious redistributive claims were made on it by government and society in the nineteenth and twentieth centuries.

Modern market capitalism also benefited, from the early nineteenth century, from the development of the rule of law and government regulation, and from the emergence of business ethics. These civilised and regularised the conflict between the different forms of capital (industrial, financial, manufacturing); and the relationships between companies and the various sections of capital. They went some way to preventing the most powerful companies, banks, etc., from taking unfair advantage of their market position, through the introduction of laws against unfair competition and monopoly (e.g. anti-trust laws). And they created a climate of certainty and predictability that enabled companies to engage, relatively safely, in activities like long-term investment planning. The state was always there as a last resort in times of crisis and recession to support the currency, to manipulate demand through taxes and other fiscal measures, to bail banks and companies out of bankruptcy and so on. In addition, the emergence of organised labour movements, particularly in the earlier stages of capitalist development, and the subsequent recognition that the concession of certain social reforms by the state would help to reduce social conflict, played a crucial part in defusing the conflict between capital and labour.

Finally, the modern market economies of Europe and the USA have had the advantage of imperial state traditions that have given them access to overseas markets and, most importantly, to foreign raw materials and labour at prices that the metropolitan capitalist countries have been able to dictate because of their power in international markets. Their ruthless exploitation of these over-seas markets has contributed to the Western standard of living enormously.

The global market is dominated by the immensely powerful economies of the USA, Japan, Germany and looks likely to remain so for the foreseeable future. These countries largely determine the rules of the international market through institutions like the IMF and the World Bank. They are already engaged in fierce competition with each other for expanding market shares in a shrinking (and increasingly impoverished) world market. Newcomers to the international markets therefore have to play by their rules or not at all as most of the countries of the Third World have discovered.

The new states of the former Soviet Union are therefore at a profound disadvantage. They cannot possibly collapse two centuries of development into a matter of years. And most of them will not be able to restructure their economies as the IMF and the capitalist countries would wish them to without considerable quantities of outside assistance. However, if they accept Western aid they will have to play by Western rules. They will almost certainly, therefore, end up joining the ranks of the Third World countries, permanently in debt to Western banks, and reduced to supplying the capitalist world with cheap labour and cheap raw materials.

Russia, at least, will be able to export its energy and raw materials, of which it has vast reserves. However, even this outcome assumes that the regions and republics of Russia where these reserves are sited would allow themselves to be exploited. By the beginning of 1992 there were already separatist movements in Siberia, the Urals, the Republic of Yakutia, opposing precisely this sort of exploitation. In March 1992, for example, the elected deputies of Siberia complained, in language reminiscent of Yeltsin's own in 1990, that Moscow was exploiting the region like a 'colony'.

However, the smaller, less well-endowed states of the CIS are in an extremely weak position. The central Asian republics, in particular, with their poor, largely agricultural economies and their small and lop-sided industrial base are in a very poor position to command Western aid, and in no position at all to bargain about its terms.

In any case, two hundred years of capitalist experience, and seventy years of Soviet experience, have demonstrated clearly for anyone who wants to see it that the old economic goal of endlessly expanding economic growth is both enormously costly in human and environmental terms and completely unsustainable in the long term. The new countries of the old Soviet Union cannot remain on this bandwagon and hope to increase the standard of living of their peoples. All the states of the former USSR would therefore be much better-off trying to find their own roads to development rather than attempting to adopt yet another completely unattainable 'model'.

Politics and power

It has been enormously difficult to preserve the fragile shoots of democracy in this chaotic, fragmented and unstable environment. It has also been enormously difficult for any government to govern.

Political turmoil in Azerbaijan (in early 1992) and Georgia (in late 1991) resulted in the overthrow of weak parliaments and dictatorial presidents elected in 1990 and 1991 and in the latter case precipitated the beginnings of a civil war that had still not fully been contained by August 1992. Popular dissatisfaction in Tadjikistan in early 1992 forced new presidential elections and also forced a political establishment still dominated by communist party officials to come to terms with the opposition parties, at the cost of an estimated seventy deaths. Popular dissatisfaction with a parliament and a government executive that were still dominated by the old *nomenklatura* was also causing political turmoil in Belarus (formerly Byelorussia). And conflict over economic policy and the management of the economic crisis had forced several governments to resign in all three Baltic states.

All the new states have been experiencing the old problem of 'dual power – dual powerlessness' in one form or another. There have been, at times, intense conflicts over power and policy between the legislatures, most of which were elected in 1990, and presidential executives, mostly elected in 1991. There have also been intense conflicts over power and policy between the institutions of central government and local authorities, many of them still dominated by old communist party officials who moved over into executive positions within the soviets during 1990 and 1991.

New political parties have emerged and there has frequently been a realignment of old political forces as different groups have struggled for power. At the same time there have been renewed restrictions on the media and limitations on political freedoms almost everywhere in one form or another.

The political situation in most of the new countries of the former USSR therefore remained highly unstable in 1992.

The problem of executive power

Unsurprisingly, there has been a pressing need to shore up and strengthen the power of the executive in order to prevent further chaos and to implement necessary reforms in almost all the new states. However, the strengthening of executive power where it has occurred has not necessarily resulted in strong or effective government. A great deal has depended on the political abilities of leading politicians and on the prevailing situation in which they have had to operate.

Both Russia and Ukraine, to take contrasting examples, created roughly the same model of a strong executive presidency in 1991 and 1992. Yeltsin began the process almost immediately after his popular election as Russian President in June 1991. Leonid Kravchuk similarly set things in motion upon his popular election as Ukrainian President in December 1991. In both cases, the two presidents managed to persuade their respective legislatures to grant them extraordinary temporary powers to issue decrees having the force of law, particularly with respect to the implementation of economic reform; to appoint members of the government directly without prior legislative approval and to establish a 'vertical' system of control over local government. This involved the appointment (by each president) of 'presidential viceroys' or governors to serve in the regions, districts and cities of Russia and Ukraine respectively as the direct representatives of executive power in the localities. In both cases, these presidential representatives became the heads of the local administration, charged with overseeing the implementation of legislation and presidential decrees. They were granted absolute executive power in their area and their decisions were binding on everyone. And they were accountable only to the President.

The outcome in the two countries was, however, rather different. This was partly to do with the sheer size and political complexity of Russia compared with Ukraine, which makes Russia much more difficult to govern, and has put Yeltsin in a much more difficult position. But it was also to do with the ways in which the two presidents handled their problems.

Ukraine

In Ukraine a number of factors contributed to its relative political stability after December 1991 and to Kravchuk's apparent success in consolidating effective executive power.

There has been an extraordinary nationalist consensus in Ukraine around the idea of an independent Ukrainian state. Over 90 per cent of the population voted for independence in the referendum on sovereignty on 1 December 1991, so the consensus also included a large part of the resident Russian population. This in turn created a relatively strong sense of national identity and nationhood. President Kravchuk, the former Secretary for Ideology of the Ukrainian Communist Party and therefore one of the more hard-line party *apparatchiks* from the old Soviet regime, cleverly exploited the nationalist card to his own advantage.

1   He stood for election as president on a platform of national independence on the day that the referendum took place. He was therefore voted into power on the coat-tails of popular support for national sovereignty with a larger share of the popular vote than Yeltsin received in Russia. This gave him a strong popular mandate that the Ukrainian opposition has not been able to challenge.

2   He cleverly manipulated relations within the CIS in order to derive maximum domestic propaganda advantage out of conflicts with Russia over such issues as control of the Black Sea Fleet and the Crimea. His insistence that Ukrainian national sovereignty is absolute and not subject to compromise earned him popular approval which has been enhanced by popular hostility to the belligerent comments of some of Russia's leading politicians about the illegitimacy of Ukrainian independence (see Chapter 14).

3   His uncompromising insistence on the absolute goal of creating a strong independent Ukrainian state also enabled Kravchuk:

(a)   To unite most of the country's political parties behind him and to split the opposition. Both the more conservative ex-communist deputies in the Supreme Soviet (elected in 1990) and the democratic forces represented by the umbrella movement *Rukh* were forced to change their priorities under the pressure of the popular consensus on independence. This also prevented the extreme fragmentation and/or polarisation of the political spectrum that has occurred in some other states like Russia, Belarus or Kazakhstan.

(b)   To push through his programme for the centralisation and concentration of power in a greatly strengthened executive presidency with considerable success. His emphasis on the importance of a strong executive both for the consolidation of Ukrainian statehood and for the implementation of necessary reforms, particularly in the economic sphere, made it virtually impossible for anyone either inside or outside the Ukrainian Supreme Soviet to argue against him without appearing to be disloyal to the cause of independence.

The result, in the eyes of the Ukrainian opposition, has been the evolution of a new authoritarianism and the re-emergence of old Communist Party structures in a new, nationalist form. For example, most of the 'presidential viceroys' in the regions, districts and cities of Ukraine are former local Communist Party committee secretaries. All the key positions in the Ukrainian leadership have been occupied by members of the old party *nomenklatura*. A great deal of the press is state owned because all the party-owned newspapers were nationalised after the events of August 1991. Censorship and news control have re-emerged and life has been made increasingly difficult for opposition politicians. And movement on economic reform has been very slow. 'In essence, everything is just like ... the good old days' as one Ukrainian journalist put it (see Ruban).

However, Kravchuk was careful to preserve the semblance of a democratic process. He made a show of consulting with all political parties and of building coalitions on major issues. For example, aspects of the new presidential apparatus were discussed publicly. The idea of a presidential State Council, for instance, was discussed at a round table of representatives from all of Ukraine's political parties, major trade unions and other groups that was held in February 1992 at Kravchuk's instigation. Kravchuk also agreed that he would appoint his 'presidential representatives' in the localities in consultation with local councils and political parties, although in the end this did not make much difference as to who was actually appointed. He also managed to divide the democratic opposition (*Rukh*) very successfully by appointing some of its leading members to the position of State Councillor in the new presidential State Council that was created in February 1992. This effectively divided *Rukh* between those who supported Kravchuk and those who decided to become a party of 'constructive opposition'. This apparently democratic and conciliatory move (Kravchuk did his best to persecute *Rukh* before the collapse of the CPSU in 1991), undermined the opposition considerably. Although *Rukh* was already weakened by the fact that with the achievement of independence it had lost most of its reason for existence. At the same time there has not been a complete clampdown on political activity and political opposition. In June 1992, a new political movement, New Ukraine, was formed which united pro-market politicians with business entre- preneurs and representatives from some of the other pro- democracy parties. This formally declared itself in opposition to the government and by August 1992 seemed to be gaining strength. So new political forces were emerging to replace the old.

On the other hand, it has been very difficult for political parties, old and new, to argue against Kravchuk's plea for national unity in defence of the new Ukrainian state at a time of crisis. His call at the end of January 1992 for all groups to put aside their 'petty' differences 'and see one and only one thing, a great thing – an independent Ukraine' (see Solchanyk) struck a chord with the population that enabled Kravchuk to dictate the terms of the political and economic debate.

Kravchuk will not be able to avoid political confrontation alto- gether. As of August 1992 Ukraine remained without a con- stitution and it was possible to forecast considerable conflict between the Supreme Soviet and the presidency over its pro- visions, in particular the powers of the presidency and the powers and functions of the Supreme Soviet itself. There is also likely to be growing conflict over the course of economic reform between the government (which was showing signs of preferring the old forms of centralised control) and new pro-market movements like New Ukraine. However, with production in Ukraine continuing to collapse (it dropped 25 per cent in the first six months of 1992), a rise in unemployment and crime and the evident failure of 'economic shock therapy' programmes in Russia, no one is in a very strong position to promote alternatives. As a consequence, no group has yet been able to seize the initiative from Kravchuk's hands and he has remained firmly in control. However, who knows, Kravchuk may yet turn out to be more of a democrat than he appears and he has at least succeeded in holding the country together during its first crucial year of independence.

Russian Federal Republic

In the Russian Federal Republic, by contrast, political instability was reaching extremely worrying levels by mid-1992. Almost all the factors that contributed to stability in Ukraine have been absent in Russia. This contributed to the continued weakness of executive power and to the reappearance of rather anti-democratic policies. And President Yeltsin was increasingly finding himself in a truly impossible position.

Unlike Ukraine, the Russian state has been suffering from an acute crisis of identity brought on by the collapse of the USSR and nationalist challenges to the federation. This has left people divided in their opinions and profoundly uncertain about the future.

Loss of national identity

The collapse of the USSR did not so much give Russia its independence as deprive it of its sense of self. The difficulty is that for seventy-odd years Russia was at the heart of the Soviet empire. For many centuries before that Russia was at the heart of an ever-expanding multi-national empire. Indeed, the term 'Russia' has scarcely ever applied to a uniquely Russian land. It almost always referred to the Russians plus others. (There are two words in the language: *russky* meaning ethnic Russians, and *rossiisky* which refers to the product of Russian ethnic culture and assimilated Turkic cultures and others). Many Russians cannot begin to imagine what would be left of Russia if its constituent republics and provinces decided to leave it. On the other hand, many of the non-Russian groups within the federation cannot see any reason why they should remain within it. The new freedom represented by the collapse of the USSR has given the chance for non-Russian nations, like the Tatars who have been part of the Russian empire since the sixteenth century, the opportunity at long last to strike out for national self-determination.

The result, on the one hand, has been profound divisions of opinion about what the Russian state is and what it should become. This has contributed to the fragmentation of the political spectrum. While, on the other hand, there has been a growing consensus among Russians at least that the federation must be held together somehow.

President Yeltsin

President Yeltsin has been unable to fill this political and ideological vacuum with anything around which people can unite or with which they can identify.

This is partly a function of the enormous complexity of the situation in which he has found himself. There are simply too many conflicting interests to be able to reconcile them all. Moreover, unlike Kravchuk who has been able to manipulate popular hostility to Russia as a means of reinforcing the national consensus on independence, Yeltsin has not had an 'external threat' to help him draw people together. On the contrary, he has been unable to defend Russia against Kravchuk's demands for fear of alienating Russian nationalists who still hope (forlornly) for Ukraine's return to Russia and therefore do not want it antagonised (see Chapter 14). And statements which appear to infringe on other states' sovereignty have also risked alienating Russia's own constituent republics even further. Consequently, President Yeltsin has found himself in the horrible position previously occupied by President Gorbachev: criticised from all sides but unable to defend himself or to promote a particular set of policies without alienating at least somebody.

However, it has also been the result of Yeltsin's failure to provide adequate ideological and political leadership.

1   Yeltsin promoted the idea of economic 'shock therapy' and a 'rapid dash to the market' in late 1991 before he had given adequate consideration to the nature of the new Russian state or the sort of society that he wanted people to create.

His calls for the creation of a market democracy were much too abstract and lacking in domestic relevance. The government, almost entirely dominated by economists, became obsessed with the mechanics and technicalities of macro-economic policy: controlling the money supply, prices etc. But it did not explain what social values and ideals were supposed to go with them. Arguments about the intricacies of fiscal policy or the importance of a multi-party system make no sense in the context of people's everyday lives and they do not provide anyone with common values, ideas or principles around which they can unite. On the contrary, to the extent that ordinary people have understood anything about either the market or democracy they have appeared to be threatening and divisive because:

(a) Both concepts are based on notions of individualism and pluralism that pit people against each other rather than uniting them. Democracy means that political parties fight each other for power, influence and popularity rather than co-operating to solve common problems. The market means that individuals compete with each other for the means of survival: jobs, profit, money. These principles look horribly divisive from the vantage point of the average Russian especially in the context of deep political, economic and federal crisis. They are also profoundly foreign to most people's cultural experience.

(b) Achieving them seems to involve massive unemployment, inequality and suffering at least for the foreseeable future with no certainty of ultimate success.

Even if people are willing to accept that economic reform is necessary and likely to hurt before things will get better, these concepts have not provided them with a new sense of identity or national belonging. On the contrary, according to the Russian social psychologist Dmitry Olshansky, Russians in particular have been left with a profound sense of loss, confusion and a sense of personal disintegration in the face of a completely uncertain future and in the face of new forms of social behaviour, the piracy and banditry of the new market, that were utterly anathemised less than ten years ago. Suicide amongst the young has jumped and in Olshansky's words 'All strata of society feel they have been deceived . . . The fight for democratic values turned out to be the old, banal struggle for survival' and people have become profoundly tired of the constant struggle just to stay alive (see Olshansky). This situation of complete social alienation provides fertile ground for the successful development of nationalist groups who can come up with alternatives based on the importance of protecting and promoting ethnic community interests. By August 1992 many people on the liberal democratic wing of the political spectrum feared that it was providing fertile ground for the emergence of fascism.

As a result the gulf between the government and the people has been growing rather than diminishing.

2   Unlike Kravchuk, Yeltsin failed, from the very beginning, even to make a show of consulting adequately either with parliament or other political parties. He failed to keep people informed about his plans and activities. He made no attempt, at least to begin with, to build political coalitions either in parliament or outside it. He even failed to co-ordinate the internal activities of the presidential apparatus adequately; to give sufficient support to the radical government that he had appointed; or to co-ordinate the activities of the government with those of the presidential apparatus or, for that matter parliament itself. The presidential apparatus, or the Office of the President as it is formally known, was built largely in secrecy from July 1991 onwards and has operated with a great deal of secrecy ever since. It has not inspired a great deal of popular confidence because it has been largely staffed by ex-communist party officials with whom Yeltsin worked closely in his days as party secretary in his home town of Sverdlovsk. And attempts to make it more accountable to parliament and the people have been largely ignored or squashed. For example, proposals in 1991 that the 'presidential representatives' in the localities should be elected were deferred (at least until 1992) on the grounds that the wrong people might get the job. Moreover, the first government that Yeltsin appointed consisted largely of young academic economists who lacked any sort of popular following either in parliament or in the country. In fact, for a politician who made his political comeback on the basis of a fine intuitive sense for popular wishes and a considerable ability to

out-manoeuvre government, Yeltsin showed a remarkable lack of political acumen once he was in power.

Yeltsin's failure to engage in the everyday practice of politics had a number of consequences.

It left him politically isolated. He has had no organised support within parliament or outside it. This made it much more difficult for his government to get its radical policies accepted. It has also made it even more difficult to pull the country together.

It generated an enormous amount of avoidable animosity towards the institution of the presidency within both the Supreme Soviet and the Congress of People's Deputies. Having granted Yeltsin extraordinary powers in October 1991, parliamentary deputies found themselves ignored and then rushed into making important legislative decisions without consultation and frequently with no more than an hour or so to look at large and important documents before they had to vote on them. Presidential relations with a Congress and a Supreme Soviet that were elected in 1990 and therefore had a heavy representation of (ex-)communist deputies were always bound to be difficult. This failure to consult, or even to make a show of consultation, made them worse.

It created competing centres of power. There were conflicts within the presidential apparatus, and between it and the government, as different groups of advisers competed for Yeltsin's ear. There were growing conflicts between the Supreme Soviet and the presidency for control over policy and control over the government as deputies grew more concerned about the direction of economic reform and their own loss of influence. By early 1992 this had turned into a real struggle for power:

(a) over the crucial question of whether Russia should become a parliamentary or a presidential republic, with the Chairman of the Supreme Soviet, Ruslan Khasbulatov, advocating the first, and President Yeltsin, naturally, advocating the second. As of August 1992 this conflict had still not been resolved with the result that Russia remained without a new constitution.

(b) over the course of government reform, the makeup of the

government itself and the powers of the president. At the
Sixth session of the Congress of People's Deputies in April
1992, deputies tried to take back all the temporary emergency
powers that had been granted to Yeltsin in October 1991;
almost forced the government to resign; and insisted on
amendments to the economic reform plans.

The confrontation between President and parliament subsided
slightly after this, largely because Yeltsin agreed to compromise
and finally acknowledged that there was a real need to consult
more widely and to engage in coalition politics which is what he
began to do from June 1991. However, the battle did not end
there. The Congress succeeded in re-affirming the temporary
nature of Yeltsin's presidential powers (they are supposed to end
in December 1992). Yeltsin retaliated by threatening to abolish
the Congress (by national referendum) and to hold new elections
for the Supreme Soviet. As of August 1992 the outcome of this
confrontation was still uncertain.

These endless conflicts between the legislature and the
executive, and between institutions within the executive itself,
created havoc with the legislative and policy-making processes at a
time of real crisis and weakened the power of the executive
enormously. People simply ignored Yeltsin's decrees as they had
ignored Gorbachev's, and many of the 'presidential representatives' in the localities, deprived of unambiguous guidance
and therefore unsure about what sort of 'order' they were supposed to be establishing, inevitably started to play their own
political and economic games. As a consequence, many local
authorities simply continued to operate as 'laws unto themselves'
and in large parts of the country Moscow remained as much of a
'distant rumour' as it had always been.

Attempts to control
In the absence of constitutional order and with the threat of
conflict and confusion growing in the country, there has been a
tendency to try to concentrate power even more and to revert to
repressive measures.

Since July 1992 Yeltsin has been concentrating executive

decision-making power in a new presidential Security Council, which consists of eight people. By the end of July and the beginning of August it was making so many decisions that it was beginning to look like an alternative government structure. Some Russian commentators interpreted this as another 'quiet coup' brought about by Yeltsin to enable him to circumvent the inefficient coalition government that was being foisted on him. It is extremely reminiscent of the old CPSU Politburo in which a tiny group of self-appointed officials made decisions for the whole country in almost complete secrecy. The fact that it has been charged with 'developing the annual presidential report, as the main programmatic document' which all executive bodies from the top to the bottom of the system will have to fulfil is also highly reminiscent of the programmatic statements that used to be issued by the CPSU General Secretary and which were mandatory for the whole party and the country at large. As one analyst remarked 'It is a return to the old model which is familiar to [Yeltsin] from his years in the CPSU Politburo' (see Kiselyov). However, this is unlikely to help Yeltsin restore the power of the executive. Nor is it likely to do anything to change the situation in the country. The difficulty, as Gorbachev before him discovered and many a party leader before *him*, lies not so much in making the decisions, although in the prevailing circumstances that is difficult enough, it lies in getting them implemented.

More generally, since about January 1992 subtle and not so subtle attempts have been made both by parliament and the government to muzzle the press, in particular the liberal press which switched from supporting Yeltsin to becoming increasingly critical of his performance and that of other 'democrats in power' both within the Supreme Soviet and outside it. The media has been under enormous financial pressure as old state subsidies disappeared and the cost of paper, and so on, became prohibitively expensive. Political pressure has made things even more difficult. The Ministry of Security (the old KGB by another name) has been growing in size and power and seems to have reverted to some of its old habits. For example, it has evidently been keeping parliamentary deputies under surveillance.

The general impression that things were beginning to revert to their old ways was also enhanced by the fact that the new 'democrats in power' took over some of the old Soviet symbols by moving themselves into former party buildings. For example, Anatoly Sobchak, the radical mayor of St Petersburg, moved the seat of the city council from its old building into the Smolny, the old Leningrad party building (and Lenin's original seat of revolutionary operations). The Russian government moved itself from the White House to the old CPSU Central Committee building in Moscow.

However, it would be a mistake to think that the clock can be turned back. Whatever the politicians may do, Russian society has changed too much and the federation has disintegrated too far for the old ways to work any longer. However, it is going to be a long time before anyone finds out what the new ways will be.

Conclusion

It is difficult to sit in judgement on politicians who have to deal with the sort of intractable problems that currently confront leaders like Yeltsin, Kravchuk or Nazarbaev. The majority of the new state leaders have only been in office for, at most, two years and they are having to deal with a legacy of multiple crisis that is necessitating extraordinarily hard decisions. Moreover, they are having to do so in the context of an international environment that is gloomy and uncertain: the global economy has been plunged into recession and international politics has been shaken to its roots by the disintegration of the Soviet superpower. No one knows what to make of the brave new world that currently confronts us all, so the leaders of these new countries are not alone.

Equally it is difficult not to sit in judgement. Much of what happens in the near future will depend on the decisions that are made now, and the successful management of crisis crucially depends on intelligent and far-sighted leadership.

President Yeltsin has probably been in the most difficult position and he had not dealt with it particularly well by August 1992.

1   He found it enormously difficult to make the transition from opposition to being in the position of ultimate power. The

destructive tactics that he used so successfully against President Gorbachev and the Soviet government were hardly appropriate when it came to governing the new Russian state or managing relations within the new Commonwealth of Independent States. Moreover, the popular coalition that had united behind him in opposition to Gorbachev and the old Soviet 'centre' could no longer be relied on once Gorbachev was gone. Yeltsin's negative tactics for building political coalitions – i.e. by uniting everyone who was *opposed* to Gorbachev, to the party, to the bureaucracy, to the 'administrative command system' – had to be replaced by a positive approach, once the central focus of everyone's hostility had disappeared. However, building positive coalitions is much more difficult because they require agreement and consensus among different interests about the goals that are to be achieved and the means that are to be used to reach them. As we have already seen, Yeltsin has not proved up to this task, and the sheer complexity of Russia may well defeat him, in just the same way that the sheer complexity of the USSR defeated Gorbachev.

2   Yeltsin tried to learn from Gorbachev's tactical mistakes. He moved quickly and decisively to produce, and get approval for, a new federal treaty for Russia. He also moved decisively, and reasonably quickly, to institute an economic reform programme.

However, he has repeated Gorbachev's strategic mistakes. Like Gorbachev before him, Yeltsin has consistently failed to appreciate that *the* fundamental problem confronting Russia on which all else hangs (even the economy), is the whole question of federal relations. Yeltsin, rather like Gorbachev, seems to have assumed that agreement on a federal treaty would, in and of itself, solve the federation's problems when, in fact, the existence or otherwise of a federal treaty is largely irrelevant if it does not deal with the *real* issues that are undermining federal relations, namely, economic and political chaos. Yeltsin will not find any solution to Russia's economic and political problems unless he puts federal issues right at the top of the agenda.

This means, first of all, as Andrei Neshchadin suggested in *Moscow News*, addressing the federal aspect of economic relations first and foremost rather than trying to reform Russia as a whole. Economic disintegration had already begun to turn Russia into a patchwork of 'mini-statelets' by August 1992. Yeltsin can no longer afford to continue alternately ignoring or repressing this process because it will continue whatever he does, for all the reasons Neshchadin cites. If Yeltsin does not want the Russian federation to disintegrate completely in a welter of acrimony and chaos, as the USSR did, then he must take the bull by the horns and do what Gorbachev refused to do: he must give the constituent republics of the Russian federation the economic freedom to reform themselves in whatever way is most appropriate for their circumstances while at the same time negotiating a new economic federation. If some republics decide to leave the federation anyway, then, as one Russian liberal remarked, 'so be it'.

It also means, secondly, that the federal aspects of political relations have to be addressed before anything else can be dealt with. Again Neshchadin's argument applies. Uniform political reform cannot be achieved in a country with so many divergent interests, nor imposed on restless peoples who are both disillusioned with the political process and, simultaneously, profoundly agitated by questions of national identity and self-determination. In this respect the conflict that has been raging between the Russian Supreme Soviet and the presidency about whether Russia should be a parliamentary or a presidential republic has been somewhat beside the point. The much more important question, which has yet to be adequately confronted, concerns what the political nature of the federation itself should be, what form the federal government should take and how political and economic relations should be combined. The peoples of Russia will take their freedom anyway whatever happens. Yeltsin should therefore learn from Gorbachev's strategic mistake and, instead of allowing political relations within the federation to fragment as a practical result of economic disintegration, pre-empt the process by beginning serious negotiations not just on a new federal treaty but on a new federation.

Thirdly, it means that Yeltsin has to address the question of Russian nationalism. Up until August 1992, he had remained rather aloof from the issue. It would be a strategic error for him to remain so. The Russian people need some sense of identity and

Yeltsin still had enough popular support to provide positive leadership on this issue. Nationalism need not be xenophobic and nasty if it is carefully managed and sensitively treated. Yeltsin cannot possibly provide the whole of Russia with a unifying ideology, but he could provide the Russian people with the sort of positive ideological leadership that might make the process of change less psychologically painful and easier to manage. If he does not, then Russian nationalism will become an increasingly dangerous political weapon that ambitious politicians, like Vice President Rutskoi, will be able to manipulate to their own advantage.

Finally, it means that President Yeltsin should stop wasting his limited time on international institutions like the IMF and the G7 Group of industrial nations, which clearly have no intention of giving him any substantial help, and devote it instead to a fundamental re-think about what the Russian federation should become and how it should get there, that is if he is really serious about wanting a democratic future for his country.

President Yeltsin has been more like Gorbachev than he knows, unsurprisingly, given their common communist party background. He has attempted to impose solutions from the top down and to repress the revolution from below that has continued to gather momentum. If he continues in this way he will be no more successful than Gorbachev was and we may all come to regret it.

Further Reading

At the time of writing there are no books available on developments in the former Soviet Union since December 1991. The best English-language source of up-to-date information and analysis is the weekly *RFE/RL Research Report* which is produced by Radio Free Europe, Radio Liberty, Inc. This is obtainable from RFE/RL Research Institute, Publications Department, Oettingenstrasse 67, W-8000 Munich 22, Germany.

The alternative is the British press and journals like *The Economist, New Statesman and Society, New Scientist*, which regularly carry articles on the former Soviet Union.

Critchlow, James, 'Kazakhstan and Nazarbaev: political prospects', *RFE/RL Research Report*, Vol. 1, No. 3, 17 January 1992, p. 32

Glezer, Oleg, 'No ethnic problems for Daghestan?', *Moscow News*, No. 2, 12–19 January 1992, p. 8

Gubarev, Vladimir, 'Deterrence factor à la Daghestan', *Moscow News*, No. 28, 12–19 July 1992, p. 4

Kiselyov, Stepan, 'Boris Yeltsin's quiet coup', *Moscow News*, No. 29, 19–26 July 1992, p. 4

Leontyev, Mikhail, 'The Russian restoration: the Pavlovites come back,' *Moscow News*, No. 33, 16–23 August 1992, p. 10

Neschadin, Andrei, 'Russian regions oppose the government on economic reforms', *Moscow News*, No. 26, 28 June–5 July 1992, p. 9

Olshansky, Dmitry, 'Cement: what is happening to us?', *Moscow News*, No. 26, 28 June–5 July, 1992

Robinson, Anthony, 'Most Muscovites set to fall below the poverty line', *Financial Times*, 3 January 1992

Ruban, Vladimir, 'Ukraine relapses into authoritarianism', *Moscow News*, No. 31, 2–9 August 1992, p. 5

Solchanyk, Roman, 'Ukraine: political reform and political change', *RFE/RL Research Report*, Vol. 1, No. 21, 22 May 1992, p.2.

Steele, Jonathan, 'The Lazarus act of the nomenklatura', *Guardian*, 30 May 1992, p. 19

14

The creation of the Commonwealth

The Commonwealth of Independent States was created out of necessity not out of choice. It is therefore a weak and rather paradoxical entity.

As we have seen, the CIS was created on 8 December 1991 by the leaders of the three Slav republics, Russia, Byelorussia (now Belarus) and Ukraine. It was subsequently enlarged on 21 December 1991 to include Kazakhstan, Armenia, Azerbaijan, Moldova (formerly Moldavia), and the four Central Asian republics of Uzbekistan, Tadjikistan, Turkmenistan and Kyrgyzstan as founder members. The only old Union-republic that did not join was Georgia (remember, the three Baltic republics had by now left the union altogether and become internationally recognised sovereign states).

At their meeting on 21 December the eleven member states of the new CIS agreed to establish a number of very limited co-ordinating structures:

1 A Council of Heads of State (which all the Presidents are supposed to attend). This is the supreme decision-making body in the CIS.
2 A Council of Heads of Government (which all the Prime Ministers are supposed to attend).
3 A number of ministerial committees which are supposed to co-ordinate activities in such areas as foreign policy, defence, the economy, transportation, social security.

They also agreed that Russia should occupy the Soviet Union's seat on the UN Security Council (thus effectively acknowledging Russia's pre-eminence as the 'successor state' to the USSR), and appointed Marshal Evgeni Shaposhnikov as commander of the armed forces at least until decisions had been taken on how the armed forces should be reorganised. In addition, the four nuclear states (Russia, Ukraine, Kazakhstan, Belarus) signed an agreement on joint measures for the management of nuclear weapons.

Since December 1991 the affairs of the CIS have been 'co-ordinated', although this is too strong a word, by informal working meetings of the heads of state or the heads of government; by periodic meetings of the Councils of Heads of State and/or of Heads of Government, sometimes separately, sometimes jointly; and by meetings of the ministerial committees (e.g. the committee of foreign ministers which attempts to co-ordinate foreign policy), often called on a very *ad hoc* basis. These meetings have been used mostly to thrash out contentious and difficult issues directly between the various state officials immediately concerned.

Meetings of the Councils have usually given rise to agreements and protocols for co-ordinating policy and action in different areas. For example, the combined meeting of the Councils of Heads of State and Heads of Government that took place in Minsk on 30 December (the first such 'summit' of all eleven member states) produced fifteen agreements, nine of which were signed by the heads of state, and six by the heads of government. These included agreements on transportation, aviation, tariffs, environmental issues, the exploration of outer space, the distribution between the member states of former Soviet property abroad, and the distribution in 1992 of food bought with foreign credits (see Sheehy, 'Commonwealth of Independent States . . .', p.3).

Weaknesses of the CIS

In practice, however, these agreements have scarcely been worth the paper they are written on, because, thus far, the CIS has been an organisation in name only. It has none of the attributes of a 'country' and, legally speaking, it has no organisational structures either.

It is not a geographic or a political state. It has no status in international law. Although each of its individual members have now received international recognition as states, the CIS itself has no such recognition. It has no central government. Consequently, it cannot act as the common representative of all the interests of its member states, either domestically or internationally. There is no CIS charter or constitution which means that the councils and committees which have been set up have no status in law and are purely provisional. There is no such thing as a commonwealth citizenship. Nor does the CIS have a central budget, so its councils and committees have no funds at their disposal. All these things are entirely the prerogative of its member states, each of which has its own constitution, its own government, its own citizenship laws, and its own budget and tax-raising powers and are gradually acquiring their own currencies.

The most that one can say positively about the CIS is that it is a very loose association of independent states that have agreed to co-operate on matters of common interest. Its continued existence therefore depends entirely on the maintenance of some consensus between these states that the CIS is necessary.

The absence of any form of central government has had serious consequences.

1   Policy making for the CIS as a whole is exercised directly by the appropriate state representatives at meetings of the Councils of Heads of State and Heads of Government. Policy making is based on the principle of 'one state one vote' and decisions are taken on the basis of consensus. This effectively gives each member state a veto on decisions. In addition, any member state can declare that it has no interest in a given issue and opt out of the discussion. For example, Ukraine, Azerbaijan and Moldova have all opted out of any declaration or agreement on conventional military forces because they want to maintain their own conventional armed forces.

This has made it extremely difficult for the member states to reach unanimous and meaningful agreement on anything, even fairly trivial issues. And it has made it nigh-on impossible to achieve unanimous agreement on fundamental issues where the national interest of each member state comes into conflict with the national interest of the others, such as the ownership and distribution of former Soviet property (particularly military property and weapons); the reorganisation of the armed forces; economic co-operation and economic reform.

2   The agreements that have been achieved only have legal force to the extent that they are signed by the individual heads of state or government and then ratified by each state's parliament. However, given the political and economic instability in most of the member states, there is no guarantee, even where heads of state or government have agreed on a course of action, that their national parliaments, or even their government colleagues, will support them. Nor is there any guarantee that consenting heads of state or government might not subsequently change their minds about implementing an agreement they have signed if domestic interests put pressure on them to go back on their word.

3   Even where agreement is achieved the CIS as a whole has no means of monitoring, or of enforcing, their implementation in the individual member states. Its agreements only have the status of 'recommendations' because the CIS has no legal authority, and because its member states are highly sensitive to anything that might infringe on their sovereignty.

4   The commonwealth as a whole does not have any means of arbitrating disagreements and differences of interest between the member states. There is no neutral body with independent authority and power of its own over and above the powers and authority of the member states. Consequently, there is no way of resolving conflicts easily or quickly because everyone is seen to be partisan by everyone else. In particular, this has made it extremely difficult for the commonwealth to do anything about the violent ethnic conflicts that have been raging in places like Nagorno-Karabakh and Moldova. Although strenuous efforts have been made to try to find negotiated solutions to all the conflicts that have been raging on the territory of the former Soviet Union in

one or two cases with some success (e.g. the conflict in Georgia over the status of the autonomous republic of South Ossetia)

5 Finally, and unsurprisingly, many of the agreements are rather vague and more like statements of intent than actual policies because vague agreements make it much easier to achieve a consensus between states who tend to be rather suspicious of each other. And, in addition, each state is very jealous of its sovereignty. Consequently, agreements between them frequently establish general principles but leave the actual details of implementation to the individual states. This means that they can usually be interpreted in a variety of (often incompatible) ways.

The inevitable outcome has been that the negotiating process between the member states has been fraught with difficulty. Very few policy areas have thus far seen successful co-operation, and, although quite a lot of agreements have been signed on less important issues (like the exploration of outer space which is economically beyond everybody's reach), the fundamental problems, like economic co-operation and economic reform, military reform, the ownership of former Soviet property, and what to do about violent ethnic conflicts or the threat of them, have remained unresolved and continue to cause very serious, sometimes even dangerous, disagreement.

The only reasonably successful co-operation that has been achieved is in those areas where individual states have signed bilateral agreements with each other (bypassing the CIS completely). For example, in January 1992 Kazakhstan (on the 16th) followed by Belarus (on the 27th) signed bilateral agreements with Russia in which the signatories agreed to preserve a common economic space and to retain the rouble as the sole currency on their territories in order to facilitate economic co-operation and trade.

Why is the CIS so weak?

Opposition to a 'centre'
The months of centre-republican wrangling and conflict that

preceded the creation of the CIS ensured that each of the former Soviet republics would be extremely jealous of its new-found autonomy and extremely suspicious of any attempts to resurrect a central government that might take some of this autonomy away.

Many republican politicians were convinced that as long as anything remotely resembling the old Soviet 'centre' continued to exist it would provide a basis for further conservative or reactionary coups and therefore pose a threat to them. In fact, rumours of a new coup (this time against Yeltsin) swept Moscow in early December 1991, in the spring of 1992 and again in mid-summer 1992.

By utterly discrediting the old central authorities, the failed August coup finally gave the republics the opportunity they had been waiting for to break away from the old Soviet Union and to destroy the old 'centre', and they took it. By October 1991, all the republics, with the exception of Russia and Kazakhstan (which waited until 16 December), had declared themselves completely independent, or had reaffirmed earlier declarations of independence. Not unnaturally, hardly any of them were interested in proposals to reimpose some sort of central control, however limited.

What sort of Union?

Nevertheless there were seven republics still actively interested in retaining some sort of union after the August coup:

1 Russia was worried about what would happen to the 26 million ethnic Russians resident in other republics, and about what would happen to the structure of its own federation, if the Union collapsed completely.
2 The four Central Asian republics were keen to retain some sort of central co-ordination because they wanted to ensure the continued flow of economic subsidies to their backward economies. (They also wanted some protection from Russian dominance, see below.)
3 Belarus and Kazakhstan were keen to maintain some form of inter-republican economic and political co-operation.

However, when the Union treaty negotiations resumed after August it quickly became clear that even these republics would not accept a Union that subordinated their interests to those of a 'centre'. Gorbachev's proposals for a 'confederative state' that would have a strong (popularly elected) Union presidency and a central government, and that would also have international status as 'a state' in its own right, did not find favour with anyone. Russia wanted, at most, a loose confederation of sovereign states that would have no Union presidency and only the most limited central co-ordinating institutions. Uzbekistan accepted the general idea of a central government but insisted that each of the states within the Union should have the right to become members of the international community and to be the subjects of international law: i.e., that each state within the Union should have all the domestic and international trappings of independence.

USSR President Gorbachev was unwilling to concede these points because as far as he was concerned any union that did not have a strong centre to which the member states were, at least, partially subordinated was a recipe for complete disaster.

As a result of these disagreements the negotiations on the new Union Treaty failed to produce a treaty that anyone would sign.

Ukrainian opposition

Another crucial stumbling block to the emergence of stronger inter-republican ties has been the attitude of the Ukrainian government under the leadership of Leonid Kravchuk.

After the coup, Ukraine wanted nothing less than complete independence. The Ukrainian Supreme Soviet declared the republic independent on 24 August 1991, and this declaration received the overwhelming support of the Ukrainian population in a referendum on 1 December (90.3 per cent voted in favour). There was also a presidential election on 1 December that Kravchuk won (with 61.5 per cent of the vote) on a nationalist independence platform. The Ukrainian government has therefore been totally unwilling to contemplate any arrangement that includes a central government. For example, at a press conference on 8 November 1991, Kravchuk declared, 'there should be no centre'. 'We will not ratify any kind of agreement that is propped up by central bodies – to any extent, however slight'. The most that Kravchuk was willing to concede was that the Ukraine would co-operate with other republics over economic and military–strategic matters, and might be willing to join a very loose 'commonwealth' (his word) of independent states.

Ukraine's position is significant because both USSR President Gorbachev and Russian President Yeltsin consistently argued that no sort of Union or association would be possible unless Ukraine, the second-largest republic in the old Union, agreed to be a member of it. Both Gorbachev and Yeltsin could contemplate the loss of peripheral non-Russian republics like the Baltic states or Georgia. But for Russians the Ukraine is at the heart of the continent and at the heart of Russia's historic identity as a state. As Russian nationalists have been fond of pointing out, the city of Kiev (capital of Ukraine) was the original foundation of the old Russian empire. Russian politicians have therefore been extremely reluctant to accept the reality of Ukrainian independence because they consider the Ukraine to be an intrinsic part of Russia. This has caused a great deal of friction between the two states. It was also one of the fundamental reasons underlying the creation of the CIS.

It was Ukraine's refusal to participate in the Union treaty negotiations that helped to precipitate their collapse and it was the Ukrainian referendum on independence that triggered the idea of the Commonwealth of Independent States. In effect, the CIS was a hasty improvisation, cobbled together in an attempt to keep Ukraine in some form of association with Russia (and anybody else who wanted to join).

These factors go a long way to explaining the organisational weaknesses of the CIS:

1   It was a rapid and improvised response to Ukraine's vote for independence on 1 December. Consequently, very little planning went into its creation.
2   The Ukrainian government has since been in a position to call the tune. It has consistently refused to contemplate any arrangements that threaten the re-creation of a centre or the emergence of the CIS as some form of state or 'super-state',

even though other member states like Russia, Belarus and Kazakhstan would like to see the development of stronger central institutions. For example, proposals for a CIS charter to be adopted at the Minsk 'summit' on 30 December were rejected by Ukraine and therefore had to be dropped. Russian proposals in January 1992 for the creation of a parliamentary assembly of all the CIS member states were also rejected by Ukraine (and Belarus) and were therefore abandoned.

It is therefore probably fair to say that the future of the CIS hinges heavily on whether Ukraine decides to remain a member of it or not. From this perspective the prospects do not look bright both because President Kravchuk has made it perfectly plain that he considers the CIS to be a transitional arrangement on the road to full economic and military independence. It is a means for achieving a 'civilised divorce' from the other states as one Ukrainian commentator put it. And because Ukraine's decision to stay or leave in turn depends crucially on the development of its relations with Russia and thus far these relations have not been good.

Russia

There was, and continues to be, deep suspicion of Russian intentions and considerable antagonism towards Russia. In the aftermath of the August coup all the non-Russian republics feared that any new central government would be dominated by Russians and by Russian interests. And many of them, particularly Ukraine, have continued to fear that the CIS would become too dominated by Russia if it were to be even slightly more centralised than it is. Russian dominance, or the threat of it, has encouraged all the member states of the CIS to assert and defend their sovereign independence very fiercely.

This antagonism is partly inevitable. The sheer size and wealth of Russia compared with its neighbours and the way in which it dominates the whole Euro-Asian landmass means that Russia's relations with all neighbouring states are always going to be difficult and delicate.

However, it is also the result of Yeltsin's cavalier and insensitive approach to Russian relations with the other republics and the outspoken statements of some Russian officials, particularly in the immediate aftermath of the coup.

Firstly, all the former Soviet republics have deeply resented the way in which Russia unilaterally took control of all Soviet property on its territory and imposed Russian appointees in all key central government positions during and after the August coup.

These Russian actions:

1   Greatly undermined the Union Treaty negotiations in the months between August and December, because from the vantage point of the other republics it looked as though any new union government would be entirely dominated by Russians. For example, according to press reports in late August 1991 President Kravchuk of Ukraine was said to be 'frightened by calls in Russia that most of the portfolios in the future Union government should go to Russian citizens', and he wasn't the only one (see Solchanyk).

2   Gave the Russian government enormous control over the old levers of power. For example, the Russian government acquired absolute control over the old USSR's only rouble printing presses. This has enabled it to manipulate the flow of roubles to the other states. It is one of the reasons why the new states of the CIS have been individually discussing the possibility of producing their own currencies and have been unable to reach agreement on maintaining a common 'rouble zone' or a common 'economic zone'. Russia also acquired considerable control over the Soviet armed forces the bulk of which are on Russian territory.

3   Pre-empted discussions about how the property and assets of the old USSR were to be divided up. This greatly embittered subsequent negotiations within the CIS on this issue. Not unnaturally, the other states saw no reason why they should not follow Russia's example and assert their sovereignty by unilaterally taking absolute control of all former Soviet assets on their territory, including military assets. It was partly this griev-ance that animated the huge row between Russia and Ukraine during 1992 over the ownership of the (former USSR) Black Sea

naval fleet which is located on Ukrainian territory.

Needless to say, such resentments have been an enormous hindrance to the development of inter-state co-operation within the CIS particularly over such issues as maintaining united CIS armed forces; the control of nuclear weapons; the servicing of the old USSR's foreign debt; and the ownership of former Soviet property abroad (e.g. embassy buildings).

Secondly, the non-Russian states have also been outraged by the often very aggressive way in which Russian government (and other leading) officials have defined and promoted Russian interests within the CIS, usually at their expense. For example:

1   Russian concern about the fate and treatment of the Russian minorities resident in the other states (all of whom have been turned into 'foreigners' now that they have lost their Soviet identity) prompted some very rash statements from the Russian side, and worries about Russian interference in their internal affairs on the part of the former republics.

For instance, President Yeltsin outraged the other republics on 26 August 1991 when he threatened to begin border renegotiations with any republic that unilaterally declared itself completely independent of the Union (in order to protect Russian minorities and bring them within the borders of the RSFSR). All the former Soviet republics, including the old Baltic republics and Georgia, have considerable Russian minorities. Most of them also have borders with Russia. This was therefore understood as a general threat because almost everyone had either declared themselves independent of the USSR, or was contemplating it, in the days after the coup. Ukrainian opinion was particularly incensed because Yeltsin's threat contradicted a formal treaty signed between Russia and Ukraine on 19 November, 1990 which, among other things, stated that their borders were inviolable (the threat only provoked greater support for independence within Ukraine).

The conflict was smoothed over and the declaration explained away as a 'mistake' but the threat has not been forgotten by anybody, least of all by Ukraine. All the states are aware that as long as the Russian troops left over from the old Soviet Red Army remain on their territory (and there are no plans to withdraw them even from the Baltic states before 1995) then Russia has the means to implement this threat even if it means war. The rise of militant Russian nationalism has also been a cause for general concern.

2   The Russian government has consistently neglected to consult adequately with the other states over the question of economic reform. It is inevitable, given Russia's enormous size and wealth, that any radical economic measures launched in Russia will have knock-on effects for the other states. The most notorious example was Yeltsin's unilateral decision to liberalise prices (which meant huge price rises) in the Russian republic in mid-December 1991. The liberalisation was postponed for two weeks (until 2 January 1992) partly as a result of protests from other states, but then went ahead anyway. Its effect was to force everyone else to liberalise (i.e. increase) their prices too because otherwise their markets would have been flooded with Russian consumers looking for goods at cheaper prices. Ukraine, in particular, complained bitterly that Russia had failed to provide it with enough roubles to compensate the Ukrainian population with increased wages.

The net effect of such Russian insensitivity, coming on top of the economic chaos that is undermining all the states of the CIS, has been to force the other states into taking even more measures to defend their economies (e.g. introducing re-usable ration coupons as substitutes for the rouble). This has made co-operation within the CIS even more difficult.

Differing interests

Finally, it is worth stressing that the members of the CIS have very different needs and interests most of which are unlikely to be met by the CIS. Virtually all of them have therefore been forced to turn outward to the international community for aid and assistance. For example:

1   All the former Soviet republics (except Georgia) have become members of the standing Conference on Security and Co-

operation in Europe (CSCE), including the central Asian republics, although there was initially some doubt as to whether these countries could properly be called European. President Yeltsin, in particular, hoped that the diplomatic and organisational structures of the CSCE might help Russia and the other states of the CIS find peaceful ways of resolving the problem of protecting the rights of the ethnic minorities on their territories as well as providing assistance in bringing an end to the wars in Moldova and Nagorno-Karabakh. Although the inability of the CSCE to intervene effectively in the bloody disintegration of Yugoslavia makes this a forlorn hope.

2 All the former republics have become members of the International Monetary Fund and the World Bank, although most of them have yet to benefit from this membership. Russia had been promised the biggest package of IMF aid but by August 1992 only 1.5 billion dollars of the promised 24 billion dollars had actually been released. The IMF was therefore doing absolutely nothing to help Russia through the first, and most painful, stages of transition.

3 The Central Asian republics have, thus far, done very badly out of the CIS. All the old economic subsidies on which they relied have gone and they find themselves badly disadvantaged by the fact that their economies (this applies especially to Uzbekistan) depend heavily on the production and export of cotton which the new states of the CIS are no longer buying in great quantities. These countries have increasingly turned to their neighbours in the east, notably Iran and Turkey, for help. In February 1992 three of the four central Asian republics (excluding Kazakhstan), plus Azerbaijan, became members of the Economic Co-operation Organisation which was founded by Turkey, Iran and Pakistan in 1963. Iran and Turkey have also been actively trying to mediate an end to the war between Azerbaijan and Armenia.

It may well be, therefore, that in the long term the CIS will quietly disintegrate because its members find it more useful to integrate themselves into multilateral organisations within the global community.

Why have a Commonwealth at all?

In some ways, the most fundamental weakness of the CIS is that it is not a voluntary association freely entered into but a 'shot-gun marriage' forced on its member states by their extraordinary levels of interdependence. As a columnist in the Russian newspaper *Izvestiya* put it in January 1992: 'the CIS arose to a large extent as a forced alliance, generated more by the impossibility of parting than a desire to continue to live together' (see Sheehy, 'Unloved, Ill-fed Infant . . .', p.1). This 'alliance' has been forced on the member states by:

Economic interdependence
This is not simply a matter of inter-republican trade. The old Soviet Union constituted one huge integrated market. This means that the fundamental infrastructure of production is spread out across the territory of the former Soviet Union with each of the republics representing a link in the chain. For example, all the non-Russian republics were heavily dependent on Russia for oil and gas. Russia, Ukraine and Kazakhstan produced 90 per cent of the country's grain. The Baltic republics dominated in the field of advanced engineering. Turkmenistan could produce raw cotton cloth but had no facilities for turning it into finished products, and so on. And in the old days these goods were traded internally at prices well below world levels.

The new states of the CIS therefore find that they are heavily dependent on each other and in particular on Russia. This has caused enormous resentment because:

1   It gives resource-rich states like Russia enormous economic power over the less well-endowed. For example, Russia has already threatened to raise the prices of its raw materials and fuel exports to world levels and to charge the former Soviet republics in foreign currency for any Russian goods they import. (The Baltic states have already discovered that this is one price of freedom). Of course, none of the former Soviet republics could possibly afford this: for instance, the inter-republican price for Russian oil was 3 per cent of the world level in January 1992! (see Bush).

2   Russia in turn resents the fact that it has been subsidising the economies of the former Soviet republics by charging below world prices for its exports to them. Some leading Russian politicians are arguing that Russia should cut its links with all the former Soviet republics completely because of this. As Ann Sheehy has put it, 'The republics cannot ignore the reality of their economic interdependence, but at the same time they resent being at one another's mercy' ('Unloved, Ill-fed Infant . . .', p. 1).

The problem of borders

As we saw in Chapter 9 very few of the old USSR's internal borders have been legally agreed or internationally recognised. They originated as administrative not state borders. Moreover, many of them were established on the basis of 'divide and rule'. This means that the populations of virtually all the new states are a heterogeneous, and potentially explosive, mixture of different ethnic groups, many of them owing their national identity to CIS states other than the one in which they are resident. Thus far the CIS has not established a formal, legal and consultative mechanism for dealing with the problem of borders or the enormously complex and inherently dangerous questions of citizenship and minority rights that it involves. Consequently, were the new states of the CIS to sever their relations completely the status of the current borders between and within the old republics would inevitably become sources of conflict. As it is these problems have already caused several conflicts, and are quite likely to generate more in the future.

Western concerns

1   Who will take responsibility for the massive Soviet foreign debt? The foreign debt of all the new states combined now stands at about 70 billion dollars. However, there has been considerable conflict within the CIS about how this enormous burden should be shared out, and there is even more uncertainty about how the resources will be found to service this debt. All the states of the CIS are economically bankrupt and simply do not have the means to meet their inherited debt obligations. However, they have at least agreed to service the debt jointly.

2   What will happen to all the international agreements to which the USSR was a signatory? The CIS collectively promised from the outset to honour all the Soviet state's international commitments. However, many of these agreements, particularly the arms control agreements, require the co-operation at least of the four 'nuclear' states of Russia, Ukraine, Belarus and Kazakhstan, and this co-operation has not always been forthcoming.

3   The fate of the Soviet nuclear arsenal and the management of the old Soviet armed forces is a further concern.

These problems have been a key source of conflict within the CIS and very little agreement has thus far been reached on how to deal with them (see Bluth).

The fundamental difficulties are that the '16th Republic' (as the armed forces became known) is vast. The military–industrial infrastructure developed to support it is immensely complex, highly integrated and thoroughly dispersed throughout the territory of the former Soviet Union (the military economy like the civilian economy was trans-republican). The resources needed to finance it are enormous. And there are a very large number of different interest groups involved. It is not just the elected republican governments who are determined to have a say. The views of the military high command, of the officer corp in the various branches (navy, airforce, etc.), and of the industrial managers in the massive armaments factories and research institutes dotted across former Soviet territory also have to be taken into account. All the elected politicians in the CIS are only too well aware that the military–industrial complex continues to pose a threat to them if only because it has weapons and organisation at its disposal.

Unfortunately for the CIS leaders Western pressure for rapid measures to ensure the security of nuclear weapons and the peaceful restructuring (and reduction) of the armed forces has been considerable. Moreover by withholding economic aid, or by making it conditional, the Western countries have an indirect but powerful means of forcing the states in the CIS to do something. It is partly this pressure and the desire for international recognition and aid that has kept Ukraine within the CIS.

For the moment the strategic armed forces (i.e. long-range weapons and forces) remain largely under central (which means mostly Russian) command. However, it is impossible to say whether things will stay that way. All the states have begun to create their own national armies and command structures, including Russia. Both Russia, Ukraine and Kazakhstan assumed authority over all Soviet military forces on their territory from the beginning – a source of enormous tension within the CIS. However, no state, with the exception of Russia has the expertise or the capability to become an independent nuclear power; and certainly no state, including Russia, has the economic means. Moreover, the strategic armed forces are being subjected to the same processes of economic and social disintegration as everyone else. Perhaps the best that Yeltsin and the other state leaders can hope for is that the old Soviet military–industrial complex will gradually atrophy as it is starved of funds and as its old trans-republican links are cut.

Whatever happens (short of war) the states of the CIS have been left with a unique, terrible and costly legacy: the dismembered remains of a military and nuclear superpower. It is hardly surprising that they cannot agree on how to deal with it.

Conclusion

It is easy to be pessimistic about the future of the CIS but we need to keep a sense of proportion.

1   Its eleven member states are struggling to establish themselves under horrendously difficult conditions. Each state has enormously complex domestic problems to deal with. At the same time they are also trying to come to terms with each other and to deal with the pressures being placed on them by the international community. Thus far they have managed to cope, with remarkably little conflict and an astonishing lack of bloodshed in the circumstances. The CIS may not really exist in anything but name as yet, and it may never become anything more, but it has at least enabled the leaders of its member states to keep talking to each other in

reasonably civil terms. For example, despite the considerable tensions between the two states, Russia established diplomatic relations with Ukraine on 14 February 1992 and there have been direct negotiations since then between Yeltsin and Kravchuk in order to try to improve relations and resolve outstanding differences. President Kravchuk himself acknowledged in April that the Ukraine was better off inside the CIS because it did at least provide a forum for discussion.

The terrible wars that have decimated what was once Yugoslavia are a terrible warning to everyone of the dangers of nationalism and of what can happen when ambitious politicians seek to exploit it for their own narrow ends.

2 Associations of states generally take a long time to develop and are usually voluntary. Even so they are rarely without 'low-intensity' conflict of one sort or another. The European Economic Community, for example, was originally formed in 1957. Most of its members are extremely wealthy and politically stable by CIS standards. However, it is still subject to considerable conflict, most recently over the formation of a single market and political union. It has also seen quite vicious (if localised) trade wars in the recent past. Sovereign states do not take easily to surrendering even a little of their power especially if they also have to bear financial costs.

The newly independent states of the CIS have only just acquired their sovereignty after decades of subordination within a highly centralised empire. It is therefore hardly surprising that they are finding it difficult to co-operate. The CIS may not last, particularly if the Russian federation itself disintegrates internally, but if it helps the republics of the former Soviet Union to achieve a civilised and peaceful divorce, as the Ukrainians hope, and/or enables them to come together again eventually in a voluntary union then it will certainly have achieved its purpose.

Further Reading

Bluth, Christoph, 'What do you do with a nuclear arsenal?.', *New Scientist*, 18 July 1992

Bush, Keith, 'Russia: Gaidar's Guidelines', *RFL/RL Research Report*, Vol. 1, No. 15, 10 April 1992, p. 24

Sheehy, Ann, 'Commonwealth of Independent States: an uneasy compromise', *RFE/RL Research Report*, Vol. 1, No. 2, 10 January 1992, p. 3

Sheehy, Ann, 'Unloved, ill-fed infant faces an uncertain future', *RFE/RL Research Report*, Vol. 1, No. 2, 10 January 1992, p. 1

Solchanyk, Roman, 'Ukraine and Russia: before and after the coup', *RFE/RL Research Report*, Vol. 3, No. 39, 27 September 1991, p. 15

Index

Abkhazia, 182
agriculture, *see* farming
Andropov, Yuri (1914–84), General
    Secretary of CPSU (1982–84), 22, 73,
    106
anti-alcohol campaign, 106–8, 114, 115,
    205, 220
anti-democratic filters, 87, 126, 129
apparatchiki, 20, 32, 73, 93, 95, 126, 155, 274
armed forces, military-industrial complex,
    13, 22, 35, 41, 47, 132, 183, 190, 211,
    254, 266, 267, 290, 291, 292, 298–9,
    300, 304–5
    and coup (1991), 228, 229, 230, 231, 237,
        238, 239, 241
    and reform, 55–6, 181, 182, 185, 200,
        214–15, 218–19, 223, 226
Armenia, 65, 84, 114, 173, 176, 179, 183,
    185, 186, 289, 301
autonomous republics, regions, areas, 25,
    26, 91, 126, 127, 168–9, 175, 179, 180,
    182, 195, 201, 240; *see also individual
    entries*
Azerbaijan, 84, 107, 168, 173, 176, 177, 251,
    271, 289, 291, 301

Baltic republics, states, 10, 43, 84, 87, 88,
    94, 170, 231, 235, 239, 253, 255, 258,
    269, 272, 296, 299, 300
    and democratisation, 142, 148, 150, 152,
        177, 179
    and sovereignty, 182, 183, 186, 218, 242,
        289; *see also individual entries*
Belarus (formerly Byelorussia), 186–7, 224,
    272, 274, 289, 290, 293, 294, 297, 304
black market, *see* second economy
blat, 54
Bolsheviks, 12–3, 23, 167

bourgeoisie, *see* middle class
Brezhnev, Leonid (1906–82), General
    Secretary of CPSU (1964–82), 21, 22,
    38, 51, 52, 73, 77, 95, 101, 102, 103,
    115, 118, 121, 184, 191, 200, 211, 226
bribery, corruption, 54, 108–10, 113, 195,
    208, 265–6, 268
budget deficit, 106–7, 114, 181, 200, 204–5,
    258–9, 263
bureaucracy, 28–9, 32–5, 63, 87, 103–5,
    111, 112, 119, 121, 144, 147, 153–4,
    285

Cabinet of Ministers (USSR), 90, 135, 136
campaigns, 105–10
campaign against unearned incomes, 77,
    108–10, 115, 116, 205
Central Asian republics, 11, 66, 152, 176,
    271, 289, 294, 301; *see also individual
    entries*
Central Committee (CPSU), 33, 81, 82, 83,
    88, 112, 115, 127, 154, 241, 284
Chechnya (formerly Checheno-Ingushetia),
    251, 252, 256
Chelyabinsk, 265, 266
Chernenko, Konstantin (1911–85), General
    Secretary of CPSU (1984–85), 22, 73
China, 3, 211, 214, 233
class system, 45–7, 49, 54
cold war, 6, 187, 212, 214, 217
Commonwealth of Independent States
    (CIS), 57, 167, 176, 187, 203–4, 208,
    239, 249, 250, 252, 271, 274, 285,
    289–306
Communist Party of the Soviet Union
    (CPSU)
    congresses, conferences; Nineteenth, 75,
        82, 84, 118, 126, 128, 174; Twenty-

seventh, 74, 97, 108, 110; Twenty-
eighth, 155
and democratisation, 85–9, 122, 124–6,
128, 129, 142, 144–57
disintegration, 88–9, 133, 150, 153–7,
158, 159–60
and ideology, 22, 36–8, 49–50, 61–4,
66–7, 131–3, 154–55, 157, 216
and law, 31, 33, 125
leading role, 29–30, 40–1, 79, 86, 88, 96,
98, 121, 124–6, 130, 143, 144, 151,
179, 185
membership and structure, 32–3, 35–6,
83, 130, **153–4**, 156, 169–70, 283
and old system, 20–22, 27–38, 40–1,
48–51, 105, 119, 150–1, 166–9, 170–2,
173, 194–5, 203
powers, 10, 11, 20, 29–33, 36–7, 146–7,
148, 150–1, 159, 161
privileges, 51–3, 63, 113
and proposed reforms, 81–3, 120–6,
130–3
and reforms of 1989–90, 85–9, 125–9,
141, 144, 150–7, 194–7
and society, 29–30, 45, 49–51, 124–6,
131–3
suspension, 53, 241–2
Congress of People's Deputies (USSR), 11,
82, 85, 86–7, 88, 90, 91, 122–3, 126–9,
132, 133–6, 142, 144–5, 147, 151, 159,
179, 181, 204
Congress of People's Deputies (Russia), 93,
123, 262, 281, 282
constitution, constitutional reform, 23,
82–3, 90, 122, 123, 124–5, 127–8, 132,
133, 135, 143, 184, 196, 233–7, 276,
281–2, 291
Council of the Federation (USSR), 134–6
Council of Heads of Government (CIS),
289–91
Council of Heads of State (CIS), 289–91
Council of Ministers (USSR), **24–7**, 30, 31,
90, 104, 112, 133–6, 160, 196
Council of Ministers (republican), 26–7, 30,
31, 168
coup (1991), 5, 13, 14, 42, 43, 53, 56, 94, 95,
134, 185, 208, 210, **222–45**, 264, 267,
275, 294, 295, 297, 298, 299
CPSU, *see* Communist Party
Crimea, 169, 170, 182, 186, 222, 229, 274

Daghestan, 251
democracy, democratisation, 10–12, 40, 88,
120–1, 160–1, 141–3, 269
and CPSU, 83–4, 88, 120, 125, 130, 150,
153, 195, 216
and federal relations, 57, 84, 174, 176,

177, 179, 187
industrial, 81, 120, 194, 199
and old system, 22, 30–1, 37–8, 62, 79
weaknesses of, 42, 82, 97, 271, 275–7,
278–80,
democratic centralism, 23, 26, 30–1, 36, 88,
96, 97, 131, 147, 152, 154, 195
dissidents, 37, 62, 66, 137, 143

Eastern Europe, 2, 3, 185, 187, 212, **216–8**,
219, 254
economy, economic system, 20–1, 27, 211,
212; disintegration, 89, 157, **190–209**,
224–5; reform, 78–9, 80–1, 100–5,
113–14, 178, 192–3, 273, 279, 300;
shock therapy, 278, 260–4, 276
egalitarianism (*uravnilovka*), 49, 50, 51, 64
elections, electoral system, 82, 93, 149; and
CPSU, 128, 130, 131–2, 144, 151–2,
155–6; and federal relations, 10, 179;
national, 85–7; old system, 31;
republican, local, 87–88; weaknesses
of, 97, 126–7, 145
Emergency Committee (State Committee
for State of Emergency), 7, 159, 185,
188, 225, 226, 229–41; membership,
56, 94, 135, 227, 234
Estonia, 10, 43, 177, 180, 185, 224, 251,
253, 261
ethnic diversity, groupings, 43–4, 141,
164–88, 250–7, 277, 299, 303
European Community, 211, 214, 217, 242,
306
factories, *see* industry
farming, 44, 48, 81, 103, 104, 109, 200–1,
203, 206, 224–5, 268
federal system, federalism (USSR), 10, 23,
38, 82, 124, 157, **166–74**, 303
federal system, federalism (Russia), 168,
250–1, 252, 256–7, 266–8, 271, 277–8,
284, 285–7, 294
five year plans, 77, 102–3, 115, 198–9

Gaidar, Yegor, Acting Prime Minister of
Russia (1992), 261, 263, 264
Georgia, 11, 42, 43, 66, 107, 156, 168, 169,
173, 176, 177, 179, 182, 183, 185, 186,
224, 254, 271, 289, 293, 296, 299, 300
glasnost, 9, 21, 42, 74, 78, 80, 83–5, 87, 103,
110–12, 114, 130–1, **136–8**, 140, 142,
151, 154, 157, 171, 176, 195, 216
Gorbachev, Mikhail (born 1931), General
Secretary of CPSU (1985–1991)
appointed, 73
and bureaucracy, 29, 103–5, 110–12,
115–16, 119
and coup (1991), 95, 185–6, 222–9, 235,

236–7, 238, 241–4
and CPSU, 10, 36–7, 41, 66–7, 96, 121,
    124–6, 130–3, 156, 216, 241
and economy, 55, 77–81, 93–4, 100,
    114–15, 158, 183, 190–208
and foreign policy, 187, 210–20
as General Secretary of CPSU, 90–1,
    95–6, 98, 100, 115, 128, 158, 220, 241
goals, 74–7, 95–8, 100, 101–2, 119–22,
    129, 130–1, 187, 192–3, 211–12
and nationalism, 167, 174–7, 184–5, 187,
    198, 295
and old system, 6, 13, 22, 29, 38, 51, 61,
    67, 96, 102, 115–16, 211, 244
as president, 91–2, 128, 133–6, 157–60,
    179, 181, 183, 186, 225, 226, 242
resignations, 187, 242
Gosagroprom, 104–5
Gosplan, 27–9, 33–4, 102, 103, 104, 178,
    190, 196, 198
Gospriemka, 105–6

hoarding, 191, 201, 202, 262

incomes, 44–7, 48–9, 50–1, 54, 57, 101–2,
    107, 204, 205, 262, 265, 266
industry, industrialisation, factories,
    production, 7, 44, 46–8, 50–1, 53, 58,
    81, 103, 114, 120, 146, 170, 178, 191,
    193, 194, 198–201, 203, 205–6, 207,
    258–9, 263, 264–5, 268–70, 276
informal groups, movements (*neformalnye*),
    65, 129, 141, 142, 148–9, 155
intelligentsia, 8, 57, 73, 138
International Monetary Fund (IMF), 258,
    260, 261, 263–4, 270, 287, 301
Interregional Group of Deputies, 129, 135,
    142, 144

Karachai-Cherkess Republic, 251
Kazakhstan, 65, 170, 224, 235, 253–4, 255,
    268, 274, 289, 290, 293, 294, 297, 301,
    302, 304–5
KGB (Committee for State Security), 56,
    87, 132, 151, 183, 185, 190, 223,
    226–7, 231, 233, 239, 241, 250, 266,
    283
Khasbulatov, Ruslan, Speaker of Russian
    Supreme Soviet, 180, 281
Khrushchev, Nikita (1894–1971), General
    Secretary of CPSU (1953–64), 22, 29,
    34, 48, 50, 98, 115, 169
kolkhozy, 47–8, 108, 109
Kozyrev, Andrei, Russian Foreign Minister,
    256–7
Kravchuk, Leonid (President of Ukraine),
    187, 252, 273–8, 280, 284, 295–7, 298,

306
Kyrgyzstan (formerly Kirgiziya), 43, 254,
    289

Latvia, 10, 43, 177, 184, 224, 228, 253, 261
law, legal system, 23, 29, 31, 33, 111, 119,
    120, 122–3, 125, 151, 177, 178, 180,
    181, 208
Law on Co-operatives (1988), 81
Law on Individual Labour Activity (1986),
    77, 104
Law on Press Freedom (1990), 137
Law on Public Associations (1990), 142
Law on the State of Emergency (1990), 226,
    234
Law on State Enterprises (1987), 81, 120,
    194, 199
left, defined, 68
Lenin, Vladimir (1870–1924), founder of
    Communist Party; Leninism, 12, 22,
    23, 61, 62, 79, 98, 111, 119, 133, 137,
    242, 284
Leningrad (St. Petersburg), 87, 144, 147,
    149, 152, 182, 231, 233, 240, 284
Ligachev, Yegor, 84, 115
Lithuania, 10, 11, 43, 94, 156, 177, 180, 185,
    198, 224, 228, 253
Lukyanov, Anatoly, 225

marketisation, market system, reform, 6–7,
    28, 42, 53, 57, 58, 68, 193, 203, 207–8,
    258–64, 265, 268, 269–70, 278–9
media, 21, 37, 94, 110, 111, 137–8, 149, 230,
    232, 239, 272, 275, 283
middle class, bourgeoisie, 8, 46
modernisation, 7–8, 44, 50–1, 166
Moldova (formerly Moldavia), 107, 183,
    185, 186, 224, 254, 255, 289, 291, 292,
    301
money, value of, 45, 107, 197, 201, 204–5,
    264–5, 267, 298
Moscow, 14, 20, 23, 27, 28, 43, 44, 88, 93,
    113, 141, 144, 146, 149, 156, 172, 182,
    185, 222, 230, 231, 238, 239, 240, 251,
    262, 267, 271, 282, 284, 294
multi-party system, 10, 87–8, 126, 129, 142,
    148–9, 155, 160–2, 272

Nagorno-Karabakh, 84, 173, 176, 251, 254,
    292, 301
nationalism, 56–7, 84–5, 149, 150, 157,
    164–88, 195, 202, 249–57, 271–8, 280,
    286–7, 306
NATO (North Atlantic Treaty
    Organisation), 210, 212, 217, 219, 220
Nazarbaev, Nursultan (President of
    Kazakhstan), 235, 253, 284

neformalnye, see informal groups
Nine Plus One talks, 95, 185
nomenklatura, 31, 35–6, 46, 52–3, 54, 56, 58,
    83, 116, 129, 131, 144, 147, 152, 154,
    160, 192, 195, 249, 259–60, 264, 265,
    266, 272, 275
North Caucasus, 107

Ossetia, 11, 293

Pavlov, Valentin, 94, 197, 225, 227, 228–9,
    236, 264
Perestroika (book by Gorbachev), 120, 215
planning, 6–7, 20–1, 27–9, 33–5, 37, 38,
    47–9, 58, 63, 101, 102–3, 146, 168,
    179, 203; and reform, 79, 80, 104–5,
    121, 193, 194, 198, 207, 258, 261
podmena, 32, 83
Politburo, 32, 33, 52, 93, 113, 115, 127, 131,
    141, 168, 283
political system, reforms, 7–8, 63–4, 80,
    81–2, 85, 89, 96–7, 118–39, 140–62,
    178, 194–7
Popular Fronts, 84, 87, 142, 148–9, 150, 179
presidency, 11, 32, 89, 90, 91, 93, 123, 128,
    133–6, 157, 159, 160, 179, 196, 226,
    235, 273, 275, 276, 280–2, 286, 295
Presidential Council, 134, 135, 136, 196
Primary Party Organisations (PPOs), 153
private cultures, 64–7
private sector, privatisation, 48, 53, 58, 67,
    81, 108–9, 191, 203, 208, 239, 249,
    258–61, 265–6
privileges, 51–3, 56, 63
Pugo, Boris, 94, 227, 229

referenda, 184, 186, 224, 242, 273–4, 295,
    296
revolution (1917), 5, 8, 12, 118–19, 167, 202
revolution (1991), *see* coup
right, defined, 68
rouble, *see* money
Rukh, 274–6
Russia (pre-1917), 5–6, 7–8, 44
Russia, Russian Soviet Federated Republic,
    RSFSR (USSR), 42, 43, 75, 92–3, 123,
    124, 148, 153, 164, 168, 169, 170,
    172–3, 178, 179, 180, 182, 185, 186–7,
    196, 202, 224, 235, 238, 240, 242,
    250
Russia, Russian Federal Republic (CIS), 57,
    169, 250–1, 252, 253, 255, 256–7, 258,
    260, 261–8, 269, 271, 273, 274, 276,
    277–87, 289, 290, 293, 294, 295,
    296–300, 301, 302–3, 304–5, 306
Russian Communist Party (founded 1990),
    92, 155, 158

Russian identity, 277–80, 286–7
Russian nationalism, 253, 256–7, 267, 278,
    286–7, 300
Russification, 172–3
Rutskoi, Alexander, Vice President of
    Russia, 256, 287
Ryzhkov, Nikolai, 90, 92, 93–4, 112, 152,
    197

Sakharov, Andrei, 143
second economy (black market), 20, 53–5,
    106, 191–2, 208, 262, 265–6
Shatalin, Stanislav, 196, 197
Shatalin Plan (500-day programme), 93,
    195, 196–7, 208, 263
Shevardnadze, Eduard, 74, 94, 227
shortages, 19–20, 52, 55, 67, 78, 85, 89, 102,
    108, 109, 113–14, 191, 198, 201, 205,
    206, 208, 225
Siberia, 44, 66, 201, 266, 271
Sobchak, Anatoly, Mayor of St. Petersburg,
    87, 230, 233, 234, 284
socialism, socialist, 19, 40, 45, 60, 63, 68, 76,
    80, 96, 98, 108, 111, 118–19, 121,
    132–3, 140–1, 157, 214, 216, 223
Solzhenitsyn, Alexander, 62
Soviet of Nationalities, 24, 169
Soviet of the Union, 24
soviets; and CPSU, 129, 131–2, 151–3, 156;
    and economy, 192, 201; and elections,
    87–88; and federal relations, 174–5,
    181; and old system, 12, 20, 23–9, 30,
    32, 38, 41, 119; and reform, 120, 121,
    122–4, 127–8, 147, 159
Stalin, Josef (1879–1953), General
    Secretary of Communist Party
    (1922–53); Stalinism, 2, 22, 34, 36, 44,
    50, 51, 52, 63, 91, 115, 118, 121, 132,
    137, 169, 170, 176, 214, 216
State Committee for the State of
    Emergency, *see* Emergency Committee
stratification, 44
Supreme Soviet (USSR, federal), 11, 24, 26,
    31, 82, 90, 91, 94, 123, 127–8, 129, 132,
    133–6, 145, 147, 159, 169, 175, 181,
    186, 196, 197, 204, 223, 228–9, 235–6,
    238, 241
Supreme Soviets (republican), 24–5, 26, 31,
    87, 123–4, 129, 147, 168, 175, 180,
    181, 231, 262, 275, 276, 281–2, 283,
    295

Tadjikistan, 43, 44, 168, 224, 252, 255, 272,
    289
Tatars, 170, 277
Tatarstan, 251, 252, 256, 266, 267
Third World, 211, 219, 270

Turkmenistan, 289, 302

Ukraine, 107, 169, 179, 182, 186–7, 202,
224, 242, 252, 261, **273–7**, 289, 290,
291, **295–7**, 298–9, 300, 302, 304–6
under class, 47
Union republics, 24, 25, 26, 27, 43, 56–7,
66, 80, 84–5, 103, 123–4, 126, 127,
134, 145, 149, 168–9, 171, 172, 193,
201–2, 207, 223–4, 252–3, 300–1,
302–3
and struggle against centre, 10–11, 89,
90–1, 95, 142, 150, 152, 156, 158–9,
160, 164, 174, 175, **177–87**, 195, 218,
294–5
and war of laws, 11, 91, **181–2**, 236, 251–2
and coup (1991), 231–2, 235–6, 238, 240,
242; *see also individual entries*
Union of Soviet Socialist Republics (Soviet
Union, USSR), 10, 19, 24, 43, 64, 81,
133, 165, 174, 175, 184, 186, 202,
218–20, 222–3, 229, 249
Union Treaty, 175, 178, 180, 183, 184–5,
222–4, 227, 229, 235, 242, 295, 296,
298
upper class, 46
Urals, 267, 271
uravnilovka, see egalitarianism
United States, USA, 34, 202, 211, 212–14,
215, 218, 220, 266, 269, 270

Uzbekistan, 43, 168, 176, 224, 249, 252,
255, 258, 261, 289, 295, 301

Warsaw Pact, 215, 217
welfare, 49, 57, 64, 204, 258–9, 260, 268,
269
West, relations with, 65, 210–20, 270, 287,
303–4
working class, 8, 46

Yakutia (Sakha), 266, 267, 271
Yanaev, Gennadi, 94, 135, 224, 226, 227,
230, 234
Yazov, Dmitri, 227, 229, 232
Yeltsin, Boris
and CIS, 187, 296, 297, 299, 300, 301
and coup (1991), 185–6, 230–1, 232, 233,
234, 235, 237–42
and CPSU, 84, 113, 156
criticism of *perestroika*, 75–6, 98
and democracy, 153, 282–4
and economic reform, 93, 183, 196, 197,
258, 261–4
and Gorbachev, 91, 93, 94, 135, 183
and old system, 52, 113, 143, 305
as president, 273, 274, 277, 278–87, 294
and republican struggle for autonomy, 95,
173, 178, 180, 199, 227, 252
and Russian federal relations, 256–7,
266–8, 271, 285–7